THE
CLIMBING
BIBLE

THE
CLIMBING
BIBLE

TECHNICAL, PHYSICAL AND MENTAL
TRAINING FOR ROCK CLIMBING

MARTIN MOBRÅTEN & STIAN CHRISTOPHERSEN

Translated by Bjørn Sætnan

Vertebrate Publishing, Sheffield
www.v-publishing.co.uk

Stian Christophersen enjoys the view from Grande Grotta, Kalymnos, Greece.

THE CLIMBING BIBLE

MARTIN MOBRÅTEN & STIAN CHRISTOPHERSEN

Translated by Bjørn Sætnan

First published in Norwegian in 2018 under the title *Klatrebibelen* by Klatreboka AS.
This English edition first published in 2020 by Vertebrate Publishing. Reprinted in 2021.

 This translation has been published with the financial support of NORLA.

Vertebrate Publishing
Omega Court, 352 Cemetery Road, Sheffield S11 8FT, United Kingdom.
www.v-publishing.co.uk

 Copyright © Martin Mobråten and Stian Christophersen 2020.
Foreword copyright © Jo Nesbø 2020.

Front cover: Mina Leslie-Wujastyk on *Clear Blue Skies* (Font 8a), Mount Evans, Colorado. Photo: David Mason.
Photography by Bård Lie Henriksen unless otherwise credited.

Martin Mobråten and Stian Christophersen have asserted their rights under the Copyright,
Designs and Patents Act 1988 to be identified as authors of this work.
A CIP catalogue record for this book is available from the British Library.

ISBN: 978-1-912560-70-7 (Paperback)
ISBN: 978-1-839810-33-6 (Ebook)

10 9 8 7 6 5 4 3

Klatrebibelen editorial:

Editor: Maria Stangeland.
Photographer: Bård Lie Henriksen.
Design and layout: Jon Tore Modell.
Editing: Elisabet Skårberg.
English translation: Bjørn Sætnan.

Vertebrate Publishing is committed to printing on paper from sustainable sources.

Printed and bound in China on behalf of Latitude Press.

Every effort has been made to achieve accuracy of the information in this guidebook. The authors, publishers and copyright owners
can take no responsibility for: loss or injury (including fatal) to persons; loss or damage to property or equipment; trespass, irresponsible
behaviour or any other mishap that may be suffered as a result of following the advice offered in this guidebook.

Climbing is an activity that carries a risk of personal injury or death. Participants must be aware of and accept that these risks are
present and they should be responsible for their own actions and involvement. Nobody involved in the writing and production of this
guidebook accepts any responsibility for any errors that it may contain, or are they liable for any injuries or damage that may arise from
its use. All climbing is inherently dangerous and the fact that individual descriptions in this volume do not point out such dangers does
not mean that they do not exist. Take care.

MARTIN

Mum and Dad, thank you for allowing me to follow my passion!
Maria, it's just awesome that I get to share climbing and the rest of my life with you!

STIAN

Thank you, Dad, for all the amazing trips and for introducing me to what has shaped
my life. Thank you, Karianne, for your patience and for always helping me when I'm
stuck. Thank you, Mum, for always believing in me, no matter what.
Kasper and Oda, this one's for you.

CONTENTS

'I REALISED, AS A FORTY-YEAR-OLD, I HAD REDISCOVERED THE FUN OF OUR CHILDHOOD GAMES. AND NOT JUST ANY GAME, BUT INDEED A GAME THAT IS MUCH MORE REAL THAN WHAT THEY CLAIM REALITY ITSELF IS.'

THE GAME

FOREWORD BY JO NESBØ

When I was young, we used to play cowboys and Indians. I was the youngest but gained respect from the older kids because of my ability to die spectacularly. I wasn't afraid to fall off branches slightly too high up the tree if I felt the need to add a certain panache for visual effect. On our way home after our battles, we passed civilians carting their baby strollers, washing their cars, mowing their lawns and performing other peaceful, meaningless and tedious tasks. And I thought: Damn it, do these people really not realise that mere metres away a war has been fought on matters of life and death?

Thirty-five years later I found myself clinging to a climbing wall, high up on the famous Thaiwand Wall at Railay in Thailand. As I looked down, 80 metres straight into the sea, I realised that if I theatrically grasped my chest, let loose my Indian-howl and fell, this time it would not only be a spectacular fall, but also a very real death. Unless of course this preposterously thin strand of rope would serve its purpose and catch me, which my future climbing buddy told me it always does, usually. I died three or four times that trip, yet always managed to claw my way back to life, fuelled by a cocktail of adrenaline, survival instinct, physical strength I didn't possess, and mental stamina previously unknown to me. Furious cursing and uninhibited roars of delight, fear and laughter, both eyes blind and sudden revelations, imminent success turned sudden panic, plans of retreat and white flags turned into a resolute struggle against limestone, demons and gravity. And on our way back from the jungle, while passing by a luxury beach speckled with tourists gleaming of sunscreen, I thought: Damn it, do these people really not realise that mere metres away a war has been fought on matters of life and death?

I realised, as a forty-year-old, I had rediscovered the fun of our childhood games. And not just any game, but indeed a game that is much more real than what they claim reality itself is.

Because climbing is of course exactly that, fun and games. We do not need to master climbing steep walls. There is no food to be found there, and hence other forms of exercise like running, swimming, riding a horse or going skiing are much more likely to bring food to the table the day the power grid shuts down. Climbing is as close to the premise of child's play as you can get – 'Hey, let's see who's able to climb up there!' And as I continued to pursue climbing, it was with a certain level of bewilderment I realised that despite the fact that it's pure fun and games, many are willing to sacrifice time, sweat and tears to become good climbers. Or at least better. Myself included. But I also realised that very few of those who were putting in the effort were basing their training on anything other than what they had picked up from other climbers, experiences from other sports and personal ideas and experiences with what seemed to provide progress with their climbing. In a time where the science of training in even the tiniest of sports has been professionalised, scrutinised and analysed – why not also climbing? As an outsider coming to climbing from other sports, it was with wonderment I came to realise that systematic training was frowned upon by a large portion of the climbing community. Perhaps related to the somewhat unclear standards of climbing – the 'real' connection with nature versus the competitive ideals of the industrial society, the natural talent versus targeted routines. But the fact is that even though the goal of these childish games is to have fun, getting better at the game is also part of the game. And I think now there is a trend towards perceiving training not just as a part of, but as an extension of the game. Most of us – we who shall not go down in climbing history – can find deep satisfaction in setting personal goals and achieving them with the means we have at our disposal, be it technical talent, strength, attitude and mentality, playfulness, discipline or sheer power of will. This is why a book addressing improving one's technique, training methods, strategy and injury prevention is welcome as an extension of this game of ours, as a tool in the challenge to see 'who's able to climb up there!'

As I'm writing this, I have just completed the hike down from Kolsåstoppen, near Oslo, after battling loose holds, basalt, and rhomb-porphyry, and have met smiling passers-by greeting me with: 'Having fun in the sun, are we?' And I have smiled back and thought: They know nothing.

Maria Davies Sandbu on *Un Petit Hueco Dans Rocklands* (Font 7b+), Rocklands, South Africa.

THE REASON WE write this book is twofold. Firstly, the interest in climbing has never been greater. While climbing as an outdoor activity used to be characterised as alternative and even a bit weird, the sport of climbing has now become commonplace. More and more people are seeking climbing as a fun and challenging activity and form of exercise, both indoors and outdoors. Secondly, after over two decades of climbing as a passion and job, we wanted to gather and present in writing our documented and experience-based knowledge to provide the tools and inspiration needed for both new and more experienced climbers to take their own climbing to new heights.

This book highlights technical, physical and mental performance factors and how these can be trained so you can raise your climbing level. Further topics are tactics, how to plan your training and injury prevention measures. Our goal is to provide you with practical tools to raise your level and to help children, adolescents and adults stay injury free and enjoy as much of this wonderful sport as we have over the last 20 years.

HOW TO READ THIS BOOK

This book is built around the three classic performance factors in climbing: technical, physical and mental. In the technique chapter, we cover various foundations for all movements on the wall and more specific techniques, before we conclude with tips on how to train these on your own. The physical training chapter focuses on specific strength, endurance and mobility training for climbing; a separate chapter is devoted to general strength and injury prevention, in which we present basic principles on how you can reduce the risk of injury, and a brief overview of common climbing-related injuries. The chapter on mental training deals with mental characteristics that are central to climbing performance and how these can be trained. The book also looks at tactics and training planning and is seasoned with shorter topics such as friction, skincare and tales about good training environments and people or stories which have inspired us.

The chapters are structured so that the most basic information comes first, before moving into more in-depth topics towards the ends of the chapters. For example, the descriptions of various techniques starts with the most basic and ends with the most advanced – which you are unlikely to need until you are climbing at a relatively high level.

Movements in climbing are varied in the sense that no two movements are ever quite the same. It is important to build a large repertoire of movements when you start climbing. We therefore recommend that less experienced climbers focus on the chapters on technique and mental training. Various techniques are presented here; when they fit and how they can be trained. Advanced climbers will find that all chapters have relevant parts, because climbing is a complex sport and it is important not to specialise too much in one area if you want to improve. Nevertheless, you should become aware of your own strengths and weaknesses and prioritise your training focus based on the area in which you want to perform. There is a big difference between training for indoor bouldering competitions and preparing for long, pumpy outdoor sport routes. By reading this book we hope to help you with this process by giving you the tools, motivation and some inspiration on your way to new heights.

At the very back of the book you'll find a list of words and expressions we climbers like to use, both at the crag and when writing books like this.

Stian Christophersen on *Trøbbel*
(Font 8a+), Harbak, Norway.

WHAT CAN HISTORY TEACH US?

Climbing today is a combination of play and training, with and without a rope, performed both indoors and outdoors. It is our clear belief that all aspects of climbing are important for maintaining motivation over time and improvement. The communities and generations that have fostered strong climbers here in Norway – because it is often a certain community or generation that has distinguished itself – have often been those who have embraced the various multitudes of climbing. They have alternated between running hard workouts and competition-like bouldering indoors, and have gone on both short and long bouldering and sport climbing trips to play on real rock both at home and abroad. They have done these activities together and helped raise each other to the next level in the process. Because if you think about it, it's hard to become a great climber on your own. Someone has to spot you and belay you, and discussing beta with a friend is a huge advantage. Your community will also push you during training and make sure you have fun when on your climbing travels.

PLAY AND TRAINING

As Jo writes in his foreword, in many ways climbing is divided between the two slightly contradictory elements of play and training. Play is perhaps the element which best characterises climbing when compared to more traditional forms of exercise like running or weightlifting. Picture your average bouldering session: you're sitting on the mat, chatting about this and that, discussing moves, and every now and then you try a boulder. You roll across the mat after failing on a dyno move while your friends are laughing. For most of us this closely resembles the play of our childhood memories. On the other hand, we typically associate training for climbing with fingerboarding, pumped forearms and stretching. You might decide to do a route five times in a row to build endurance for the project you're working on. This is tiresome and painful, and most people would not consider this playing.

Many climbers prefer playing and try really hard to avoid what they consider training, while other climbers love to train and forget to play all together. Because you are reading this book you probably have the intention to improve as a climber. To achieve this you must train, but you should also not forget to play. Playing is just as important in order to improve as a climber as it is to crimp on the fingerboard or repeat routes until you're pumped. It's typically when you're playing that you learn new intricacies of technical movements, and playing will keep climbing from becoming boring and monotonous like other forms of training might be. At the same time, by training specifically on technical, mental and physical factors, you'll be more consciously aware of how you're moving on the wall, and increase both your physical and mental fitness. Combining targeted training and play will make you a better climber, and they should not be seen as contradicting elements, but instead as symbiotic building blocks.

And remember, even the more traditional forms of training can be made to feel more like play. Many of the best athletes credit their performance to having fun all the time, even when training. So play and have fun every time you train!

ABOUT TRAINING PHILOSOPHY

In many countries there has been quite a physical focus on training philosophy for many years. In countries such as Japan, a focus on playing with movements is stronger, and there is less focus on the physical. We might be going out on a limb here, but we believe that some climbers have placed too much emphasis on physical training and this is reflected in their climbing – we often see climbers with poor technique. From our own time as competition climbers in Norway, we were told that we had to distinguish between training and climbing. This is a logical distinction, but it is important to emphasise that one should not exclude the other. You can distinguish between sessions where the focus is more on play and sessions where you train specifically, but do not focus on one at the expense of the other.

The lack of good holds for hands and feet emphasises the importance of good technique. Siri Olimb Myhre gliding up *Oppvarmingseggen* (Font 6c+), Harbak, Norway.

PHOTO: BJØRN HELGE RØNNING

CHAPTER 1

TECHNIQUE

CLIMBING IS DEFINED as a technical strength sport. In other words, technique is one of the most important elements to master, but for many it will also be the most difficult. So, what is technique, and, perhaps more importantly, what is good technique? If you see a child who has never moved up a wall before, it will have an intuitive understanding of maintaining balance on the wall. This is an example of good technique. Similarly, we often see that beginner climbers who have a good physical foundation tend to rely on their arms to get up the wall. This is an example of poor technique. Technique therefore has to do with maintaining balance and conserving power. But is this all, and is there a universal answer to what is good technique? We want to argue that there are a number of basic movements and positions that are universal. At the same time, physical and mental abilities and limitations will allow for great variation in how the various techniques are used.

This chapter presents grip positions, footwork, foundations and specific techniques. We also look at which of these are suitable for different types of climbing. Finally, there are tips on how to train technique.

GRIP POSITIONS

It's important for us as climbers to master the different types of grip positions. Holds, like slopers, pockets and crimps – and how best to grab them – vary greatly. Many routes and boulder problems demand use of several, if not all, of the different grip positions. We have chosen to categorise grip positions into the following types:

- open hand
- pinch
- half crimp
- crimp

Some grip positions are more aggressive than others. An aggressive grip position means that the middle joint in the fingers is bent at an angle of 90 degrees or more, which leads to a greater activation of the shoulders and arms. An aggressive grip position allows for bigger and more explosive movements, while a less aggressive grip lends itself to more careful and precise climbing. The grip position is often dictated by the hold, but the use of different types of grip position on the same hold can also allow for different ways of moving your body.

Stian Christophersen om *Fokus* (Font 8a+), Harbak, Norway. Stian is crimping hard with his left hand while reaching for the crux pinch.

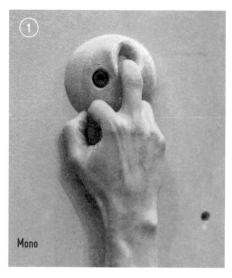

Mono

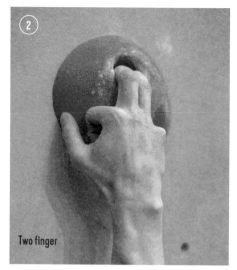

Two finger

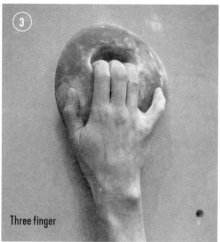

Three finger

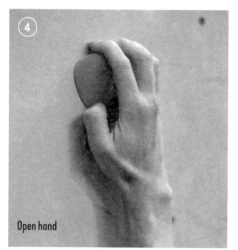

Open hand

Holds 1–3 are what we call pockets.

OPEN HAND

This is the most common grip position and it can be used on most holds. Most of the flexion and load is focused on the outermost joint. Climbers can use one to four fingers in this position. The number of fingers engaged is usually based on the shape and size of the hold.

It's worth noting that once you add the pinkie finger to this grip position, you engage your arm and shoulders and the grip position becomes more aggressive. This is because when you engage the pinkie the angle of the middle joint on the other three fingers is reduced.

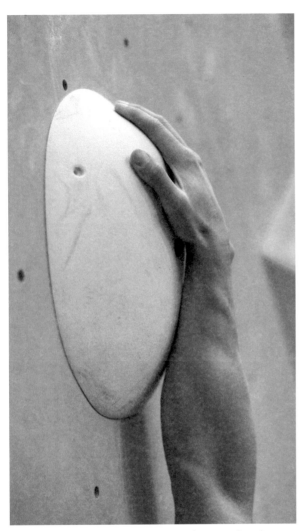

This photo shows the correct grip position on a sloper, providing a large contact area between the hold and the hand, and hence more friction.

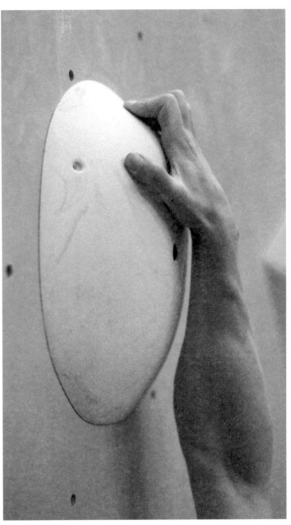

This photo shows a half-crimp grip position on a sloper, which reduces the contact area and therefore the friction.

The open-hand grip position is especially handy for large holds and pockets, but can also be used for smaller edges as long they aren't too thin. Open hand grip is the preferred grip position for lead climbing as the physical cost is lower than with other types of grip position. It is assumed that the fingers are less prone to injuries when using an open-hand grip position instead of more aggressive grip positions.

When climbing on slopers, as in holds that have a negative angle, a variant of the open-hand grip position is usually used. The goal is to maximise the contact area between the hold and the hand and fingers. More contact area means more friction, as demonstrated in the photos above.

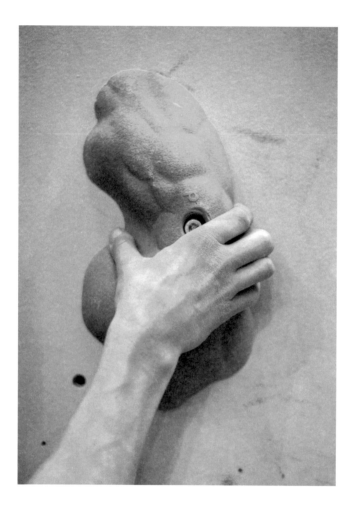

PINCH

As the name implies, this grip position is for when you have to pinch around both sides of a hold. Your thumb is on one side while your other fingers are countering on the other side. By squeezing the hold like this you can keep body tension on the wall in ways which other grip positions won't allow. But pinching requires strength and many climbers struggle with this grip position.

On indoor climbing walls the holds are mounted in such a way that they protrude from the wall and this allows climbers to pinch almost any indoor hold. Some types of rock, like limestone with tufa features, also allow for pinching to be used outside.

HALF CRIMP

The half crimp is suitable for smaller holds and edges. The middle joint of the fingers is bent, and the outer joint is straight. The half crimp is a more aggressive grip position than the open hand and is better suited for when the moves are long or the wall is steep and the positions demanding. Half crimp is commonly used in bouldering and for crux sections when lead climbing. Using a half crimp is more physically taxing than climbing with an open hand because more muscles are involved, but it also allows for a higher exertion of force.

CRIMP

Crimping is suited to really small edges and when moving explosively between small holds. The grip position is similar to the half crimp, but you also engage the thumb to lock the fingers in a bent position. This is the most aggressive grip position and it should only be used when necessary.

It might seem that this should be the preferred grip position for any situation, and for many climbers it is. The catch is that crimping is the most aggressive type of grip position, and it is closely related to injuries to pulleys, cartilage, bones and sinews. Crimping with care and learning how and when to use the other types of grip positions can reduce the chance of injuries, and as the crimp has some clear performance advantages we are going to cover the topic and keep on crimping.

Children and adolescents whose finger joints are still developing should not crimp.

WHY DO WE CRIMP?

Have you ever wondered how bats manage to hang upside down when they sleep? And what does this have to do with crimping?

As many of you have probably experienced, it's easier to hold on to smaller holds when you lock your thumb over the outermost part of the index finger than if you use an open hand or half crimp. Many also resort to crimping when they are getting pumped, so it's obvious that this grip position provides some advantages. But why?

There are several reasons why we might choose to crimp small holds. First and foremost, we get help from an extra finger, the thumb, to generate force in the crimp. By crimping instead of using an open-hand grip position, we also increase the contact area between the hold and the fingertips, providing better friction and allowing us to hang on to smaller holds and in-cuts. These two factors can explain why we choose to crimp, but there is more. When crimping, the angle of the finger joints is in a better position for exerting power than when using an open hand. In addition, the friction between the tendon and the tendon sheath will increase, and this friction is estimated to account for up to nine per cent of the force exerted at the middle joint of the finger. This means that we can either relieve the musculature by nine per cent or get nine per cent more power in a grip position at maximum muscular exertion. This mechanism is called the Tendon Locking Mechanism (TLM) and is the main reason why bats can hang by their toes and sleep with the minimal use of muscular forces.

VARYING GRIPS

Many climbers favour a particular type of grip position and this often has to do with genetic factors. Climbers with small hands prefer edges and crimps and will be at a disadvantage on wide pinches where large hands are an advantage. It is important to train and practise with all the different grip positions in order to be able to adapt to the various challenges you'll face on the wall. That being said, many climbers are also able to use their favourite grip position on most holds. Climbers who spend a lot of their time outdoors often resort to crimping, even when they venture indoors. This is not necessarily wrong, but anyone who wants to become a complete climber should clearly train and practise all the different grip positions. Because of the risk of injury, children and beginners should avoid crimping.

FOOTWORK

Your legs and feet can and should take a large part of the force needed to keep you on the wall. This requires proper positioning of the feet. There is a big difference between how you should place your feet when smearing your shoes on a sloper or edging your toes on a small edge, and walls at different angles add to the complexity. There are also different shoes designed for different applications.

First and foremost, it is important to place your foot precisely on the foothold. It is important that you as a climber look at your foot as you place it. Too often, we see climbers falling because their foot slipped after they placed it haphazardly without looking. Particularly for beginners, this is a recurring problem. It is easy to forget about your feet because you are looking up and focusing on the next handhold. And when nerves or stamina starts to become an issue, imprecise footwork is common. Remember that a small foothold can have a tiny recess that's hard to spot, which can be crucial for whether your foot will stick or slip. In other words, footwork requires precision and focus. Take a moment to observe experienced climbers on the wall; it is often impossible to hear when they place their foot on a hold. Their footwork is extremely precise so that they can get the most out of their feet.

- Look at the foothold and place your foot gently and with precision.
- Lower both your body and your heel when smearing on larger holds.

It's important to lower both your body and your heel when smearing on volumes or larger holds in order to increase the contact area, and hence the friction, between the hold and your shoe.

Both the inside and the outside edge of the shoe, as well as the tip, can be used for edging on small holds.

1. EDGING

On small edges it is important to use the edging properties of your climbing shoes. Climbing shoes are relatively stiff, and by precisely placing the edge of the shoe you can quite securely stand on holds that are just a few millimetres deep. You can edge with the outside edge, the inside edge and the tip of the shoes. Which technique is best depends on your body position and the foothold. If you're standing sideways against the wall, use the outside edge or the tip of your shoe. If you are facing the wall, use the inside edge or the tip of your shoe. On very small footholds it will be best to use the tip of your shoe as this is what most shoes are designed for. Not all shoes are created equal, and which model and brand is best for which purpose will vary, but as long as the shoes aren't too soft, most shoes will provide good support on small footholds. But be aware that old and worn shoes will have lost much of their edging properties, so if you know you're going to be climbing on the edge you should think about which shoes to use.

2. SMEARING

When standing on slopers, volumes or directly on the wall, it is the friction between your shoe and the foothold that enables you to stand. This is known as smearing. Imagine trying to rub or smear the rubber of your shoes on the foothold. The contact area between your shoe and the foothold is crucial for how well your foot will be able to stick to the foothold. Lowering your heel will increase the shoe's surface area in contact with the foothold. If you try to use the edge of your climbing shoe, the contact area will be smaller which will increase the risk of your shoe losing grip and slipping off. You can smear on basically any surface, and the technique is often used to maintain balance and as an intermediate step when moving your feet up to better footholds.

3. VOLUMES AND LARGE FOOTHOLDS

When standing on a large foothold that protrudes significantly from the wall, it is advantageous to stand as far out on the foothold as possible. The reason for this is that you can lean more towards the wall and the load on the handholds is therefore lower. Very often we see inexperienced climbers place their feet closer to the wall when standing on volumes because this feels safer. This greatly increases the load on the fingers and arms as, in practice, you're making the wall steeper.

CLIMBING SHOES

The steepness of the wall will often dictate how you use your feet. If the angle of the wall is less than 90 degrees (a slab), it is generally better to use soft shoes so that you get the full effect of the rubber smearing on the wall. On vertical walls, stiffer shoes with good edging qualities are more appropriate. On steep overhangs, aggressive shoes will allow you to pull on the footholds with your toes. Aggressive shoes have a downturned, banana-like shape that helps translate force from your foot on to the foothold.

Indoors, and on most occasions outdoors, it's necessary to have shoes that offer both edging and smearing capabilities. Many shoe models combine these qualities well, and they are well suited for beginners and indoor climbers. As you gain more experience, it can be wise to carry several different models in your bag for different applications. An aggressive shoe for steep climbing, a soft shoe for smearing indoors and a rigid shoe for outdoor climbing.

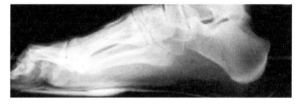

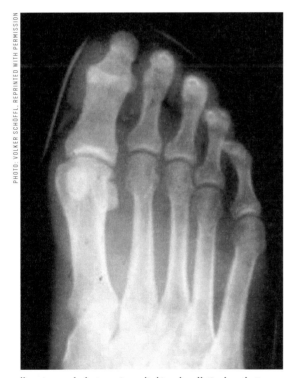

PHOTO: VOLKER SCHÖFFL, REPRINTED WITH PERMISSION

X-ray image of a foot wearing a climbing shoe. Notice how the toes are squeezed together by the tight-fitting shoe. Find a shoe that fits your foot, and let your feet rest by regularly taking your shoes off during your training or climbing session.

BUYING SHOES

The number one factor when buying shoes is the fit! The fit of climbing shoes varies wildly between different brands and models. Be the annoying customer in the shop and try on all the different models they stock in order to make sure you find the shoe that best fits your foot. Climbing shoes will adapt to your foot and expand somewhat with use, but it is important that your foot fills the entire volume of the shoe, both in the toe box and in the heel cup. It's also important that the shoes aren't too small – too often beginners are advised to get the smallest shoes they can fit their feet into, and that pain is to be expected. The point of tight-fitting shoes is to maintain a stiff front tip, which is only really necessary when climbing outdoors on really tiny footholds. The smearing capabilities are also reduced if the shoe is too small.

THE FUNDAMENTALS

The fundamentals are the founding principles to which we must always adhere, regardless of what type of movement we are about to execute. We have chosen to define the following fundamentals:

- balance and weight distribution
- force vector and tension
- static and dynamic climbing styles.

Our reason for choosing these three is that they are essential for any movement we perform on the wall. No matter how we move, there's a redistribution of weight, and there's always a choice between doing a move with speed (dynamically) or by locking off (static). In order to use a hold in the best possible way, we're dependent on the force acting in the correct direction. Often we also utilise the force acting between two points of contact on the wall, for example between two handholds or between a handhold and a foothold. This is what we call tension.

The climber lowers her body underneath the handhold in order to relieve the arms and achieve a better angle relative to the handhold.

The centre of gravity is centred between a relatively wide area of support.

1. BALANCE AND WEIGHT DISTRIBUTION

It's important to keep your balance in order to expend as little energy as possible. In sports science we define the athlete to be in balance when the centre of gravity is centred on the area of support. The centre of gravity is the point where the weight of your body is centred, usually just below the navel. The area of support is the area between the points of your body touching the ground. If you're standing on the ground and place your legs on each side of your body you'll be standing safe and securely because your centre of gravity is centred on your area of support. If, on the other hand, your centre of gravity is outside your area of support, you'll be off balance. A wider area of support will give you more room to move without losing your balance. The traction of your points of contact will also increase the amount of movement you can perform securely without losing balance: for example, it's easier to maintain your balance during challenging movements when standing on concrete compared to when standing on ice.

As with any other sport, the climber is in balance when the centre of gravity is confined within the area of support. The area of support for a climber is defined by the contact points on the climbing wall. This includes not just your two feet, but also your hands. A stable balance is best achieved by centring the centre of gravity on the area of support. In order to maintain balance try to always have four points of contact (two hands and two feet) on the wall before initiating a move, and three points when executing a move. In effect, this means that if you want to move one hand, you should have a secure grip position with your other hand and both your feet. A better hold will also increase your ability to move freely on the wall. When climbing on large and positive holds you can lean out from the wall and from side to side. This means you can compensate for poor balance by using better holds, but this isn't possible when using smaller and less positive holds.

In order to maintain good balance, the climber moves her body to the right before she moves her right arm.

As a general rule you should lean in to the wall and below the handholds as much as the available footholds allow. By lowering your body underneath the handholds you will lessen the load on your arms and your body will have a better angle in relation to the handholds. In order to avoid getting more fatigued than is necessary, it is best to hang with your arms straight whenever possible.

Weight transfer is the principle of positioning the body, especially the hips, so that the centre of gravity remains centred on the area of support as we move. The most common form of weight transfer is to move the centre of gravity to the right when moving the right hand, and vice versa. Maintaining your balance usually doesn't require large movements. Quite often, just shifting your hips to the side by a few centimetres is all it takes to stay in balance. By proficient use of weight transfer, you will achieve better balance when moving, increase reach and waste less energy. Weight transfer is the principle behind a large proportion of the techniques we use when climbing and is a basic skill to practise.

Remember that you can place a foot anywhere on the wall to increase the area of support and achieve better balance.

It is important to remember that you must position your body so that it is in balance for the position it will be in *after* you have made a move. Your body may well be in balance as you start a move, but this is of little help if your body is unbalanced when the move is completed. The clearest example of this is the 'barn door' – when the climber loses balance and swings out from the wall.

SIDEPULL EXERCISE

The exercise consists of one right-facing sidepull and three footholds. The three footholds should be evenly spaced horizontally: one foothold directly below the sidepull, and one foothold on each side. Hold the sidepull with your right hand and use only your right foot to stand on the wall. Do not flag with your left foot or use other tricks. It will be easy to maintain balance if you stand on the foothold to the right. You'll also be able to maintain balance when standing on the middle foothold. But you'll lose balance if you stand on the foothold to the left of the sidepull.

Hannah Midtbø using opposing forces between holds to climb a steep boulder problem.

2. DIRECTION OF FORCE AND TENSION

It is only possible to use many of the holds we use when we're climbing because we can apply force in the right direction. Consider a sidepull. If we try to use it like a normal hold and pull straight down, we can't hang on. Instead we have to try to position ourselves so that the force is acting perpendicular to the grip surface. In the same way we have to step up high with our feet in order to use an undercling. Only when we get enough force acting up into the hold are we able to effectively use the undercling.

Sometimes we can use the force acting between holds. We call this tension, which is a term covering all situations where the body is maintaining tension or forces between different points of contact. This can be between two handholds, but also between a handhold and a foothold.

Picture yourself squeezing together two opposing sidepulls in order to achieve tension. We call this compressing between holds, or compression climbing, and this is particularly important when climbing on slopers.

Tension gives us many more options for climbing on holds that wouldn't normally be good enough to hang.

Synnøve Berg Nesheim using a toe hook to create enough tension on a left-hand sidepull.

When climbing overhangs you need to maintain tension all the way through your body, from your fingers to your toes. Understanding how to optimise this tension is difficult. You have to pull with your arms – but not too much or you'll lose contact with your feet! To understand this balance it can be helpful to think of your feet as claws that pull down at the same time as your arms are pulling up.

Your body is stronger than your fingers! If you are exerting more force with your body than is necessary to maintain your position, you might unnecessarily increase the load on your fingers. Optimal load balance requires experience and a lot of time on the wall, and emphasises the importance of practising as much as possible on all kinds of holds and angles.

A static movement pattern is the style of choice when the moves need to be precise and the holds are hard to hit.

3. STATIC AND DYNAMIC CLIMBING STYLE

One of our old climbing coaches and a legend of competition climbing in Norway, Chris Fossli, once said that all movements should optimally be dynamic, but that our 'poor' dynamic abilities inhibit them from being so. This is probably at least partly correct, and we should strive to perform most moves with at least some dynamic elements in order to minimise energy waste. Despite this, where a static style might require a certain level of strength in order to make a move slowly, faster and more dynamic moves will require a faster rate of force development, coordination of arms, legs and body, spatial awareness, and contact strength.

A static move is where one arm is held statically in place without changing its angle, while the other arm moves to the next hold. By definition, all moves are dynamic, but in climbing we use the term dynamic to refer to moves that are quick, and where both arms are in motion. In the same way we use the terms static and dynamic climbing style to describe the way different climbers tend to move on the wall. Static climbers like to move slowly and controlled, while dynamic climbers move faster and 'bounce' between holds. Static climbing is useful when the holds are small or hard to hit, or when climbing on sight when you don't know what and where the next hold is. You reduce the chance of missing the hold, but often end up using more power to lock off. A static style is often preferred on vertical and less steep climbing. In these cases, it's often the size of the holds and the balance required that makes the climbing challenging, and this is more easily overcome with a static and controlled style. Static climbing requires more body strength because you must lock your body in different positions, and climbers with a strong core and shoulders are better suited to this style of climbing.

Big moves are usually performed dynamically.

By executing a move dynamically we can exploit the speed generated at the beginning of a move, without stopping and using unnecessary energy. This is especially relevant for steep climbing. In these cases it is usually the longer moves that are the most challenging, and maintaining the elusive balance is perhaps less crucial. What's more, climbing statically through steep terrain is a lot more physically challenging as it requires more energy to maintain a stable body position during moves.

Climbing dynamically can also be quite effective on slopers. If you pull yourself up slowly on a sloper, your centre of gravity will gradually move away from the wall and the friction will worsen. By dynamically making a move between slopers, you can initiate the move from below, where the angle in relation to the hold is more positive and the friction is better. The principle is the same with poor and slopey footholds. If you pull up, your heels lift, the contact area decreases, and you risk slipping off the foothold. When moving from slopey footholds you should therefore move dynamically and initiate the move from below.

A quick and dynamic move is recognised by a starting phase, a floating phase and a stopping phase, similar to when performing a high jump, or shooting a bullet into the sky. In the starting phase you want to create force using the big muscle groups in your legs and core, but the arms also help to initiate the movement, and guide you in the right direction. It's important that your arms pull your body towards the wall, so that when you grab the next hold your body isn't already moving away from the wall. In the floating phase the arm and the hand must be coordinated in order to precisely hit the next hold.

Deadpointing slopers: the movement starts from below; the centre of gravity is then moved over the left leg and in towards the wall. This allows the left leg to straighten and create an upwards motion, while the right hand maintains grip and keeps the centre of gravity close to the wall. With enough power generated early, more strenuous body positions are bypassed and the next hold is reached at the apex of the move.

A dynamic move obviously needs to be stopped when the next hold is reached. By adapting the amount and direction of power in the starting phase, less energy is needed to stop the movement. A bullet fired straight up into the air will, in principle, be weightless at the apex of its trajectory before it starts to fall back down again. We call this the deadpoint of the trajectory, and it is the preferred time to stop a move. In any case the movement has to be stopped, which requires contact strength. Contact strength is the ability to quickly generate enough power to maintain grip on the next hold and stop the move. Sticking a dynamic move might also require tension in order to lock the body position. Especially if the handholds are poor.

Many climbers find dynamic climbing to be mentally challenging. It's difficult to truly let go and go all-in for the next hold. It feels much safer to make a move statically and with control. This is especially common in the world of sport climbing because of the fear of falling. Dynamic climbing is something that can and should be practised. Especially for shorter climbers, dynamic climbing can be essential, as some moves can be quite reachy. Remember, getting used to a more dynamic style can take time. We have worked with many climbers who are uncomfortable with the risk involved in doing a move more dynamically, and therefore prefer a more static and controlled style. Yet we find these athletes raise their level significantly when adopting a more dynamic climbing style.

PHOTO: GETTY IMAGES

GERMAN DYNAMICS

When climbing dynamically, the movement tends to flow from one hold to another. Udo Neumann, a former coach of the German national team, likens dynamic climbing to the way a monkey swings from branch to branch. They use the transition between the swings in a perfect way when each pendulum movement flows into the next without visible interruptions. In the same way you as a climber can use the energy generated from a move to keep the momentum going into the next move. Most of us have probably experienced stopping and losing all momentum after a dynamic move, and then having to start again from scratch to generate speed for the next big move, but we often see skilled climbers carrying the speed from one move into the next. There are of course many complicating factors, one being that vines aren't climbing holds, but the principle is the same – use the least amount of energy to execute a move! This means dynamic moves and fluid transitions between each move. *'The perfect combination between fast and slow, aka flow.'* – T. Landman.

SPECIFIC TECHNIQUES

In this section we present the specific techniques which are based on the fundamentals presented in the last section. We as climbers strive to choose the different techniques that – based on the challenges we're currently facing on the wall – allow us to use the least amount of energy as possible.

FRONTING

The most common climbing technique is what we call fronting. As the name implies, the chest should be facing the wall, knees pointing out to each side and the hips close to the wall. When moving your right hand, you should first move your hips sideways to the right to maintain balance, and vice versa when moving the left hand. When fronting, it's usually advantageous to lower your body to shift as much weight as possible on to your feet and get a better angle in relation to the handholds. This requires flexible hips. If you try to lower your body without being sufficiently flexible in your hips your centre of gravity will be pushed out from the wall which in turn will increase the load on your fingers. If the handholds are poor you will in most cases lose grip and fall. If the holds are positive you'll have more room to move around, but with your centre of gravity too far out from the wall you will be forced to expend more energy than is necessary. Fronting is the best technique for understanding the importance of weight distribution and balance, where small shifts in body position can greatly influence your balance.

To improve at fronting it is a good idea to train on a vertical wall. You should be using poor handholds and relatively good footholds, and move from side to side to get a feel for when you are in and out of balance. Try to find the position which requires the least amount of energy to stay on the wall.

This technique can be used whether you choose to do a move statically or dynamically. Particularly when making harder and longer moves, doing the move dynamically can be wise in order to save energy. In this case try to use speed to transfer your centre of gravity above your hips and move easily to the next hold without using your arms too much. Fronting is often the technique of choice on vertical walls where the holds are bad and a static style is more appropriate.

ROCKOVER

Rocking over is a specific type of fronting. This technique is useful when moving on to a high foothold and is performed by leaning your hips sideways over the foot, with your knee fully bent. By shifting your centre of gravity over your foot you'll reduce the load on your arms and keep your body up against the wall. This allows you to maintain grip on small and poor handholds. If you're not flexible enough to keep your body up against the wall it can help to place your heel on the foothold instead of your toes. This requires less hip flexibility, but does require a larger foothold. Rocking over is usually done statically and in control, when the holds you're moving from or to are very bad.

TWISTING

As an alternative to fronting, twisting shifts your hips sideways and positions your body to the side of the holds when doing a move. When moving your right hand, your right hip twists in towards the wall, and vice versa.

It's usually easier to reach further when twisting (right) than when fronting.

Twisting has three advantages:
- effective weight transfer on steep terrain
- 'fuel efficient' climbing
- increased reach.

This technique is frequently used when the wall is steeper than vertical. If we observe experienced climbers on steep terrain, we often see them twisting from side to side on every move. By twisting their hips into the wall, they increase their reach without having to pull themselves up with their arms, something which is of obvious advantage on steep walls. Twisting can also be used for vertical climbing, especially by those who aren't flexible enough to get their body close enough to the wall by fronting.

An extreme example of twisting is the drop knee. Drop knee is when we're twisting even further, sometimes even pushing the knee below the level of the foothold. This can be a useful technique when using a high foothold. The alternative would be to front, but using a drop knee requires less power to keep the body close to the wall and the centre of gravity centred on the area of support.

An example of a drop knee.

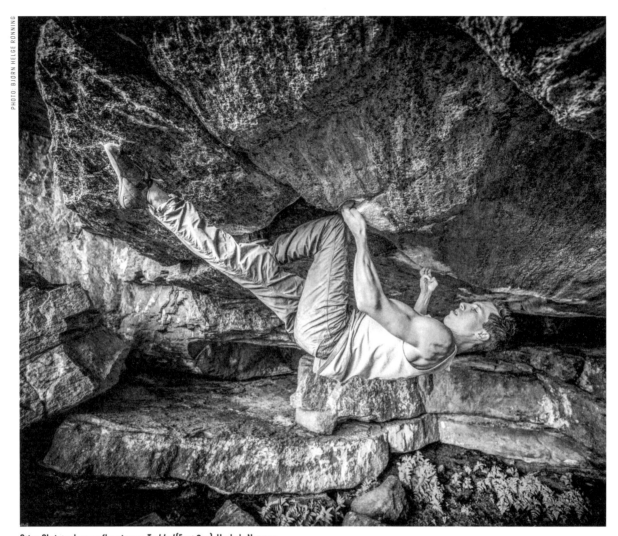

PHOTO: BJØRN HELGE RØNNING

Stian Christophersen flagging on *Trøbbel* (Font 8a+), Harbak, Norway.

FLAGGING

'Flag like a nationalist' is how Mats Peder Mosti describes the beta on his classic boulder problem *Trøbbel* at Harbak outside Trondheim in Norway.

Flagging is an alternative to twisting for finding balance through a move. Flagging is when you cross your free leg behind or in front of the leg you're standing on. Which way you flag will depend on the height of the foothold. Flagging can be used on both vertical and overhanging climbing to create a larger area of support and to balance your centre of gravity.

In most cases where flagging is an option it will also be possible to match your feet and twist your hips in, but this might be difficult if the footholds are small, and it's usually more efficient to just cross your legs and flag. Flagging is a very useful technique on all wall angles as you can spend less energy doing moves.

PHOTO: BJØRN HELGE RØNNING

Hannah Midtbø winning the 2017 Nordic Bouldering Championship in Oslo.

The grip surface is the side of the hold you grip. The grip surface of a right-hand sidepull is on the right side. It's important to direct the force towards the grip surface, in this case towards the left.

SIDEPULLS, GASTONS AND UNDERCLINGS

In order to exert any force to the hold when climbing on sidepulls, it's important to find footholds which push or pull your centre of gravity to the opposite side of the grip surface. This ensures the direction of the force is directed on to the grip surface, allowing you to use the hold. It's helpful to try different foot placements to see how this affects your balance; it's often possible to find your balance by shifting your weight distribution, and you can switch between twisting and fronting when using sidepulls.

A gaston, or shoulder press, is when you use the opposite hand from that which you would normally use on a sidepull. This flips the script when it comes to body placement and balance. When using a gaston, your centre of gravity should be on the same side of the hold as the grip surface. This allows you to generate force and 'push' away from the hold. Your centre of gravity will then shift away from the handhold as you do the move. It is most common to front when using a gaston, but twisting can sometimes be the way to go. Using a gaston is physically demanding and requires strength in your shoulders and arms.

Joakim Louis Sæther has positioned his body so that he can use a left shoulder press to push himself to the right towards the next hold.

These three examples show the same move from an undercling but using a foothold at three different heights. In the first example the foothold is too low for the climber to be able to comfortably reach the next handhold, and in the second example the foothold is too high, pushing the climber's centre of gravity out from the wall. Example three shows the ideal foot placement.

An undercling is where the grip surface is underneath the hold. These holds can be used when there is a foothold below that allows force to be directed up into the handhold. In general, it's easier to use underclings if the footholds are higher, rather than lower, in relation to the handhold. This is because you can generate more power, and hence increase use of the undercling as your centre of gravity moves upwards. If your centre of gravity passes above the undercling, things start to get harder, as your weight is forced out from the wall. When making long moves which shift your centre of gravity above the undercling, it's advantageous to do these dynamically in order to minimise the time your body is in this physically demanding position.

LAYBACK

When climbing along an edge or a crack, or when using multiple sidepulls in sequence, it's impossible to ignore the technique known as laybacking. Laybacking is when you lean back and away from the holds. In the same way as when using a normal sidepull, your centre of gravity must be on the opposite side to the grip surface. The most common method is to twist and place your hips sideways against the wall, but laybacking can also be done by fronting. The position of the footholds will dictate the best way.

This balancing act is usually best performed statically. As your centre of gravity will always be near the perimeter of the area of support when laybacking, maintaining balance is a continuous challenge. In order to avoid swinging out like a barn door, we sometimes have to compensate by doing a move dynamically.

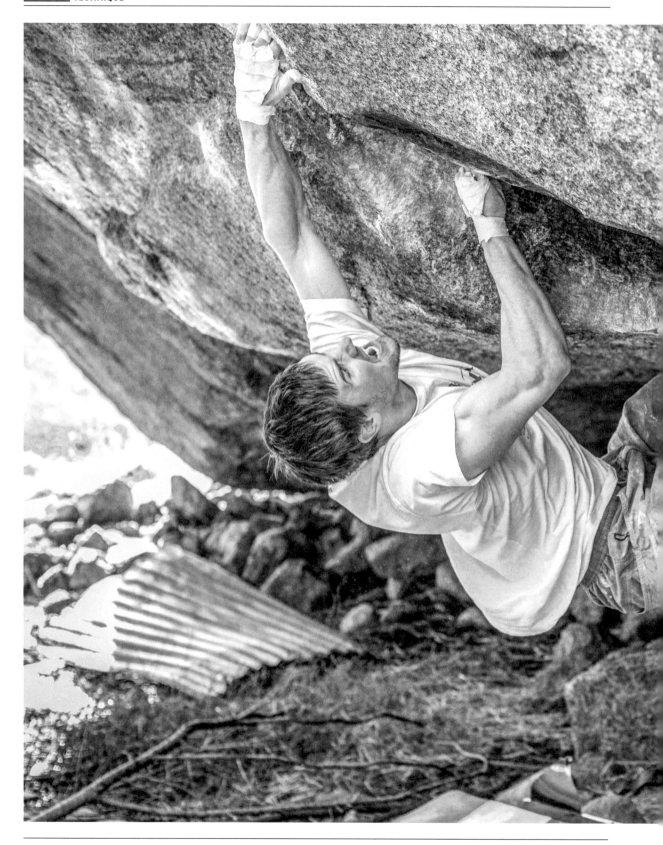

Joakim Louis Sæther jamming on the *Cellar Project* (Font 7c+), Rogaland, Norway.

LOUIS' SCHOOL OF JAMMING

JAMMING IS WHEN you literally jam your hands, fingers or feet into cracks. This technique is most commonly used when climbing cracks outdoors. As we're not expert crack climbers, we've asked Joakim Louis Sæther to write some words about jamming:

Jamming hurts, but mastering this technique can be essential for sending certain routes and boulder problems. Jamming correctly is less painful, but it's still a good idea to tape your hands before you start. The following is a list of some different types of jams:

- finger jam
- hand jam
- fist jam
- stacking
- foot jam.

FINGER JAM

The best finger jams are also the scariest: this is when you can wedge your knuckles into a V-shape (a constriction) in the crack. Finger jams can be placed in many different ways. The thumb can be pointing either up or down, and you can use either one or more fingers in the crack. You should place your fingers into the crack with your elbow pointing out to the side, then twist your elbow down and along the crack. This way you can lock your fingers in place in a parallel crack without getting them completely stuck.

HAND JAM

Pretend to be Master Yoda about to karate chop a rock into two pieces.

Place your flat hand into the crack, fold your thumb in towards your palm and flex your thumb muscle as hard as you can while pressing the tips of your fingers against the inside of the crack. This might hurt a little, but with the proper technique a good hand jam should feel like the best jug in the world! Twist your elbow down along the crack to secure the jam.

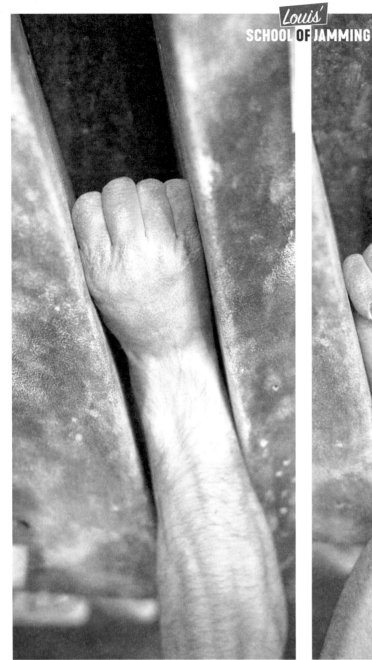

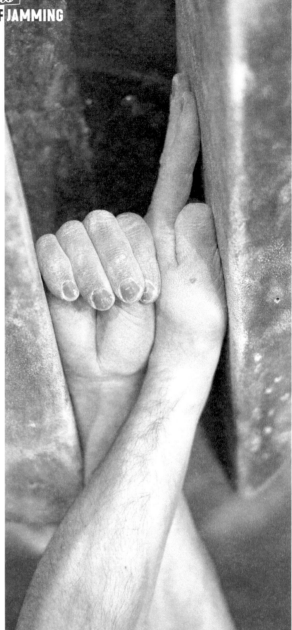

FIST JAM

Have you ever been so angry that you've clenched your fists, ready to throw punches?

Place your fist in an appropriately sized crack. Clench your fist and squeeze so that both sides of your hand expand and push against the sides of the crack. A fist jam is usually more painful than a hand jam. Again, twist your elbow in to secure the jam.

STACKING (COMBINATION JAMS)

If the crack is wider than a fist – usually called an offwidth crack – then you need to combine the different techniques. For example, you can stack two hands, or a hand and a fist, against one another. Which option you choose will depend on the size of the crack.

To find out more about how to climb cracks, check out Pete Whittaker's book *Crack Climbing.*

PETE WHITTAKER

CRACK CLIMBING

FOOT JAM

Easy, but painful! The most common way is to place your foot in the crack sideways with the pinkie toe facing down, and then twist your knee back up along the crack.

The climber lowers herself below the sloper to improve the angle and maximise friction.

She has to shift her centre of gravity out from the wall slightly in order to generate speed towards the next hold. It's important to move out of this position quickly.

CLIMBING ON SLOPERS

Many climbers find climbing on slopers to be the most challenging type of climbing. This is because it requires a great deal of skill when it comes to balance and weight transfer, and often in combination with dynamic moves. There are two factors that are especially important when climbing on slopers:

- The centre of gravity should be kept low and close to the wall.
- Movements should start from below and be dynamic.

Slopers have a negative angle and the force required to execute a move has to be generated from a position where the grip is at its best. This position is below the hold and close to the wall. If we try to pull up statically on a sloper, our centre of gravity will move out from the wall, resulting in a decrease in friction between hand and hold, with falling off being the consequence.

PHOTO: BÅRD LIE HENRIKSEN

The sit-start to *Oppvarmingseggen* (Font 6c+) at Harbak, Norway, is a classic compression problem on slopers.

The optimal way to move between slopers is to use the principle of the deadpoint. As we discussed in the section about dynamics, deadpointing is when you're able to stop at the apex of the move, when your body is 'weightless' and your centre of gravity is close to the wall. When done right, the move is executed from below, where the position is best, and uses as little energy as possible to reach the next hold. Stopping the motion at the deadpoint also minimises the strength required to hang on to the next hold.

As also described earlier, the force created between the points of contact on the wall is what we call tension, and this is central to climbing on slopers. By using slopers with the grip surface in opposing directions we can squeeze our hands together and thereby create more force and increase friction, which is essential to climbing on holds with a negative angle. This is known as compression climbing, and we often hear about 'compression boulder problems', or 'compression moves' when this is the defining attribute of a route or boulder problem. Compression climbing requires a strong upper body, as we use muscles in the upper arms, chest and shoulders to compress between the holds.

STEMMING

Stemming is a technique usually used when climbing inside corners (also known as dihedrals) and it works by pushing your arms and legs against two opposing faces. The angle of the corner influences how much of your weight can be shifted on to your feet. In narrow corners, at angles smaller than 90 degrees, we can almost solely rely on the friction created between hands, shoes and the wall, without the need for positive holds. At angles greater than 90 degrees, the difficulty increases, as does the need for handholds and footholds. The further away from the corner you place your hands and feet when stemming, the better. With a wide stance, you can often rest without using your hands at all. This does require a certain level of hip flexibility.

Climbing corners is usually a static endeavour, where time is spent finding the right placements with enough friction for your hands and feet.

MANTELING

To mantel – or mantelshelf – means to push your body up above your arm(s).
This is particularly useful in two scenarios:

- when topping out a boulder problem or wall
- when scaling large features on the wall, such as a ledge or volume.

You can mantel by using both hands to raise your body over a ledge or feature so that you can get your feet up on to the same hold.

Manteling using only one hand can be a useful technique on large features, allowing you to reach up high to the next hold.

Manteling can be done by only using your arms, or more commonly with your feet as well. When performing a mantel it is essential to have your centre of gravity centred on the area of support. When manteling on to your right hand it's common to place your left foot high and to the left, and vice versa. Good hip flexibility is helpful as it will help you keep your body close to the wall. If you lose balance, there are no positive holds to help keep your body close to the wall. Manteling is usually done statically, but it can sometimes be helpful to start with a bit of speed to help you 'stand' with your arms.

Remember to angle your knee outwards to generate force inwards.

HEEL HOOK

Heel hooking is when you pull in with your heel instead of pushing on the hold with your toe, as you would normally. The two most common uses are:
- high footholds, especially on steep terrain
- to improve the direction of force on the handhold you're using.

You can heel hook around a corner in order to shift your weight sideways and maintain balance.

You can use your heel to relieve some tension and rest your arms when climbing steep walls where the foothold is high.

When climbing steep walls you can often place your heel on holds, as long as they are large enough. This will relieve tension and allow you to rest your arms on steep routes and boulder problems. When the foothold is high you can also use the heel hook to pull your body up and close to the wall, instead of standing on your toe. The heel hook can further be used to alter your balance and the direction you're pulling on a hold, for example, when you're heel hooking with your right foot while pulling on a left hand sidepull.

CHOOSING SHOES FOR HEEL HOOKS

In the same way that some shoes are made for tiny edges and others are more suited to smearing, there are also different types of shoes for different types of heel hooks. A round heel with a large surface is better for heel hooks on larger, more rounded holds, while a narrow heel is better for hooking on edges.

TOE HOOK

Toe hooking is, as the name implies, when you hook your toe around or underneath holds, edges and features. The two most common uses are:
- to improve the direction of force on the handhold you're using
- to keep your feet on the wall on steep terrain.

Synnøve Berg Nesheim uses a toe hook to pull her body rightwards and away from the left hand sidepull.

As with heel hooking, you can use toe hooks to improve the direction of force on the hold you are hanging on. For example, you can use a right foot toe hook to pull your body to the right when you're holding a sidepull with your left hand.

Toe and heel hooks can be used interchangeably, but toe hooks often allow for a longer reach and require less hip flexibility.

By locking your toe underneath holds on overhangs you'll use much less energy keeping your feet on the wall. You can improve the grip of a toe hook by counteracting with your other foot on top of the same or a nearby hold; this is known as bicycling.

In order for a toe hook to work you need to actively use your arms and body to pull your centre of gravity away from the toe hook, and at the same counteract by pulling your body away from the handholds with your toe hook. It is the resulting tension between hands and toe hook that allows us to keep hanging on.

If we lose tension between the holds, the toe hook, the hand, or both, we will most likely slip. Toe hooking requires a great deal of both arm and core strength.

Bicycling.

CHOOSING SHOES FOR TOE HOOKS

Different shoes will work with different types of toe hooks. In general, you want a flat shoe with as much of the upper covered with rubber as possible. Aggressive down-turned shoes often don't have a large enough contact surface. Soft shoes can work well, especially if they are soft enough for the toes to be able to curl up slightly.

DYNO

We define a dyno as a move where you're off the wall with at least three points of contact as you go for the next handhold. This technique requires a lot of strength and coordination and many find it mentally challenging.

In order to create enough energy to do a big dyno it's important to start the movement in the legs. In practice, this means lowering your body and straightening your arms as much as the position allows for, and then pushing off with your legs. The energy has to be directed towards the next hold, and in a way that keeps your body as close to the wall as possible as you reach the next hold. This is accomplished by using your arms to pull your body close to the wall and steer you in the right direction as you launch with your legs.

It can be physically challenging to hang on after sticking a dyno because of the resulting swing. It's therefore important to have good contact strength in the fingers and arms when doing dynos. Good contact strength will help you pull up as you land the next hold. This can help reduce the swing, which will make it easier to hang on and not lose grip.

Dynos require coordination, and it's important to practise regularly. By practising moves like these, over time your body will learn the nuances which separate success from failure.

Continuously exposing yourself to the mental challenges of dynos and dynamic climbing can build the confidence needed for such moves. Time and time again we've seen climbers who initially struggle with dynos and dynamic moves get better and better as they keep challenging themselves. It's important that coaches and climbing partners do not push too hard, and instead let the climber control the rate of their own progression. Remember that some prefer to climb with less risk involved, while others jump right into things without much thinking.

POGO

The pogo – or ninja-kick as it is also known – uses one of your legs as a pendulum to create extra momentum to help you do a dynamic move. By swinging your foot down and behind you before exploding up and forwards, and at the same time pulling your body up and in towards the wall with your arms, you can do big moves from low body positions. And it's in these exact situations where this technique is useful: when the footholds and your body are so low that you can't create enough upwards momentum by doing an ordinary dyno.

The pogo is a complicated technique to master. It requires a great deal of coordination to pull it off correctly, but when done right it can provide the solution to an otherwise impossible move.

Hannah Midtbø 'flicks' her left hand from the starting hold to the pyramid. This way she prevents the barn door effect which would otherwise have swung her off the wall had she only used her right hand.

FLICK, CLUTCH AND MODERN BOULDERING MOVES

Flick and clutch moves have become popular in bouldering competitions as they require a high level of coordination and they look spectacular. The holds have to be placed in exact positions in relation to one other for it to be necessary to do these moves. It's therefore quite rare to encounter moves like this outdoors.

A flick is when you immediately turn your first hand, the one left behind on the starting hold, just as your second hand hits the next hold. This can be necessary when the position your body ends up in as you get to the next hold is impossible to maintain.

An alternative to the flick is to immediately match on the foothold and move your feet as you land the next handhold. As illustrated in the example above, by moving her feet to the next foothold and thereby increasing her area of support, the climber is able to maintain balance as she grabs the handhold with her right hand.

A classic example is when you do a dynamic move to a sidepull and at the same time jump your feet out to a volume to obtain balance as you grab the handhold.

A clutch move is when you immediately continue onwards with either one or both hands to the next hold, if the first hold reached isn't good enough on its own. For example, on a dyno, where the first hold you jump to is too poor to hold, but you continue the momentum up and go for the next and better hold.

Indoor bouldering (especially bouldering competitions) has proven a popular scene for challenging climbers with a combination of moves like the ones described above. A dyno, a clutch and multiple foot matches can all be combined into one single 'move'. The combinations are endless. Modern bouldering competitions are starting to resemble parkour or circus acts, and the 'tricks' described here require a lot of coordination to pull off. You should practise these techniques if you want to be a competition climber, but these skills are rarely needed in outdoor climbing. You should decide what type of climber you want to be, and plan your training accordingly.

PHOTO: BJØRN HELGE RØNNING

WALL ANGLES AND TECHNIQUE

In this section we will describe the fundamentals and techniques that are most useful for different angles of wall. This will be helpful in understanding which techniques will be most useful before you throw yourself at slabs and steep overhangs. We will also provide a useful overview of the different techniques used indoors vs outdoors.

Gina Didriksen stays calm on a tricky slab at Harbak, Norway.

SLABS

'On slabs we are all equal.' This is a well-known saying in the world of climbing, meaning that a big and strong upper body is of no help on slabs.

Slabs are walls with an angle of less than 90 degrees (0 degrees being flat ground). Minute differences in angle on different sections of a wall can greatly impact the climbing experience. Indoor slabs usually have an angle of 87 to 83 degrees, but outdoors you'll find slabs as easy-angled as 70 degrees. This translates to a 'strenuous walk', where your hands are used only for support and balance. When climbing on slabs it's important to lower your heels to maximise the friction between your shoes and the wall. Friction is, as previously mentioned, dependent on the contact surface, and a lowered heel increases the contact surface between your shoe and the wall.

Climbing outdoor slabs is mostly about trusting the friction between your shoes and the wall. You have to climb with confidence, and lower your body and poke your rear away from the wall a little in order to achieve optimal friction. Climbing slowly and taking your time to find your balance is usually the best approach. Most times you will want to be fronting, and only rarely is it necessary to twist your hips in. Indoor slabs often feature dynamic moves that require coordination.

Remember to use soft shoes and to take your time.

VERTICAL CLIMBING

Vertical walls have an angle of exactly 90 degrees. Balance and weight transfer are truly crucial elements, and vertical climbing usually demands a relatively calm and controlled style. This is because the difficulty of vertical climbs is often a result of the size and shape of the holds, requiring us to continuously seek positions that reduce the load on our fingers and arms. Even though most moves will be static, some will require a more dynamic approach. Remember that in these cases you have to be very precise, as the holds can be rather small. More often than not it's better to be fronting on the wall, as long as your flexibility is not a hindrance.

The most common rock type here in Norway is granite. Granite usually involves clean lines and small edges for hands and feet. In order to use such holds efficiently you'll need to climb with precision and use shoes with stiff edges that allow you to stand in a stable position and relax your fingers and hands as much as possible. Other rock types and indoor holds are often less positive, but larger in size. This type of climbing is more dynamic and softer shoes allow you to smear the footholds.

Shift your body weight on to your feet, and be precise when placing your hands and feet.

Theo Moore going for the on-sight on *The Minotaur* (E5 6a), Huntsman's Leap, Pembroke, Wales.

OVERHANGS

Overhangs are walls with an angle which is steeper than 90 degrees. The steeper the wall, the more physically demanding the climbing will be; using techniques that lessen the physical impact is essential. Examples include the toe and heel hook, twisting in, and a dynamic climbing style.

The holds are often bigger in overhangs than on vertical walls, and it is usually the distance between the holds that dictates the difficulty of a climb. This favours a dynamic movement pattern. When the climbing gets steeper, twisting in becomes the technique of choice as this reduces the physical impact. Heel hooks and toe hooks are often really useful. A well-placed heel hook can provide a rest for your arms, and both heel and toe hooks can be used to keep your body close to the wall and to better align the direction of force on the holds.

When climbing overhangs it's important to maintain body tension in order to keep pressure on the footholds as you climb. As discussed earlier, we use the term tension to describe the force acting between the different points of contact on the wall. On an overhang it's vital to maintain tension between hands and feet. We often see climbers focus only on the tension between their hands, which results in a loss of pressure on the footholds as they pull their body up. You should instead try to 'pull' your body down using your toes to maintain pressure. To help you maintain this pressure we highly recommend aggressive shoes with down-turned toes. Some shoes are so soft that you can curl your toes behind the hold where possible. Legendary American climber Dave Graham says he regards his feet as claws, gripping the footholds to keep his feet on the wall.

 Twist in, maintain pressure through your feet and move swiftly!

PHOTO: MIKE HUTTON

Tom Randall on *The Spider* (F8a),
Chee Dale, Peak District, England.

Mari Augusta Salvesen dispatches
The Rhino (Font 7b+), Rocklands, South Africa.

ROOFS

Roof climbing is, as the name implies, climbing on walls with an angle that is near horizontal (180 degrees). This is the most physically demanding type of climbing, but luckily there are some tricks you can use. Just like when climbing overhangs, there's less of a need for techniques that focus on balance. The focus is instead on dynamic climbing and trying to reduce the load on your fingers and arms.

When climbing roofs you should actively use toe and heel hooks to unload fingers and to avoid big swings that will inevitably occur if you lose tension on the footholds. Bicycling footholds is especially common to keep your feet on the wall and to make the climbing less physical. Twisting in is, for the same reason, the technique of choice.

As with overhangs, soft and aggressive shoes are the best for climbing roofs as they allow you to curl your toes behind footholds, thus helping you keep your feet on the wall.

Use any trick in the book to keep your feet on the wall!

'LEARN TO DO BY KNOWING
AND TO KNOW BY DOING.'
JOHN DEWEY

TECHNIQUE TRAINING

In a way, we are all training our technique every time we go climbing. Every time we put on our climbing shoes and move around on the wall we're practising different techniques and constantly assessing whether to move dynamically or statically, and how to adjust our balance. But you should still set aside some sessions to focus specifically on certain techniques to ensure the quality of the training. Such sessions should follow these guidelines:

- You should be well rested, motivated and curious.
- You should define focus areas in advance.
- During the session, maintain focus:
  - *How should the move be executed?*
  - *How am I executing the move?*
  - *How can I improve the execution?*

The first point is perhaps the most simple. Yet we still see many climbers fall victim of the temptation to train hard and physical when they feel fit and rested. Technique can be trained on its own or as part of a climbing session, but it should never immediately follow a physically demanding session as you will be less focused. Technique training is about discovering new movement patterns and nuances of your already established techniques. You need to be fresh, motivated and curious to challenge the status quo, and be open to new ideas from your peers.

For technique training to be effective you should define one or more focus areas. These should be based on your weaknesses as a climber. Some climbers are well aware of their strengths and weaknesses, while others are not. Those of you who are unaware should seek help from either a close friend or an experienced coach who can point out areas you should focus on. It's important that the person giving you this feedback knows you as a climber and spends some climbing time with you. An experienced coach will, within a few hours of varied and challenging climbing, be able to point out your strengths and weaknesses.

Most larger commercial climbing walls will have experienced coaches available to help you with such an evaluation. Alternatively, you can test yourself on different boulder problems and routes and see if you can spot a pattern and assess which types of problems or routes you find easy or hard.

One of the biggest challenges of identifying strengths and weaknesses is that it's often possible to climb a boulder or route in the style that suits you the most. For example, a static climber will often be able to do a move statically, even if this move should ideally be performed dynamically. Being made aware of this makes it possible for the climber to plan sessions where the focus is primarily on dynamic climbing. By starting a process where they continually challenge themselves in a structured manner, dynamic moves will over time become a part of their normal movement pattern. This way they're not only practising dynamic moves when specifically training them, but also when they're 'just' climbing.

When training specific moves and techniques, it's important to have a clear picture of how a move should be executed and how you're actually doing it. Try paying really close attention to how other climbers are doing it, especially those who are doing it correctly. To understand how you yourself are doing a move it's helpful to discuss with others and to film yourself climbing. Having an experienced climber or coach point out strengths and faults in your execution at the same time as watching a video of yourself climbing is a powerful tool in understanding and developing your technique. Remember, it takes a trained eye to spot the minute details of climbing techniques, and whoever you're discussing it with should be experienced in coaching climbers and know your strengths and weaknesses. At the same time you need to be open to new ideas and spend time in the ongoing process.

STAGES OF DEVELOPING TECHNIQUE

Learning a new technique takes time and effort. When describing the progression of learning a certain technique, it is common to look at technique training as a repetitive exercise where you go through different stages:

FAMILIARISATION

Here you get an overview of how the technique is performed. This usually starts with watching other climbers before trying it yourself. When you try to perform the technique yourself it can be a good idea to divide the technique into familiarisation exercises which contain elements of it. This will make it easier to combine all the different elements into one movement. Using deadpointing as an example, the familiarisation exercises could be:

* finding the starting position for the move
* deciding the direction of the movement
* defining the optimal position on the wall at the end of the move.

Becoming comfortable with these three elements will make it easier to start trying the whole movement and to enter the next stage.

COARSE COORDINATION

Here you practise the moves until you can consistently repeat them. At this stage it's reasonable to pick three to five boulder problems or challenging individual moves that require the chosen technique for this training session. Get help from a coach or an experienced climber who can define the moves, or find a suitable boulder problem at your local climbing wall. It's important to be conscious of what makes a move harder or easier, and to get feedback from others on your execution. Filming yourself climbing is an important tool at this stage.

FINE COORDINATION

Here you focus on the details of the movement. It's important to have a high number of repetitions and to really fine tune the moves until they are executed to perfection. At this stage the feedback you get from your own body is more important than what others tell you.

This is because it's difficult for others to pinpoint the details that make something feel right or wrong for you individually. Filming yourself in slow motion can help give you an even better understanding.

AUTOMATION

At this stage your body should be on autopilot and you should be climbing without thinking about the move itself – as long as the conditions are similar. But just because a move is automatic doesn't necessarily mean it's also optimised. Most moves have some scope for variation, but only one way is the optimal way. This means that even though you have learned a new technique, it's important to stay curious in order to optimise it. Getting feedback from others, filming yourself and listening to your body when climbing are the most important ways to improve.

ADAPTATION

This is perhaps the biggest challenge for us as climbers. There will always be small differences between different wall angles, formations, and types and sizes of holds. Even if a certain technique is automatic on a particular boulder problem or route, you will still have to adapt it when you come across similar moves. Experienced climbers often look like they're climbing purely on intuition. This is a result of them mastering different techniques and not having to stop and think every time they're about to do a move. They recognise and initiate the moves automatically.

External factors also play a role. For example, it can be quite difficult to climb with perfect technique during a competition with lots of spectators, or when you're run out far above the last piece of gear or bolt on a route. External factors will always affect your climbing. You should be prepared for this and minimise the effect it has on your technical execution.

There are large differences in the complexity of different techniques. More complex techniques require a lot more coordination and demand higher precision. These techniques require many familiarisation exercises and much training before they can be mastered. They will also be difficult to reproduce in new situations. Some techniques might only be suited to one single move on one single boulder problem. Others can be useful just about all the time.

Beginners and intermediate climbers should therefore focus on the techniques they will need the most often – those regarding balance, and simple dynamic techniques.

Remember that technique training is like anything else: practice makes perfect. If you want to become better at lead climbing on vertical walls, you need to practise the techniques needed for that style of climbing. If, on the other hand, you want to become a competition climber you should focus on coordination moves and dynamic climbing.

LEAD VS BOULDERING

Lead climbing is all about finding your flow and using the minimum amount of energy so you can hold on for as long as possible. In bouldering, the difficulty often lies in doing just a single move, challenging your strength, coordination or balance to the limit. This begs the question: should you train for both lead and bouldering if you're mostly going to do one or the other? If you ask us, the answer is yes. Climbing technique is complex: there's always something to learn from another branch of climbing.

Despite there being short bouldery routes and long boulder problems, there are several reasons that those seeking progression should train both lead climbing and bouldering and focus on multiple facets of technique training – those associated with bouldering and those associated with lead climbing. This is regardless of whether you want to excel at one or both genres, because some techniques are easier to learn when climbing on a rope, and others are easier to learn when bouldering.

In general, we recommend that you do more of the specific technique training when you're bouldering. It's easier to design specifically themed challenges on the bouldering wall than on the rope wall. There is also less of a mental aspect, which is especially important when training dynamic techniques. By practising these techniques when bouldering you'll become comfortable with them and over time include them as a natural part of your repertoire, enabling you to do difficult and challenging moves when roped up. Yet there are some techniques that are easier to understand when climbing on a rope – especially techniques involving weight transfer and balance. This is a result of your arms getting tired and being unable to pull hard, which forces you to lower your body, find the balance and shift as much of your weight as possible on to your feet. Way too often we see

PHOTO: BJØRNAR SMESTAD

boulderers fail to master these techniques. Their tendency is to grip harder than they need to and overuse their arms. This results in loss of pressure on the footholds and an increased risk of falling. By doing more roped climbing, boulderers can learn the importance of balance and energy-efficient climbing – also significant aspects when bouldering.

We must also not forget that maybe the most exciting – and also the most challenging – part of climbing is the fact that we never practise the exact same move. There's always a level of improvisation in the movements we do as we have not done this exact move before. This means we need a large repertoire of moves to choose from, to ease the adaptation and improvisation needed for doing new moves. By climbing as many routes and boulder problems as possible, we are constantly adding to our movement library and making it easier to improvise every time we try something new. The more routes and boulder problems we climb, the better.

Kilian Fischhuber, one of the most decorated competition boulderers of all time, claimed he was never the strongest or most technical climber. His biggest advantage was that he was extremely skilled at regulating his stress level. He always knew exactly how much he could relax in a given position, or how hard he had to pull in another. He conserved his strength where he could, and used just the right amount of power when he needed to explode off a hold. He only competed in bouldering, but much of his training was done on the rope wall.

CLIPPING THE ROPE

Anybody who has been through the process of learning to clip the rope into quickdraws knows how frustrating this process can be. Not only are you now standing far above the last bolt, but you've also pulled up an extra length of rope to reach the karabiner, which could potentially result in a long fall. You start to fumble with the 'biner, the rope is twisting away and you can't get it to slip into the gate (the part that opens). You're standing slightly off balance, and the arm that's keeping you from falling is getting tired. It feels like your foot is starting to slip and you're just fumbling even more with the quickdraw. Sound familiar?

For an ascent to be considered valid it has to be done on lead, and having an efficient way of clipping the rope into the karabiner is an essential part of whether you succeed or not. As with learning any technique, clipping must also be practised. Start in safe and controlled situations: there's nothing wrong with standing on the ground and practising clipping a low quickdraw over and over until you get the hang of it. Continue by moving on to lead climbing an easy route, where you have enough margin to take your time with every clip. As you keep practising you'll progress naturally and become more comfortable with climbing harder lead climbs, clipping from smaller holds and more strenuous positions, and with an increasing level of pump in your forearms. On really hard routes, clipping the rope can be the hardest part of the climb, and being as efficient as possible when clipping is crucial.

Below are the most common techniques for clipping the rope. Experiment with all of them to find the one that works best for you and then optimise it; but we recommend you learn all the different techniques well enough so that you can adapt your choice based on what you encounter on different routes.

FOREHAND

When the gate of the karabiner is facing the same side as the hand you're clipping the rope with (for example, the gate is facing left and you are clipping with your left hand, as illustrated in the photos, right), it's efficient to let the rope run from your harness, up through your hand and over your index finger. This way you can hold the karabiner with your thumb, open the gate with your index finger and the rope, and drop the rope through the opening.

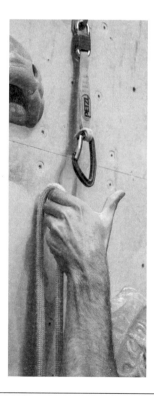

BACKHAND

When the gate of the karabiner is facing away from the hand you're using to clip with (for example, the gate is facing left and you are clipping with your right hand, as illustrated in the photos, below), it's common to use one of two techniques:

1. Hold the rope between your thumb and index finger. Hold the karabiner steady by pulling down on it with the tip of your middle finger. Use your thumb and index finger to guide the rope and push it through the gate with your thumb. This is an effective technique for slabs and vertical climbing, as you can use your middle finger to lift the karabiner away from the wall slightly to add some space for the rope between the karabiner and the wall. It's also useful when clipping up high or reaching out to the side, as you can maximise reach by using your middle finger to reach the karabiner. Keeping the karabiner steady can be challenging, particularly on steep terrain where you can't rest your hand against the wall behind the karabiner.

2. Let the rope run from your harness and over your palm between your thumb and index finger. Grab the quickdraw directly at the lower karabiner with your index and middle fingers to hold it steady. Twist the karabiner into your palm and use the meaty part of your thumb to squeeze the rope through the gate. This is an efficient technique when climbing on steep terrain where the quickdraw is hanging freely below the overhanging wall, as it helps you hold the karabiner steady. You will lose a bit of reach though when compared to the first technique, above, and it's therefore not as efficient when you have to reach up high or out to the side.

  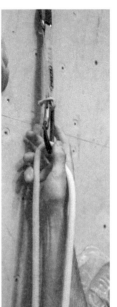

PHOTO: BJØRNAR SMESTAD

READING ROUTES AND BOULDER PROBLEMS

When you're visualising, you can picture how to climb a route, make a plan and execute it. This gives you a good understanding of technique. Discuss the plan with your peers to get their input, as other climbers might have completely different ideas on how to solve a move or section of climbing. It's important to imagine how to use both handholds and footholds, where to move fast, and where to move with more control. It can be hard to read the whole route when outdoors, but indoors you can usually see all of the holds. When reading routes indoors it can be a good idea to put yourself in the route setter's shoes. If there's a foothold out left, it's probably there for a reason. Route setters don't put holds up at random in the hope that someone will find a way up; they plan for a certain sequence and to force the climber into specific positions. By picturing how your body must be placed in relation to a given set of handholds and footholds, you're making a more conscious decision about how to climb than if you were climbing purely by intuition. This will, in turn, improve your intuitive climbing. Visualisation is important to improve your technical abilities, but it's also an important mental tool. We'll dive deeper into this in the chapter on mental performance factors.

What happens if you read a climb incorrectly? Unfortunately, this happens quite often, and it can be hard to reset and improvise when the challenge you face is completely different from the one you prepared for. You have to think quickly so as not to get tired, and go for a new solution. Sometimes a new solution will present itself, and sometimes you have to stop and think before continuing the climb. Some climbers train specifically for these situations. They have sessions where they don't read a route before starting to climb, forcing the whole route to be climbed by improvisation. This can also be trained when climbing on sight outdoors, as you can see less of the holds from the ground which makes reading the whole route difficult or even impossible.

Stian Christophersen flashing
Special Edition (Font 7c+),
Brione, Switzerland.

SET YOUR OWN ROUTES AND BOULDER PROBLEMS

THE DEVELOPMENT OF larger commercial climbing walls has greatly reduced the need to invent your own routes and boulder problems. These gyms have their own professional route setters who work to provide you with different routes for training anything from strength to endurance to technique. This is, of course, a good thing, but making your own routes and boulder problems is an important part of becoming a better climber because it forces you to become more conscious of why you move a certain way when climbing. By setting your own problems you're guaranteed to also become better at solving them, which is such an important part of climbing, and you'll be able to set problems with the perfect level of difficulty and technical focus for the exact training session you're about to have. When to start setting your own problems is dependent on your own development as a climber and on your local climbing wall. If your climbing wall is rather small, with just a small bouldering wall with lots of random, unmarked holds, it will be natural for you to start setting your own problems earlier than if you normally go to a large commercial climbing wall.

You'll need to set boulder problems with specific technical themes. If, for example, you're going to challenge yourself with a deadpoint move, you need to consider which holds to use and where to place them in relation to one other to force the deadpoint move. You will also need to set problems and circuits to ensure the quality of your physical training. To complete a bouldering session which targets finger strength and static strength, you need good quality problems on small holds suited to your strength and height.

Setting your own problems is harder than you'd think. We asked one of Norway's top route setters, Kenneth Elvegård, to give us some tips:

- Set your own variants of existing problems. You can subtract or add holds to change the character or adjust the difficulty level. Many shorter climbers can, for example, add an extra foothold to make a height-dependent problem possible.
- Set your own problems on a wall which is littered with holds. The classic training wall is normally packed with holds. This gives you endless combinations to choose from and is a good place to start.
- Start by choosing which handholds to use.
- You can choose to use all holds for feet, just a selection, any tiny foot jib, only the same holds as you used as handholds, or any variation thereof. Using only the same holds for feet as for hands is called trailing, and is suitable for problems that don't traverse sideways too much. If you're traversing you might have to include some extra footholds or jibs. Jibs are small footholds set on the wall to be used solely as footholds. They are usually too small to be used as handholds and are often attached using screws instead of bolts.
- Decide up front what you want to set, and don't give up until you've accomplished your goal. You can start by setting just one move, and then take it from there. Remember to keep testing each move. Route setting consists of setting, testing, tweaking and retesting.

We have on multiple occasions observed the Kolsås Climbing Club youth group training here in Norway. The kids are encouraged to set problems for themselves and each other at an early stage. Over time they develop their skills and achieve a good understanding of climbing. They intuitively understand how to move on the wall, and how to solve a problem by looking at it.

When training your technique, you should choose a wall with the appropriate steepness for the technique that you're going to focus on. For precise footwork, and balance and static climbing it's better to choose a vertical wall, while overhanging walls are better for dynamic and flowy moves. Tension and directing force is needed on any wall angle, but more so on steep prows, where you compress together with both hands and feet, or on steep overhangs with poor holds, where tension is needed from head to toe. Here are some tips:

- To train weight transfer you should use large protruding footholds, and small, preferably poor, handholds. Set a problem that traverses sideways slightly, so as to feel the subtle differences of placing your hips slightly more to the left or right.
- Precision footwork is best trained on small footholds or footholds that require you to place your foot in exactly the right spot. You can use slightly better handholds, but not so good that you can afford for your feet to slip.
- Static climbing is best trained on small holds that are difficult to stick at speed, such as small edges or pockets. Footholds that are large and positive are well suited, as they allow you to pull with your arms without your feet slipping because of reduced friction.
- When training dynamic moves you should either make the moves longer and/or the holds worse. Longer moves are harder to do statically, and slopey holds get worse as you pull yourself higher. Both force you to start the movement from a low position. Try using volumes for feet. If these aren't too positive, they will often force a dynamic move.
- For directing force and maintaining tension you need holds that are too poor to hold individually. Try experimenting by holding the smallest holds possible on each side of a prow. By exploiting the opposing forces you generate, you can use much smaller holds than you might think. When climbing an overhang, try also using holds that are so small that you'll fall if your foot slips. You can start with a larger hold, and work your way down to smaller footholds as you improve.

Physical routes and boulder problems are easier to set than technical ones, as they don't require the same level of precision. Here are some tips to help you set physical problems:

- Try to avoid dirty tricks when setting physical problems. We recommend fronting as much as possible, and no twisting, heel hooking or matching on too many holds. The point of physical training is to train your physique, and using advanced techniques that reduce the load will defeat this purpose.
- If you're working your finger strength on a five-move boulder probem, you should use holds that are so bad that you can only manage to do just those five moves. If, instead, you want to do a 50-move endurance circuit, you need to use holds that will enable you to do those 50 moves.
- For arm and upper body strength training, you should use larger holds and do bigger moves. It's OK to cut loose with your feet now and then, but try to avoid excessive flailing.
- For finger strength, you obviously need small handholds, but you can vary the hold size somewhat, by dynoing to slightly larger holds and going static between smaller holds without cutting your feet.
- Always test the boulders before you start training to ensure that they fit your programme.

OTHER PEOPLE'S PROBLEMS SHOULD BE YOUR PROBLEMS TOO

Most of us have a tendency to only climb boulder problems that suit our style. By trying problems which other climbers have set, and preferably climbers with a different style than your own, you'll also be training your weaknesses. This is a good way to become more conscious of your own strengths and weaknesses. If parts of a boulder problem are impossible because of height/reach or the like, try adding a foothold or changing that part of the problem.

HANNAH MIDTBØ:
Progression takes time and effort. If you're investing time and effort, make sure your training is varied.

INDOORS VS OUTDOORS

Too many climbers favour either indoor or outdoor climbing, without reflecting on the elements that they're missing out on by not including all forms of climbing in their training. Sure, a competition climber should focus their training indoors, just as a trad climber loyal to outdoor cracks might not benefit too much from jumping around on volumes indoors, but as we've mentioned previously, climbing is about using the techniques we have in our arsenal to improvise in new situations. We should therefore always seek to challenge and increase our repertoire as much as possible.

An indoor climber will benefit from climbing outdoors because:

- outdoor climbing quite often involves moving around on smaller and poorer holds for both hands and feet. This requires precision and sensitive climbing, which is hard to replicate and train indoors. Many climbers who only train indoors don't have a good understanding of weight transfer and keeping a low centre of gravity, as the holds indoors are usually not conducive to such types of moves.
- outdoor climbing can sometimes involve painful and awkward holds and moves, which route setters usually try to avoid with indoor climbing. If we recognise the value and importance of having a large repertoire of moves, we can't deny ourselves the opportunity to learn something new, just because it feels uncomfortable or because the holds take too much skin.

An outdoor climber will benefit from climbing indoors because:

- indoor climbing, especially bouldering, makes it easy to train specific techniques. Whether it is routes set by others, or a problem where you define what holds to use yourself, it will be easier to try one or a combination of moves repeatedly and evaluate the process.
- indoor climbing is often more dynamic and requires more tension, which is difficult to adequately train outdoors.

BETA OR NOT?

Most climbers today will have seen another climber on their route or boulder problem before they try it, or they will have received some information on how to do it. This information is known as 'beta'. Having beta can be both good and bad for developing your technique. Beta is positive in that it can serve as inspiration for trying new boulder problems and new techniques. But it can also have a negative effect as it simplifies the process of problem-solving. Climbing is problem-solving, and you won't improve if you don't actually practise solving problems.

We didn't use to have the enormous database of online climbing videos that we have today. When climbers went out to try a problem, they usually had to figure things out themselves. This turned them into inventive and resourceful problem-solvers. Many climbers today lack this ability and perhaps also the motivation needed to solve these problems. They want to get to the top as quickly and easily as possible, which of course makes beta invaluable. This takes some of the magic away from climbing. Part of what makes climbing so exciting and unique is that we don't practise predefined moves, but use our own body, skill and experience to solve these problems.

During one of our trips to Rocklands in South Africa, we had a chat on this subject with one of the best competition climbers of all time, Kilian Fischhuber. We wanted to convince Kilian to come to Norway for some climbing and were wondering if he had seen any of the videos we had made. He responded that he almost never watched climbing videos. This piqued our interest, as a world without climbing movies sounded terribly sad to us, so we asked him why. He said he didn't want to know how a boulder problem should be solved, as this took away from his interest in doing it. To Kilian, climbing was solely about problem-solving.

 Challenge yourself by hitting the climbing wall and trying as many problems as you can without watching anybody else try them before you. Experience the joy and sense of achievement from solving problems on your own. For us, this process is always rewarding, and we're convinced it has improved our technique.

SUMMARY

In this chapter we've presented fundamentals and techniques we feel are universal and useful for any and all climbers. Yet there will always be individual differences, and your physical abilities and attributes will affect which techniques will suit you better. This means that the way you and your climbing partner solve the same boulder problem or route might be drastically different, without one way necessarily being any more correct than the other.

A common example of this is the difference between slender and powerful climbers. Slender climbers usually have quite strong fingers relative to their body weight. They will, therefore, be able to do moves on smaller holds which heavier climbers cannot. A larger climber might prefer to do bigger moves on bigger holds. The lighter climber will over time develop the skill to keep their feet on the wall because they don't have the upper body strength to hold on and stop a swing. One of the world's most well-known climbers, Dave Graham, belongs to this category. He has said he thinks of his toes as claws that keep his feet latched on to holds. If his feet slip, he falls. 'Skeleton style', as he himself calls it, works well for him, and there are very few routes or boulder problems he cannot climb. Chris Sharma, on the other hand, is much more of a powerful type of climber, and he's used to jumping to holds, cutting his feet and taking the swing. He's strong enough to climb with this style, but he's also heavier, which means he has to climb faster so as to not get too tired. 'Skip the bad holds, go for the good ones,' he says in the climbing movie *Dosage 3*. Both Dave and Chris have developed and perfected their styles over time. Both could have trained to become more like the other, and to a certain extent they probably have, but Dave's style wouldn't work for Chris, and vice versa. They both have a technique which is perfectly suited to their body.

Progressing your technique involves more than just knowing about the different fundamentals and techniques. You need to stay curious to find the optimal solution for you, learning from the feedback your body and your peers give you, and be conscious not just of *if* you get up a climb, but *how* you got up it.

CHAPTER 2

PHYSICAL TRAINING

OUT OF ALL the different factors influencing a climbing achievement, the physical aspect is perhaps the most talked about. And not without reason. As climbing becomes progressively harder, the holds get worse and further apart. Walls get steeper and the cruxes more sustained. This places increasing demands on physical factors like finger strength, arm strength, core strength, endurance and mobility. These are factors that are relatively easy to train, and progression can be just as easily measured. If we look at the traditional approach of splitting climbing performance into three, the physical factors are considered to be more important for performance than the technical and mental factors.

This chapter starts by looking at what defines 'the climbing body'. Next up is the different physical performance factors within strength, endurance and mobility, and how these can be trained.

Martin Mobråten on *Spectre* (Font 8b), Bishop, USA.

Kenneth Elvegård and Adam Pustelnik
are both skilled climbers with different
physical attributes.

THE CLIMBING BODY

Every climber has different physical proportions and attributes, yet to this day these seem not to make much difference to a climber's performance. Even at the elite level, there are huge differences in height, arm length and body weight, evidence that trainable traits are more important to performance than how a climber's body is put together anatomically. Still, climbing does favour a relatively slender body type with a particular distribution of muscle mass – the bulk of the muscle in the upper body rather than the legs. This is why climbing can be seen as a weight-dependent sport, where a lower body weight will allow a climber to hold on to smaller holds since they have fewer kilos to haul.

It can therefore be tempting to lose weight in order to improve performance, rather than exercising to improve the correlation between strength and body weight. This weight loss has traditionally been common in climbing. Nevertheless, we have in recent years seen a shift towards steeper climbing, bouldering and an increased focus on technically complex and demanding climbing. We don't doubt that losing weight is performance enhancing, but shedding pounds can also have a negative effect, as less muscle mass will make it harder for you to do physically hard moves on steep terrain. Also, it won't be of any help to be thin and lightweight if you're not technically adept enough to do tricky moves, and you'll probably be just as scared when you're 10 feet above the last bolt no matter how much you weigh! For adult climbers, a reduction in weight can be an important performance variable, but we recommend you focus more on developing your technical, tactical, physical and mental abilities before you consider losing weight to boost your performance. Losing weight also means you'll be training with an energy deficit for a period of time, and this will make it difficult to lay down the right amount of quality training you need, which is what you should be focusing on. The effect of a reduction in weight will also be much higher if your skills are already at a high level, so instead, consider losing weight only as a last tweak of form before a project or competition, and only after you're at a stable and acceptable performance level. In addition, for younger athletes, there are some obvious health risks associated with losing weight, and on a general basis, we recommend that young climbers don't lose weight in order to increase performance. We'll cover this in greater detail in Chapter 5.

Our unconditional recommendation is to 'climb with the body you've got' and to get to know the strengths and weaknesses of your body. Tall climbers are at a clear advantage when it comes to reachy moves, but will find steep compression climbing more challenging. On the other hand, shorter climbers have to compensate for their lack of reach by being more dynamic in style but will be at an advantage when the climbing is steep and/or features more compression. Heavier climbers will often also have more muscle mass, which will give them an advantage on physically hard climbs, while a lighter climber might find it easier to hang on to smaller holds, as they have a higher finger strength to weight ratio.

'IF YOU CAN'T DO THE MOVE, THERE IS
NOTHING TO ENDURE.'

TONI YANIRO

PHOTO: MIKE MULLINS

STRENGTH

As the walls get steeper, the holds smaller and the moves bigger, the need for a strong core, strong arms and strong fingers increases. This is what we call climbing-specific strength.

It's easy to forget how specific training actually is when getting lost in the myriad of training videos, articles, blogs and interviews. For example, if you're doing pull-ups on good holds, you'll get good at doing pull-ups on good holds. And if you're exercising your core by doing the plank, you'll get better at doing the plank. It is an oversimplification to say that general exercise doesn't have an effect, but the direct transfer value to climbing can in many cases be marginal. We must, therefore, focus our strength training on the specific performance factors – finger, arm and upper body strength.

Stian Christophersen
on the first ascent of
Lierpillaren Direkte (F8b+),
Bergfladt, Norway.

FINGER STRENGTH

Finger strength, as in what is the smallest hold you can still hang on to, is the most important performance factor in climbing. We can compensate quite a bit with good technique, but it's obvious that the best climbers also have the strongest fingers. Finger strength has proven to be a good indicator of what level of climbing you are at and will be a deciding factor for how hard you can pull on a route or boulder problem.

Strong fingers also correlate with good endurance. Put simply, the stronger your fingers are, the poorer the holds you can hold, and the less you'll use of your maximum strength per hold, which all means it will take longer for your forearm muscles to tire. Of course, every time you're climbing, you're also training finger strength, but the best way to get strong fingers specifically is by doing so-called deadhangs.

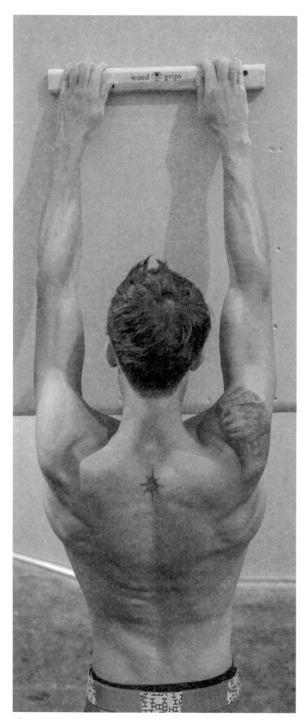

It's important to lower your shoulders and slightly rotate your elbows in towards each other.

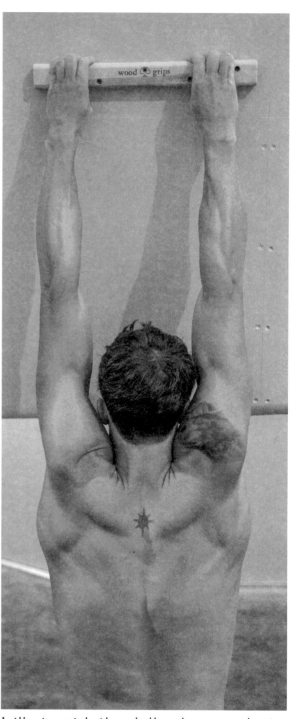

Avoid hanging passively with your shoulders up by your ears, as shown in the picture above.

DEADHANGS

Finger strength has always been regarded as important, but it is only in recent years that specific finger strength training has gained any real traction in the climbing community in general. Spanish climber and researcher Eva López deserves much of the credit for the increase in knowledge on the subject of finger strength training. Her PhD on the subject brought forth simple and effective training methods by using deadhangs on fingerboards to improve finger strength. The advantage of deadhangs is that the load is easily adjusted based on the level of the climber, and progression is easily tracked. The load is adjusted by increasing/decreasing the size of the hold, by adding/subtracting weight and by adjusting the hang time.

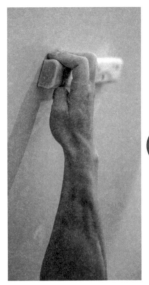

The most useful grip position when training finger strength is the half crimp. Your front three fingers should be bent at 90 degrees at the middle joint, and all four fingers should be engaged on the hold.

 If your hand opens, let go. This means the load is too high and you're at risk of injury.

1. SIZE OF THE HOLD

It will be progressively harder to hang a given time interval as the hold becomes shallower. Down to a certain point, around 2 to 4 millimetres, the depth of the hold can be a measure of how strong your fingers are. On shallower holds than this, the anatomy of your fingers and the friction will decide if you can hang or not, and reducing the hold size won't give an increase in muscular training effect.

2. TOTAL WEIGHT

If it's too hard for you to hang with the full weight of your body, you can start by subtracting from your body weight by using an elastic band or a rope pulley system with weights. Stronger, more experienced climbers might have to add extra weight, as they're already accustomed to hanging on small holds with the full load of their body weight.

3. HANG TIME

The smaller the hold you use or the more weight you add, the shorter the time you'll be able to hang on. A shorter hang time with more added weight or a smaller edge size will cause some specific adaptions in muscles, tendons and connective tissues, while longer hang times with less load and a bigger edge size will cause others. It's important to note that you will also have gains in strength with longer hang times as long as you hang on close to failure; strength gains do not only come from short and heavy hangs. To use hang time as a variable, it's easier to vary your training and train with different methods to meet the training goals you've set for yourself.

We recommend using primarily the half crimp grip position. This is the grip position that provides the highest muscular load to the forearms, and it is also of value for other grip positions. But it's important to remember that whatever grip position you're training is also the grip position you'll get strongest at. So, if you want to improve your pulling power on slopers or pockets, then the grip positions you are training should reflect this. It's also important to maintain control of your hang posture. You should pull your shoulders down and back, with your arms straight, and the inside of your elbows facing each other.

KEEP THIS IN MIND!

Deadhanging is specific strength training for your fingers, and the climbing community has traditionally regarded finger-specific training as putting climbers at an increased risk of injury. The recommendation is usually that you should have a certain training base before starting with this method. This base is built through general climbing, and you could also argue that it builds other performance factors rather than just pure finger strength. Working on all factors of your climbing is where your focus should be at the start of your climbing career.

Still, it's important to point out that deadhanging is by no means more stressful for the fingers than hard, fingery bouldering sessions, and well-controlled, specific strength training for the fingers could actually mitigate the risk of finger injuries in the future. It is much easier to regulate the load when doing deadhangs than during a bouldering session, and because strength training, in general, is regarded as one of the single most important factors for reducing the risk of injury across any sport, it's natural to assume that it's possible to achieve a similar effect with specific finger strength training.

Special care must be taken regarding finger-specific training for younger athletes. Because of skeletal development throughout childhood and adolescence, younger athletes may be more susceptible to skeletal injuries following high-intensity finger training methods on fingerboards, campus boards and on the bouldering wall.

DEADHANG TRAINING METHODS

Here are the three methods we recommend for deadhang finger strength training.

1. HANG ON

HANG TIME	REST	REPETITIONS	SETS	BUFFER	GRIP POSITION
30 seconds	3 minutes	1	8	None: hang on until failure*	Vary between half crimp, open hand, pinch and sloper

This is an easy starting point for many climbers. We're using hang time to failure to set the load, meaning that on the given hold you must be able to hold the grip for over 30 seconds. You can use bigger holds or even a pull-up bar, or take some weight off with a band or a pulley system, to enable you to hold on for the 30 seconds. If you can hang on for a substantially longer period of time (such as 40 seconds or more) you need to use smaller holds or add weight. We find this deadhang method relevant for training all the different grip positions except full crimp. We recommend that you vary between different grip positions during the session.

Start with one session per week and progress to two sessions per week after three to four weeks of training. As you go several times to failure, this session should be done as a standalone session in combination with complementary strength training.

*Failure also means technical failure. If you lose form in your hang posture or can't maintain your finger position, you've reached technical failure and should step off.

2. STRENGTH HANGS

HANG TIME	REST	REPETITIONS	SETS	REST BETWEEN SETS	GRIP POSITION
10 seconds	5 seconds	4–5	4–5	1 minute	Half crimp

This method is similar to traditional strength training, where each set is close to maximum effort by combining both intensity (hold size and total weight) and volume (number of repetitions). Resting time between sets is short enough not to allow complete recovery between each set, and this helps to fatigue the muscles throughout the session. In practice, this means you should only just complete – or just fail to complete – the last hang of each set, and you should maintain this intensity throughout the whole session.

It should be easy to adjust the size of the hold during the session so that you're able to complete the correct number of reps and sets. If you're unable to hang for the 10-second repetition, it's important that you take some weight off or use bigger holds so that you maintain control for every set. Advanced climbers can also adjust the load by adding extra weight.

Start with one session per week, either as a stand-alone session or after warming up for a regular climbing session. You can do both bouldering or roped climbing after this session, but take into consideration that your forearms and fingers will be fatigued and so you shouldn't overload them during the rest of your climbing session. After three to four weeks you can increase to two sessions per week, with a minimum of two rest days between each deadhang session, and then go on gradually reducing the hold size to maintain a steady training progression. Our advice is to complete one training cycle of the Hang On method before progressing to this method.

3. MAX HANGS

HANG TIME	REST	REPETITIONS	SETS	BUFFER	GRIP POSITION
10 seconds	3 minutes	1	4–5	1–3 seconds	Half crimp

The premise of this exercise is to hang in control for 10 seconds per repetition. Between each hang, you rest for 3 minutes and then repeat for four to five sets. The buffer gives you an indication of how close you are to maximum effort, independent of any reduced or added weight. With a buffer of three seconds, you should be able to hang for a maximum of 13 seconds, but still let go after 10 seconds. The shorter the buffer, the closer you are to maximum effort, but there's still a reasonable training effect with a buffer of up to 3 seconds. This buffer also makes the training a lot safer with regards to injuries as it avoids you just barely being able to hang for 10 seconds or, even worse, falling off uncontrolled.

This method is very well suited to improving your maximum finger strength as the load is high, there are fewer repetitions and the rests are longer. This means you will improve the ability of your muscles and nervous system to develop and sustain force. It's a natural progression to start with one or more cycles of the Hang On method and continue through one or more cycles of Strength Hangs before commencing a cycle of Max Hangs.

As the Max Hang method only involves a few repetitions, and even though the load per hang is high, it allows for the exercise to be combined with a regular climbing session afterwards. We recommend starting with one session per week, then upping to two sessions per week after about four weeks, or when you feel progression in your training. Further progression is easily promoted by adding extra weight.

Deadhanging is a safe and efficient way to train finger strength, but it lacks the aspect of movement which after all is what climbing is all about, and a downside to training deadhangs is that you're only really training to hang. When we're climbing, we're moving between holds, which means we also have to have good arm and upper body strength.

PHOTO: ERICK VIGOUROUX

INTERVIEW WITH
EVA LÓPEZ

Spanish climber and researcher Eva López wrote her PhD on using deadhangs for finger strength training. She compared the effect that two different approaches had on finger strength and endurance.

THESE METHODS WERE named MAW (Maximum Added Weight) and MED (Minimum Edge Depth). The MAW method involved hanging in control for 10 seconds on an 18-millimetre-deep edge with as much added weight as possible, and with a safety buffer of 3 seconds. The hang was repeated four to five times with a 3-minute rest in between each hang, two times per week. The MED method consisted of hanging with no added weight on the smallest hold possible for 10 seconds, plus a 3-second buffer, again repeated four to five times with a 3-minute rest in between each hang, two times per week. The participants in the study warmed up before doing the deadhangs and followed the session with a regular climbing session afterwards.

The training lasted for eight weeks, where one group completed four weeks of MAW followed by four weeks of MED, while the other group did the opposite, namely four weeks of MED followed by four weeks of MAW. The result was that group one (the MAW-MED group) performed better on both strength and endurance tests than group two. Group one had an increase in maximum strength of 10 per cent after four weeks, while group two increased their maximum strength by 2 per cent. This effect did reduce a few weeks after the training period, but even so, this is a significant increase in maximum strength, especially considering that most of the participants were already experienced climbers with an average level of F8a+.

'AS LONG AS YOU'RE PROGRESSING IN YOUR TRAINING, IT SEEMS TO BE BENEFICIAL TO ALTER BETWEEN PERIODS OF MAW AND MED, WHILE ALSO ADJUSTING THE INTENSITY AND HANG TIME.'

Eva López training on the Transgression fingerboard.

When training methods are presented in scientific articles, there are often many questions that arise and nuances that should be highlighted. We asked Eva some questions regarding deadhanging and her research.

Is it important to switch from MAW to MED after four weeks?

First of all, it's important to point out that the training needs to be adjusted to a climber's individual needs, goals and abilities. Every climber – and coach – needs to choose a method, and decide how to incorporate this method into their training plan, based on their training experience, finger strength, goals and so on. This is why I'm reluctant to lay down specific rules, but it's reasonable to say that an advanced-level climber shouldn't use the MAW method before she has completed a moderate-intensity period of MED. For example, she can start with a 15-second hang time with a 5-second buffer for two to three sets the first week, and then increase to four to five sets the fourth week. I've covered this in detail in both my articles and my blog, and I would encourage anyone interested in deadhang training to get acquainted with the material we have gathered.[1, 2] I also have a YouTube channel where we explain different training methods and hang technique.[3]

On a general basis, I would always recommend the easiest and least intensive training method and periodisation that still yields an effect. This is an effective, safe and sound way to train. Regarding the specific question, it's logical that after a training period on relatively deep holds with added weight, you'll be ready to train on the smallest holds possible without added weight. As an apropos, hanging on thin edges without added weight is one of the more specific aspects of climbing, and progression in specificity is one of the founding training principles. During our study, we noticed that the increase in finger strength after a period of MAW training continued even after switching to the MED method, even though the strength test was performed on a 15-millimetre edge. Our hypothesis is that the strength increase after four weeks of MAW training enables the climber to use even smaller holds in the following four-week period of MED, which in turn leads to a further increase in finger strength.

As long as you're progressing in your training, it seems to be beneficial to alter between periods of MAW and MED, while also adjusting the intensity and hang time. This is especially the case when starting with deadhang training, and then you can experiment by altering between MAW, MED and other deadhang methods.

On this basis, I would say that going from MAW to MED isn't a general rule, but just one of many strategies for periodisation to choose from. We need to look to the training literature, which states that the stronger and more advanced an athlete is, the higher the training dosage needs to be, and the more we need to vary the training methods, choice of exercises, and periodisation strategies in order to create new stimuli and further development. This way we avoid stagnation and reduced motivation.

1 López-Rivera, E. and González-Badillo, J.J. (2012). *The effects of two maximum grip strength training methods using the same effort duration and different edge depth on grip endurance in elite climbers.* Sport Technology 5: 1–11. López-Rivera, E., and González-Badillo, J.J. (2016). *Comparison of the Effects of Three Hangboard Training Programs on Maximal Finger Strength in Rock Climbers.* In Northern Michigan University (Ed.), 3rd International Rock Climbing Research Congress, Telluride, USA 5th-7th August 2016. Telluride (Colorado, USA): IRCRA.
2 http://en-eva-lopez.blogspot.com.es/search/label/Finger%20training
3 evalopeztraining

'ON A GENERAL BASIS, I WOULD ALWAYS RECOMMEND THE EASIEST AND LEAST INTENSIVE TRAINING METHOD AND PERIODISATION THAT STILL YIELDS AN EFFECT.'

Why have you chosen to use the half crimp as the grip type?
Are there any added benefits of varying between different grip positions?
I would like to clear up a misunderstanding I experience that many have regarding my work. In experimental research, it's obvious that all variables need to be standardised, and we're therefore forced to choose one out of several possible variables. We chose the half crimp because both we and other researchers, and also the climbers themselves, claim this grip position to be the most common for small holds, and small holds are the most common feature on the hardest sections on a route together with the shape and texture of the hold. This doesn't mean that you only have to train the half crimp. I have never made this claim. The circumstances surrounding an experimental study is one thing, but these are not directly transferable to all types and levels of climbing.

It is a well-known fact that isometric [static] training yields a specific strength effect at the joint angle you're training at, and as long as you have enough time to train, you should train all grip positions if you want to become a well-rounded climber. If you're climbing at an advanced level, at a minimum you should be training both the half crimp and the open hand grip through specific training methods like deadhangs. If you have a lot of time for training, or there are specific grip positions on a project or a crag you wish to train for, you could also use equipment like pinch blocks or hooks for isolated finger training without hanging.

On a general basis, all climbers should train all grip positions through climbing different boulders and routes, and advanced climbers can implement the more specific finger strength training methods in their weekly training. For this group, it will be important to moderate the training volume during the climbing week so they can maintain a high level of quality for the specific exercises.

Are there other finger strength and endurance training methods that are as good or even more effective than the MAW–MED method?
There are, but whether these methods actually give a significant, positive effect will depend on many factors like training experience, periodisation strategies and load control, to mention a few.

With that in mind, we can use training methods and exercises like endurance-oriented deadhangs (intermittent deadhangs), one arm deadhangs (maximum strength training), contrast training (weighted deadhangs followed by explosive deadhangs) and campus boarding, without forgetting climbing on different routes and boulder problems with specific requirements to grip size and wall angles, as well as training with MAW and MED. In addition, we should vary the hang time and intensity for the maximum strength methods and the volume and time for the power endurance methods. Based on this, I recommend alternating between the different parameters and methods every four to eight weeks.

There is a risk involved in having an excessive focus on strengthening the arms and upper body, as this type of training often involves muscular growth and hence an increase in body weight. We should try to train with high load and relatively few repetitions to maximise strength while at the same time limiting muscle growth. Implementing this training into more general climbing training requires planning so that the fingers are able to adapt to the increased load from stronger arms and upper body, and potentially a heavier body as a result of increased muscle mass.

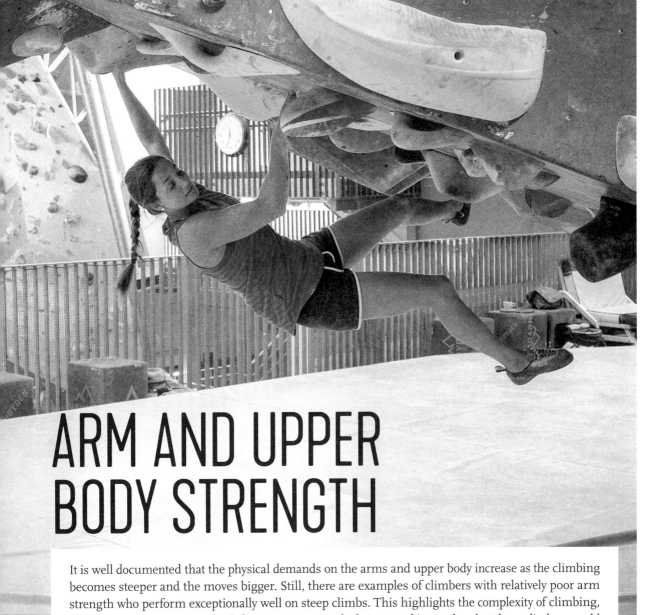

ARM AND UPPER BODY STRENGTH

It is well documented that the physical demands on the arms and upper body increase as the climbing becomes steeper and the moves bigger. Still, there are examples of climbers with relatively poor arm strength who perform exceptionally well on steep climbs. This highlights the complexity of climbing, where you can compensate for deficiency in one area by being good in another; but these climbers could perhaps raise their level even higher by training their arm and upper body strength.

At lower levels, bouldering and steep routes can provide enough strength training for the arms and upper body, and through this lay a good foundation for the more specific training to come later. Wall angles are a useful indicator of load, as the climbing becomes more physically challenging as the walls get steeper. A clear advantage of using climbing as a training method is, as previously mentioned, that you also train all the other factors that impact your performance.

Still, we recommend you add some specific strength training on top of what you would otherwise get through just regular climbing. Variations on pull-ups and lock-offs are the best options to add.

PULL-UPS

Pull-ups are the most common and simplest way to train your pulling apparatus, and for many, this is the first exercise to add in a specific strength training programme. The movement starts with the arms straight, then you pull your shoulders down, rotate your elbows toward each other and bend your elbows all the way until your chin is level with your hands. Try to do the pull-up calmly and smoothly, and don't cheat by 'kipping' and using your legs. If you find doing a pull-up is too hard, then you can use a bungee (as in the photos above) or a partner to help you take some of the load off. To begin with, you can try to do as many pull-ups as you can in one go, rest for 2 to 3 minutes, and repeat for three to four sets. When you're able to do more than six repetitions per set, it's time to up the difficulty, either by adding extra weight or by using an offset grip position – meaning one hand is lower than the other. Adjust the difficulty so you're only able to do three to four reps per set, and work your way back up six reps before upping the difficulty yet again. We recommend varying your pull-up training by alternating between added weight and offset grips; this mimics the varied movement patterns of climbing.

Strong, advanced climbers can also try doing one-arm pull-ups. When transitioning from regular pull-ups to one-arm pull-ups, it can be helpful to adjust the load with a bungee cord. This enables the movement to be performed with sufficient quality and allows a gradual progression in the training.

LOCK-OFFS

It's important to be able to lock your arm and body off in different positions, for example when doing a static move or when clipping a quickdraw. Specific lock-off training can be done with one or both arms, depending on your level. Beginners can train by doing so-called 'Frenchies' – locking off during a pull-up at three different stages, for example when your elbow is bent at 45, 90 and 120 degrees. Advanced climbers can do the same exercise with just one arm, and hold each position for 3 to 5 seconds. When transitioning from being able to do regular Frenchies on both arms to doing them with just one arm, try using a bungee cord or get help from a partner. It's important to be aware that training static positions will only make you stronger at holding that exact position, plus or minus a few degrees, so it's important to vary the angle of your elbows to build static strength throughout the range.

COMBINING FINGER, ARM AND UPPER BODY STRENGTH

Up until this point we have looked at how we can specifically train our fingers, arms and the upper body, and we will now look at how we can combine these elements in our training. This kind of combination training is important to make our strength training specific enough to the movement tempo and pattern we face when we're climbing.

We must always position our body in order to maximise the use of the holds. This means we have to create force in different directions as we move between the holds, and that we have to use different grip positions depending on how the holds are shaped. Hanging on edges and training pull-ups and lock-offs is good strength training but it excludes the wide variety of movement patterns we face when climbing.

The strength of a muscle is not the same as how fast it can generate force. What makes hard strength training challenging for your arms and upper body is the fact that the movements are rather slow. And even though it's important to have the strength to maintain a body position or climb slowly, climbers, and especially boulderers, need to be able to generate power quickly, an ability best developed through explosive strength training. In short, the way to train this is by doing these moves as quickly as possible. We differentiate between strength and explosiveness in the fingers in the same way that we do with the arms and the upper body. We need finger strength so we can hang on to holds, but we also need the muscles in the forearm to generate power quickly enough for us to achieve maximum power on a hold in a very short amount of time. This ability is known as contact strength.

By combining campusing (climbing without feet) and campus boarding, we will, in addition to increasing the speed of our arm movements, challenge the contact strength of our fingers even more so than by doing deadhang training. Bouldering will give us a large variation in the types of moves that we do. Through this, we train both slowly generating maximum power when moving statically for a bad hold or maintaining a body position, and also rapid generation of power when moving fast.

BOULDERING

Our experience is that bouldering on progressively smaller holds and steeper walls provides a very good training effect for finger, arm, and upper body strength, and should be considered the most important training method for climbers at any level. We could, for example, mention the fact that both of us were Font 8b boulderers and F8c route climbers before starting with systematic finger strength training. To get the most out of a bouldering session they have to be planned in advance to ensure you're training the specific abilities that you want to develop. Most importantly, plan which type of boulder problems you want to work with, and make sure to get enough rest in between each attempt so that it's actually a strength training session and not about endurance.

It'll take some experimentation to find the right problems for a specific session, so we recommend that you use some sessions to put together a good selection of different boulder problems. Physically, you'll get more out of the training if you remove the technical tricks you can use to take some of the load off of your fingers – like heel and toe hooks and twisting in. On a general basis, we consider the physical effect on your fingers, arms and upper body to be higher if you front the wall and use small footholds.

1. MAXIMUM INTENSITY BOULDERING

Choose four to five boulder problems close to your maximum level, with four to five moves per problem. Repeat each problem two to three times with at least 3 minutes of rest in between each attempt. If the main goal of the session is targeting explosiveness, each boulder problem should consist mainly of large moves that require rapid development of force both to start and to stop the movement. Alternatively, when targeting finger, arm and upper body strength, it's usually sufficient that the wall is steep and the holds are relatively small, without placing too much emphasis on the distance between the holds.

2. PYRAMIDS

An alternative to the session described above is to build the difficulty of the problems like a pyramid, which will have you doing more boulder problems. This is a common way to structure a session, but it's important to know that it's the hardest problem that will have the greatest effect on your strength. As above, you should decide if you want to challenge your explosiveness or your strength.

A pyramids bouldering session might look something like this:

6a	6b	6c	6b	6a
3 problems	2	1 (two tries)	2	3

Choose different types of boulder problems, and don't have more than two attempts on each problem. Rest for at least 3 minutes between each attempt. Adjust the difficulty of the boulder problems to your individual level. We recommend that the hardest problem is one to two grades below your maximum. So, if your personal best is a Font 7b, make the hardest problem in the pyramid a 7a or 7a+.

3. MOONBOARD

Developed by climbing legend Ben Moon, the Moonboard is perhaps the most commonly used system training wall around today. It is 40 degrees overhanging and features boulder problems set using a systemised grid of small, positive holds. You'll find suggestions for problems in the Moonboard app, which lets you climb on thousands of predefined problems at all levels of difficulty. A bouldering session on the Moonboard is very good training for your finger, arm and upper body strength, and it lets you do both maximum intensity sessions and pyramid training.

GOING FOOTLESS

Footless climbing, or campusing, involves doing climbing moves without using your feet. This is great training for your fingers, arms and upper body, as you're not using your legs to help. To begin with, you should focus on landing the holds with your arms bent and maintaining control over your body to avoid taking any unnecessary swings on straight arms – so start your campus training with good holds and easy moves. Start by doing three to four moves per problem, and increase to six to eight moves as you progress. A positive aspect of campusing is that you can vary the moves and vary between doing them slowly for strength or fast for explosiveness. When training explosiveness, we recommend doing fewer, but bigger moves; ideally no more than two to three moves per problem. Advanced climbers can reduce the hold size for an even greater finger strength training effect.

THE CAMPUS BOARD

The campus board is one of the earliest forms of training installations developed especially for climbing. It was designed by Wolfgang Güllich as part of his systematic training for the first ascent of *Action Direct* – the first 9a route in the world – in the Frankenjura, Germany, in 1991. The name of the board comes from the college gym it was first installed in – the Campus Gym. The campus board consists of wooden edges in different sizes, mounted on an overhanging wooden board, and allows for different methods of training finger and arm strength. The advantage of campus boarding when compared to deadhangs is that it involves arm movement – meaning you go from one edge to another and therefore let go of one hold to grab another, just like regular climbing. This results in a very specific training effect for fingers, arms and upper body, in addition to training technical elements like coordination and dynamics. The challenge with campus boarding is the high risk of injury to fingers, elbows and shoulders. Younger athletes should postpone campus board training until their bodies are fully developed so as to avoid risking injuries to the skeletal structure in their fingers.

Fully developed climbers can stay safe and injury free on the campus board by using proper technique and a sensible progression. First and foremost, it's important to learn how to properly move on the campus board, and for many, the best way to do this is by practising the moves while keeping the feet on footholds placed below the board. Start by doing shorter moves on the deepest edges, progress by skipping holds and making bigger moves, and then move on to smaller holds as your technique improves.

Campus training should be done at the beginning of your training session so that you're well rested and can maintain quality in your training.

1. TRADITIONAL CAMPUS BOARDING

It's important to maintain control of the movement so that you land each edge with four fingers in a half crimp grip position and avoid landing on a straight arm. To achieve this, these exercises are targeted towards strength training rather than explosiveness, and will therefore build a foundation for the more explosive campus training.

1. Up-down (1-2-1, alternating hands)
2. 1-2 match, 2-1 match
3. 1-2-3 match, 3-2-1 match
4. 1-2-4 match
5. 1-3-4 match

When you feel ready to increase the difficulty, you can do the same exercises but without your feet on the wall below. When you're comfortable going footless, increase the distance between the edges, and then choose smaller edges. Here are some examples to try:

1. 1-3-5
2. 1-3-6
3. 1-4-7
4. 1-5-8

EXAMPLE OF A CAMPUS BOARD SESSION

Warm up by doing some exercises with your feet on the wall.

First set:

1-3-5 x3 per arm, with 1 minute of rest between each repetition. Rest for 3 minutes.

Second set:

1-3-6 x2 per arm, with 1 minute of rest between each repetition. No rest.

Third set:

1-2-3-4-5-6-7 x3 with 1 minute of rest between each repetition.

2. EXPLOSIVE CAMPUS BOARDING

When doing campus moves to train explosive strength and finger contact strength, each move should be as big as possible. Again, we must point out that this is not a suitable training method for younger climbers because of the risk of injury. Exercises we recommend are:

1. 1 to maximum height with one hand
2. 1 to maximum height with both hands
3. 1-2-3-4-5-6 maximum speed one hand at a time
4. 1-3-2-4-3-5 dyno both hands at the same time (double dyno)
5. 3-1-4 double dyno

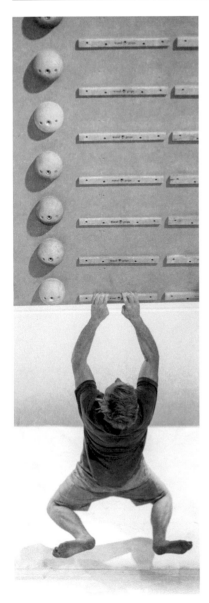  

Double dynoing on the campus board is one of the hardest and most challenging moves you can do, and when stringing together several double dynos in a row you have to slow your body down before starting up again every time. This form of training can be very effective but it is also closely related to the risk of injury. We recommend that double dynoing is reserved for advanced climbers with an established training base and experience with systematic, traditional campus board training.

EXAMPLE OF A CAMPUS BOARD SESSION

Start with exercise 1:
Three repetitions per arm, with a 2-minute rest between each repetition.
Then do exercise 2:
Four repetitions, with a 2-minute rest between each repetition.
Finish with exercise 3:
Two repetitions, with a 2-minute rest between each repetition.

CORE TRAINING

Several of the exercises described previously will train your stomach and back – what we call the core muscles – while in parallel also training your arms and upper body. But still, it can do you good to also focus more specifically on your core muscles, as a strong stomach and back is important for several reasons: to maintain body position when moving an arm or a leg; to maintain pressure on footholds during steep climbing; and to stop a swing when your feet do slip during steep climbing.

The most important thing to understand about training your core is that – as we've mentioned previously – training is specific. This means that the training you do has to resemble as closely as possible the movement patterns of the climbing you'll be doing, and this is where your average core workout won't give the desired effect. An obvious example of this is hanging exercises vs floor exercises: the former has the potential to be climbing specific, but the latter does not. In addition, hanging exercises have the added benefit of training your arms and upper body, which allows you to combine multiple elements in your training.

Common for all the following exercises is that you're moving your legs and body from a hanging position. To increase the difficulty of an exercise, you can make the holds worse or try to move your feet further away from your body.

For most of us, a session will be limited by how tired we get in the fingers and forearms while still having plenty left in the bigger muscle groups. Adding two or three of the following exercises to your climbing sessions, two to three times per week, can be an effective way of maximising the time you have available for training, and increase the training yield per workout. Vary between different exercises for each week.

FOOT PLACEMENT

Being able to place your feet on holds from a hanging position is important on steep walls. It is also important that you are able to maintain your body position when your feet are finally back on the wall. Here are two specific exercises to train this ability:

1. TIC-TAC

Choose two good holds that enable you to hang for 30 seconds without using your feet. Choose three footholds on each side of your fall line – one low, one knee high and one at hip height. Place your right foot on the bottom right hold, let go and drop your foot back down, place it on the middle right hold, drop it back down, and then go for the top right hold. Repeat this with your left foot before taking a two-minute rest, and then repeat the full set two to four times.

As an alternative to Tic-Tac, you can hang in the same position but cross your legs over to the other side, so your right foot goes for holds on your left side, and vice versa.

2. DIAGONAL

Hang from one good hold with both hands and place your right foot on a hold far down to your right. Let go with your right hand and hold this position for about five seconds. Repeat on your left side and do three to four repetitions per side, and two to four sets.

Progression for both of these exercises is controlled by the size of the handholds and how steep the wall is. Less experienced climbers can start by using good holds on a 30-degree overhanging wall and move on to a steeper wall before using poorer holds. You can also adjust the difficulty by moving the footholds further away and making them smaller.

HANGING EXERCISES

The following exercises are performed from a hanging position. To ensure the focus is on core strength it's best if they are done using really good handholds, so that finger strength isn't the limiting factor.

1. L-SIT

Start this exercise by pulling yourself up slightly, as when initiating a pull-up, and lifting your legs so that your body looks like the letter L. Many of you might struggle a bit with hanging with your elbows slightly bent. In this case, you can use a bungee to take some of the load off your arms so you're able to hold the position.

To make it even easier, if you're unable to keep your legs pointing straight out, you can bend your knees, or get help from a partner to lift your legs and then try to hold back as they drift back down.

Alternatively, you can hang with your arms completely straight to further isolate the lower part of your stomach. For climbers who are comfortable with the L-sit, this can be a good way to vary the exercise. For further progression with the L-sit, try swinging one leg out to the side while keeping the other leg pointing straight ahead, then switching back and forth from side to side.

We recommend doing eight to ten repetitions for three sets where each set should last until exhaustion, with 3 minutes of rest between each set.

2. ROOF TOUCH

The roof touch is similar to the L-sit, but here your arms should be straight as you lift your feet all the way up until they're level with your hands. When you're comfortable doing the L-sit without any help and you have energy to spare after each set it's time to progress to the roof touch. You can add variation to the roof touch by alternating between lifting your legs straight up and diagonally – meaning your right leg should be on top when rotating to the left and vice versa. This exercise is significantly harder than the L-sit, and we recommend three sets of four to six repetitions, with 3 minutes of rest between each set.

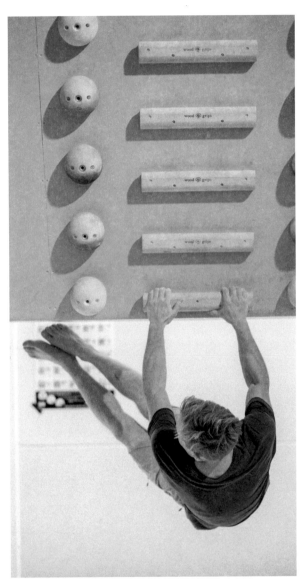
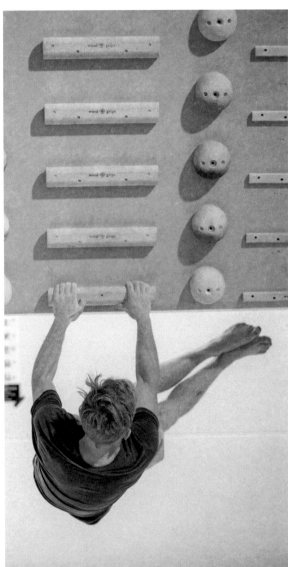

3. WINDSCREEN WIPERS

For this exercise, start by doing a roof touch, and then lower your legs by rotating sideways until they are horizontal. Continue by rotating back and forth to both sides. As with the roof touch, this is a challenging exercise, and we recommend three sets of four to six repetitions, with a 3-minute rest between each set.

FRONT LEVER

This is perhaps the most well-known strength exercise for climbing and it's definitely one of the hardest. To do a perfect front lever your arms and legs should be completely straight and your body horizontal. To get to this level we can divide the progression ladder into multiple steps:

1. ASSISTED FRONT LEVER

Lift your legs up and get into the front lever position. Use a bungee or a partner to help you keep your hips up and hold this position for 3 to 5 seconds. Repeat for three to four sets.

Getting assistance like this is of course also an option for the one-legged front lever.

2. ONE-LEGGED FRONT LEVER

Lean back and lift your hips up towards the roof. Extend one leg forwards horizontally, but tuck your other leg up towards your chest to reduce the load. Hold this position for 3 to 5 seconds before dropping down. Repeat three to four times for each leg.

Do the exercises with your arms slightly bent to start with, and straighten them as you progress.

3. FRONT LEVER

You're now hanging horizontally, and both your arms and your body should be straight. If you've got this far, try working on holding the position for longer, or even adding extra weight around your feet to make it harder still.

The most challenging part of the front lever is stopping your hips from dropping. The goal of this exercise is to keep your hips level with your shoulders and your body horizontal. There's nothing wrong with training for the full front lever if you can't yet manage the one-legged front lever without your hips dropping, but keeping your hips up is where your focus should lie. Using a bungee or a training partner can be very helpful to ensure you're doing the exercise correctly.

STRENGTH TRAINING TERMS

THERE ARE A plethora of different terms within strength training and it can be useful to know some of them in order to understand the effects of different training methods. We have tried not to use too many technical terms, but some are too important to pass by so we will explain them here.

STRENGTH TRAINING

We train muscle strength to generate more force. How much force a muscle can generate is dependent on:

- the size and number of individual muscle fibres. This is known as the muscular cross-sectional area.
- the degree to which we can activate each muscle fibre. Voluntary muscle contractions are caused by sending signals from the brain via the nervous system as electrical impulses. The number of impulses reaching the muscles over a given time interval will decide how much of the muscular cross-sectional area gets activated and hence the total force generated. The last 20 per cent of maximum muscle contraction is a direct result of this ability.
- anatomy. Where the muscle is attached via ligaments to the bones will affect the torque lever and therefore the actual force output, which can vary from individual to individual. A person with a longer torque lever will be able to output a higher force with less muscle mass than a person with more muscle mass but with a shorter torque lever.

Strength training is all about improving the first two qualities – namely muscle size and activation. Most climbers will benefit from focusing on getting stronger without getting bigger, and their training should, therefore, be targeted more towards improving their muscle fibre activation, and less on increasing the muscular cross-sectional area.

STATIC STRENGTH TRAINING

Static strength is when a muscle is generating power without creating motion.

The muscles related to finger and wrist strength are working mostly statically when gripping a hold, and sometimes we will do a move with an arm or a foot while the rest of our body is working statically to maintain the body position. We measure the static work by multiplying the hold time by the load.

When training fingers, the load is our body weight +/- added weight, and the hold time is usually 7 to 10 seconds for most methods of static finger strength training.

DYNAMIC STRENGTH TRAINING

Dynamic strength is when the musculature is generating force and thereby creating movement. This is the most common form of strength training, and in climbing the primary focus for dynamic strength training is to improve the strength of the pulling apparatus in the arms and upper body. The training load of dynamic strength training is measured in volume, which is the product of total weight lifted multiplied by the number of repetitions.

When doing pull-ups the training load equals your body weight +/- added weight multiplied by the number of repetitions multiplied by the number of sets.

CONCENTRIC

Muscles contract to create movement and to stabilise joints. A muscle contracting is in what is known as the lifting phase in strength training.

Lifting your body when doing a pull-up is the concentric phase of the movement.

ECCENTRIC

Using your muscles to slow down a movement is what we call eccentric training. When you're lowering yourself after doing a pull-up you're in the eccentric phase – also known as the breaking phase – of the movement. We will always be able to absorb more force than we can generate, and eccentric strength training can, therefore, be an effective method of strength training.

It's important to remember though that this is a very stressful training method with a high risk of injury.

Eccentric strength training requires experience with strength training and a good training foundation to reduce the risk of injury. It will also lead to increased muscle soreness in the following days, which can negatively affect the quality of your other training.

PLYOMETRIC

Initiating a concentric phase by starting with an eccentric phase is known as plyometric strength training. Picture how you might dip low before exploding into a pull-up. Setting up the move like this exploits the elastic energy created in the eccentric phase and enables us to develop more power in the concentric phase.

HYPERTROPHY TRAINING

The goal of hypertrophy training is to increase the muscular cross-sectional area. The size of a muscle has a significant impact on how much force it can generate, but in weight-dependent sports, like climbing, having overly large muscle volume is not advantageous. The way to increase muscle volume is through high training volume. This means training with a relatively low load per repetition, but increasing the number of repetitions to reach exhaustion for each set, or to train with a relatively high load and fewer repetitions per set. A normal dosage would be three to four sets of eight to twelve repetitions, with a resting period of 2 to 3 minutes between each set.

MAXIMUM STRENGTH TRAINING

The goal of maximum strength training is, as the name implies, to increase your maximum muscle strength. This type of training involves maximising the load for one to three repetitions. This will stimulate the activation of muscle fibres via the nervous system, more so than when doing hypertrophy training. For the last 20 per cent of a maximum muscle contraction, you're dependent on being able to activate all muscle fibres, and by prioritising this training method you'll be able to generate more force from the same muscular cross-sectional area,

which, as a climber, is what you want. It's important to emphasise that the amount of force a muscle can generate is dependent on both the muscle size and the degree of activation, and most strength training programmes will, therefore, have a progression from hypertrophy training to maximum strength training.

Maximum strength training usually consists of three to five sets of three to five repetitions, with 3 minutes of rest between each set. More experienced athletes can train by doing four to six sets of one to three repetitions.

EXPLOSIVE STRENGTH

How much force a muscle can generate through a movement is dependent on how quickly it contracts. This is known as the rate of contraction. A muscle being strong is not the same as a muscle being able to generate force quickly, and it is essential for boulderers to train the ability of the muscles in the arms and upper body to contract quickly. Explosive strength training is characterised by relatively low loads – between 0 per cent and 60 per cent of max load – and with the fastest execution possible.

The most common regime is three to four sets of three to six repetitions, with a 3-minute rest between sets. Fast pull-ups, double dynos and big moves on the campus board are examples of climbing-specific explosive strength training.

RATE OF FORCE DEVELOPMENT

Rate of Force Development (RFD) is a measure of how quickly a muscle can go from zero to maximum force and is an important attribute of the muscles in the forearm for all kinds of climbing. This is an especially important attribute for bouldering and hard crux sections on routes, where you have to be able to quickly generate the force needed to hang on to small holds. We refer to this ability as contact strength. In climbing, we train this ability through maximum strength training like dead hangs, hard bouldering and campusing.

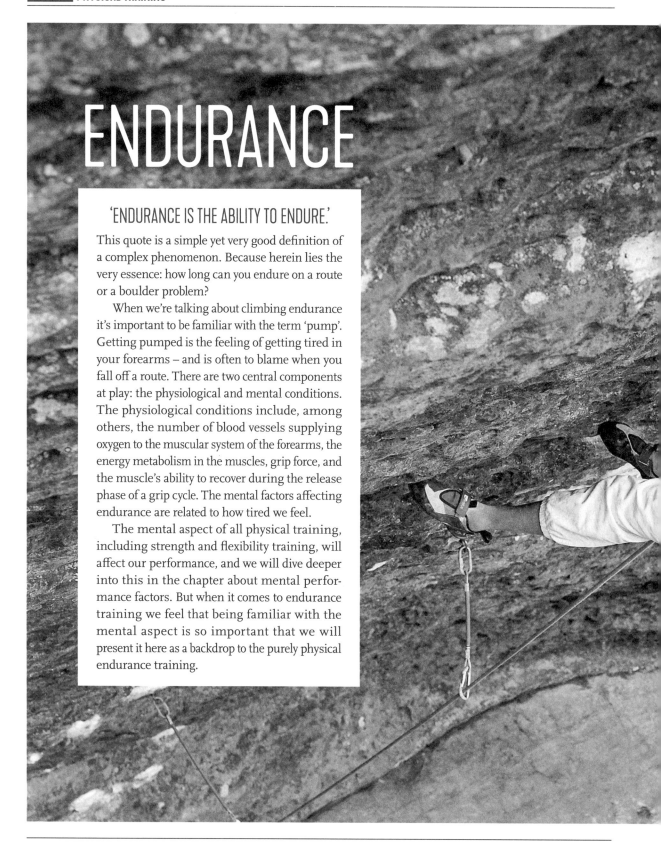

ENDURANCE

'ENDURANCE IS THE ABILITY TO ENDURE.'

This quote is a simple yet very good definition of a complex phenomenon. Because herein lies the very essence: how long can you endure on a route or a boulder problem?

When we're talking about climbing endurance it's important to be familiar with the term 'pump'. Getting pumped is the feeling of getting tired in your forearms – and is often to blame when you fall off a route. There are two central components at play: the physiological and mental conditions. The physiological conditions include, among others, the number of blood vessels supplying oxygen to the muscular system of the forearms, the energy metabolism in the muscles, grip force, and the muscle's ability to recover during the release phase of a grip cycle. The mental factors affecting endurance are related to how tired we feel.

The mental aspect of all physical training, including strength and flexibility training, will affect our performance, and we will dive deeper into this in the chapter about mental performance factors. But when it comes to endurance training we feel that being familiar with the mental aspect is so important that we will present it here as a backdrop to the purely physical endurance training.

Maria Davies Sandbu gets a taste of the pump at Red River Gorge, USA.

MENTAL ASPECTS

The concept of the central governor model emerged as a response to what is known as an energy model to explain endurance performance. The energy model says, in short, that performance declines with the increasing degree of muscular fatigue throughout the activity, but what the model has trouble explaining is, for example, how the final kilometre of a 10-kilometre race is the fastest when world records are set. Or how we can be physically fit, but still end up getting pumped at the second bolt, long before the crux of our project. Because, strictly speaking, the pump is nothing but a sensation. Who hasn't approached the crux of a route, thinking only about how pumped their forearms are? Or wondered if they can clip the rope in time as their left hand crimp starts to open a little? Or experienced how quickly the pump seeps into their arms as they stand a few metres above the previous bolt, reluctant to fall?

Our brains are lazy and overprotective by nature and basically don't want us to get tired on a route. The feeling of being exhausted therefore arises significantly earlier than our capacity suggests and an important part of endurance training is to get to know this feeling. The thought patterns, 'Now I'm pumped, this will never go', and, 'Now I'm pumped, so I'll give it beans', will in all likelihood produce two different results, even though the physical conditions are the same. Being used to climbing with pumped forearms, knowing that you are able to still clip the quickdraws, daring to do a few more moves, knowing that you are able to stop and shake out some of the pump, that you are capable of doing hard moves even when pumped – these are all important mental attributes that constitute endurance performance. Being aware of these elements during training and actual attempts on a route will raise the quality of your climbing, and will eventually provide you with certainty as to what the pump means for you. And it is this confidence that will allow you to go all-in – or *a muerte*, as the Spanish say – on every single attempt.

An important element of the central governor model is also the expectation you have for the activity. For example, it is easier to endure climbing with pumped forearms if you know you are coming to a good rest in three moves, versus on an on-sight when you don't know what's in store after the next three moves. Of course, there is a lot of training behind managing expectations, whether it is the result of working on a route, general endurance training or good mental preparation. And it's exactly these preparations that are so important for your expectations, both the physical and the mental. For it is beyond any doubt that physical attributes are crucial to endurance performance, and these are trained through physical conditioning. The mental preparations lie in coping with climbing while pumped, visualising how the sequences on the route are best solved and how they will feel, and finding the correct level of arousal. These are elements we will discuss in more detail in the chapter on mental performance factors.

Rannveig Aamodt on-sighting
in Red River Gorge, USA.

PHYSICAL ASPECTS

The mental aspects of endurance are gaining increasing attention, but there is a broad consensus that we must be physically fit enough to produce good endurance performances.

When doing repetitive movements, such as gripping and letting go when climbing, the metabolism in the muscles determines how many repetitions we can manage, and this can be simplified into two forms: with and without an adequate supply of oxygen. This is called aerobic and anaerobic metabolism, respectively. Oxygen is transported from the lungs via the blood to the muscles at work. For several traditional endurance sports, such as running and cross-country skiing, the circulation system, oxygen uptake and utilisation rate are considered important factors. Metabolism is primarily aerobic when working at lower intensities and with a well-developed circulation system. When working harder and at higher intensities, anaerobic metabolism is required to maintain the muscular work. Degradation of nutrients such as glycogen and creatine phosphate in the muscles is then the primary source of energy, a by-product of which is lactate, also known as lactic acid. The accumulation of lactate that we are unable to dispose of in the muscles is considered a decisive factor in our reduction of intensity, and will also have consequences for both fine coordination and how quickly the muscles can contract. This has obvious consequences for our climbing performance, as both being able to coordinate a move and being able to quickly close the grip on the next hold is crucial to whether we fall or not.

Climbing is not, in principle, a sport that places any special demands on oxygen uptake or the circulatory system. It is nevertheless difficult to argue against it being advantageous to be in generally good physical shape given the capacity we have to endure training and how quickly we recover. Still, we won't improve our climbing-specific endurance by only running intervals. Climbing places significantly greater demands on the local conditions of the forearm muscles, including the number of blood vessels in the muscles, the ability of the muscles for anaerobic metabolism, and maximum finger strength.

The number of blood vessels in the muscles is important for transporting oxygen to the forearm muscles. As we grip harder, we will increasingly shut off blood circulation in the forearms. It is estimated that with a grip load between 40 and 75 per cent of maximum finger strength, we have completely shut off the blood supply. At lower loads, however, it's still possible for blood to circulate to the forearm muscles, and the number of blood vessels will then be crucial for nourishing the working muscles. Even more important, however, is the blood circulation in the muscles as we release the grip. This removes the by-products from anaerobic metabolism and ensures that we recover more efficiently between each gripping phase. Exactly this trait appears to be crucial for endurance performance in climbing. Since a climbing route will involve repeated grip and release phases, our ability to recover in the release phases is important for how many moves we can do.

Good maximum finger strength gives us a better margin per grip and allows the blood to circulate also during the grip phase, allowing the muscles to last longer before they tire. This is even more important on more intense routes that leave little room for rest in the release phases, as a release phase shorter than three seconds is not enough for the muscles to recover.

Stian Christophersen climbing into the sunset in Kalymnos, Greece.

PHOTO: CHRIS BURKHARD

Since routes of this type will provide inadequate muscle recovery, the muscles' ability for anaerobic metabolism will be crucial. There are two simple methods for testing this ability:

1. Use an edge you can hang on to for at least 15 seconds. Hang in intervals of 10 seconds, with a 3-second rest between each interval, for as long as you can. This will give you an indication of how well you can recover during the release phase. The edge depth provides an indirect measure of your finger strength.

2. Use an edge you can hang on to for at least 15 seconds. Hang until exhaustion. This will give you an indication of how well your muscles are working anaerobically and an indirect measure of your finger strength.

It is important to distinguish these two traits in training as they are trained in different ways. The ability to recover in the release phase and increasing the number of blood vessels in the muscles are trained at a lower intensity for a longer duration, while how well the muscle works anaerobically is trained at high to maximum intensity and a duration of 30 to 120 seconds. These two training methods train your endurance and your power endurance, respectively. To determine the intensity of the workout, we use a five-step scale from no pump to maximum pump, and the different methods can be divided according to this scale:

ENDURANCE	INTENSITY LEVEL 1–5		POWER ENDURANCE
Arc and continuous	1	3–5	Circuits
Circles	1–3	4–5	4 x 4 boulders
Yo-yo	2–3	4–5	The McClure Method
3 x 5 routes	2–3	4–5	Deadhangs
2 x 4 routes	3	4–5	1 x 4 routes

LEVEL 1: No pump, endurance
LEVEL 2: Slight pump, endurance
LEVEL 3: Moderately pumped, endurance
LEVEL 4: Very pumped, power endurance
LEVEL 5: Extremely pumped, power endurance

ENDURANCE TRAINING

By training endurance, we will increase the number of routes we can do in one day or in one session, and how many easier moves we can do in a row without getting drained. The training helps us preserve our strength during longer, easier sections of a route and helps us recover during a climb. Because endurance training also gives us a high volume of moves, it will also build a foundation to endure more and harder training in the future. All together, we can say that endurance training enhances our capacity, both on the wall and in our training.

Common to these training methods is that they have a high volume – the number of moves or the number of minutes on the wall – and low intensity. Here are six methods for training endurance.

1. ARC (AEROBIC ENERGY RESTORATION AND CAPILLARISATION)

This method is comparable to mellow long-distance running. The advantage of this method is that it builds your capacity to endure training and to recover on the wall during a climb, but the disadvantage is that it takes both a long time and is at a level so far below your own maximum level that it might not be very technically demanding. The most rewarding way to train this, we think, is to do lots of easier routes outdoors, for example as an active rest day, as this provides a greater benefit for your technique than a corresponding indoor session.

2. CONTINUOUS

This training method is aimed at the formation of new blood vessels in the muscles and to build a base for more intensive training. It involves being on the wall continuously for over 10 minutes at a sufficiently low intensity so that you do not exceed level 2 on the 'pump scale'. As your endurance progresses you can continue climbing beyond the initial 10 minutes, but one repetition is enough per session.

3. CIRCLES

Circle training is a popular method based on interval principles. This means periods of work and periods of rest where the intensity per circle, the rest time between the circles and the total number of circles determine how hard the training will be. When endurance training at lower intensities (levels 2 to 3), each circle can be between 4 and 10 minutes long, and involve trying not to get pumped while climbing. Here you can easily insert some harder sections followed by easier sections and a rest so that you get variation through the circle and allow the pump to come and go, a bit like when you're running in hilly terrain. You can start with two circles per session with a 2- to 3-minute break between each circle and increase both the number of circles and the time per circle as your endurance improves. The easiest approach is to use a training wall with lots of holds and use any handholds and footholds, but you can also get your training partner to point out which holds to use as you climb.

4. YO-YO

Climb a route on lead, then down-climb the same route, and then climb back up a second route on top rope. The total time should be 5 to 7 minutes on the wall per set. The difficulty level per route and the number of sets in total determines how hard the session is, but for endurance training, the focus should be on easier routes and more sets. Yo-yo sessions are easier with a climbing partner who is doing the same session as you, so that the rest period is roughly equal to the climbing time. Begin training with two to three sets and increase to five sets before making each route a little harder.

5. 2 x 4

Choose two routes where the first one is a little harder than the second and lead them one after the other. Done correctly, you should be able to complete the first route by a small margin, with a moderate forearm pump, and you should be able to recover on route two. Repeat in sets of four with a rest period equal to climbing time. If possible, it is good to vary the routes in the sets in order to maximise the variation in your climbing.

6. 3 x 5

Choose three routes that are roughly equally hard and lead them one after the other. Repeat five sets, and adjust the resting period to match the climbing time. If possible, it is good to vary the routes in the sets in order to maximise the variation in your climbing. The goal is to keep the pump at an acceptable level so that you can complete the exercise with only a light to moderate pump. A common mistake is to start too hard; our recommendation is to choose routes that are a tad easier than you think will allow you to complete the session.

You will climb faster on circles that you're familiar with, so make your own circles longer than when your partner is pointing them out while you're climbing.

POWER ENDURANCE TRAINING

Power endurance is a key quality for managing hard routes. While we have the opportunity for longer release phases and even rests on easier moves and sections on a route, harder sections – or short and hard routes – do not allow for this in the same way. As mentioned earlier, the muscles will not be able to recover during hard climbing and must work with an ever-increasing accumulation of lactate and other by-products from anaerobic metabolism that occurs during the grip phases. This gives us an increasing degree of pump and muscular fatigue which not only weakens the muscles physiologically but also weakens our mental ability to maintain intensity. This demands that we train not only the physiological properties to cope with this, but also our mental ability to climb with pumped forearms. Learning to climb in a technically correct way and making good tactical choices on a route while the forearms are burning is just as important as training for physiological adaptations in the muscles. The basic principle of power endurance training is therefore that it is performed with high intensity: high up on the pump scale and with a lower volume, which means fewer moves or minutes on the wall.

1. CIRCLES

Here are two methods for training power endurance using circles:
- **POINT IT OUT**. Have your climbing partner or coach point out holds for you. This requires being familiar with the wall, the holds on the wall and the level of the climber so that you reach the required number of moves or minutes on the wall. If the moves are too hard, each circle will be broken up by too many falls and short sections, while if the moves are too easy you won't achieve a high enough intensity. The climb should last for about 90 to 180 seconds, which is somewhere between 25 and 50 moves, depending on how fast you climb. You should do four to six circles per session with 3 to 5 minutes of rest between each circle.
- **REDPOINT**. Here you can create your own route with defined handholds and footholds. The climbing time should be around 90 to 180 seconds, or 40 to 60 moves. You can also simulate the type of climbing that you are training for. So, if you're training for a particular route, you can create a circle that simulates both the number of moves and how the sections are put together. For example, if there are three crux sections with rests in between, your circle can reflect this. If the route is more homogeneous with little or no rest, the circle can be created to simulate this. Making these circles yourself is also great training for your technique since you have to test and adjust the moves, handholds, and footholds several times to get it to work. You can vary the sessions by having two to four attempts on very hard circles with a long (over 10 minutes) rest between each attempt, and having slightly easier circles, resting for 3 to 5 minutes with a total of four to six attempts.

Vary the length of the circles, both during a session and between each session.

2. 4 x 4 BOULDERING

Choose four different boulder problems which force you to try hard, yet are still relatively manageable. Each problem is repeated four times in a row without rest, which amounts to one set. Then rest for 3 minutes before repeating this for the next three problems. We recommend choosing relatively sustained problems with between 8 and 12 moves. The problems should be on overhanging walls and not too technically demanding.

3. THE McCLURE METHOD

This method gets its name from British climbing legend Steve McClure, who uses it as one of his exercises to prepare for hard and intense redpoints and on-sights. The exercise is done on the campus board with the legs either on a chair or a foothold, and you go up and down continuously – for example, 1-2-1 or 1-2-3-2-1 – for 60 to 120 seconds. If you manage more than 120 seconds, adjust the foot position to make it more difficult. This is then repeated for five to six sets with a 2- to 3-minute break between each set.

4. 1 x 4 ROUTES

Here you choose four different routes which are so hard that there is a high chance that you will fall at the top. They should also be as sustained as possible. You should climb until you fall, and the goal is to go all-in on every attempt. Rest for 10 minutes and move on to the next route. If there aren't enough routes at your climbing wall you can have four attempts on the same route.

5. DEADHANGS

Deadhanging is a simple and effective high-intensity endurance training method because we can customise how long the grip and release phases are for each set.

To make this training specific enough, we need to look at how long the grip and release phases are when climbing.

Observational studies have shown that the average grip phase in competition lead climbing lasts for about 7 seconds. As mentioned earlier, the release phase must last for more than 3 seconds in order for us to recover during a climb. When we put this together for a deadhang session, it can look something like this:

Hang time	Rest between reps	Repetitions	Sets	Rest between sets
7 seconds	3 seconds	7	7 to 14	2 minutes

Hanging and resting times are adapted to the grip and release phase during climbing. The goal of the session is to train each set to exhaustion, to the point where the fingers start to open. In order to have progression and variation in your training, you should use different grip positions and edge depths.

Start with one session per week and increase to two sessions with a minimum of two days of rest between each session after four to six weeks of exercise. Since these sessions are both load and volume intensive, it is recommended that you don't combine them with regular climbing in the same session.

BEASTMAKER

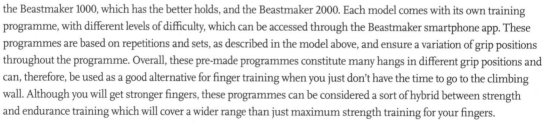

Beastmaker is a fingerboard developed by British climbers. It is available in two models, the Beastmaker 1000, which has the better holds, and the Beastmaker 2000. Each model comes with its own training programme, with different levels of difficulty, which can be accessed through the Beastmaker smartphone app. These programmes are based on repetitions and sets, as described in the model above, and ensure a variation of grip positions throughout the programme. Overall, these pre-made programmes constitute many hangs in different grip positions and can, therefore, be used as a good alternative for finger training when you just don't have the time to go to the climbing wall. Although you will get stronger fingers, these programmes can be considered a sort of hybrid between strength and endurance training which will cover a wider range than just maximum strength training for your fingers.

Our experience with the app is that the exercises described are often hard to complete according to the climbing grade they are associated with. Therefore, go down one grade compared to what you normally climb, and complete the entire programme before considering whether to increase the level of difficulty. These programmes train you to exhaustion, and the goal of each session is to complete all the hangs as prescribed. When you find that you can complete a session with a fair margin, you can try to go up one level.

CHICKEN WINGS

Have you wondered why we climbers raise our elbows when we're getting pumped? This strange phenomenon we call chicken winging is caused by us automatically trying to find a better angle on the handholds for the flexor muscles of the fingers. As the muscles tire when climbing, the elbows start to rise and bend backward in relation to the wrists, and it looks like we have chicken wings.

So now you can at least see when your partner is about to fall and give him the scientific explanation for his chicken wings when you've lowered him to the ground – though that's probably the last thing he'll want to hear about at that point ... !

DIFFERING PERFORMANCE FACTORS BETWEEN BOULDERERS AND LEAD CLIMBERS

THERE IS STILL a lot we do not know about the physical differences between boulderers and lead climbers, but some elements are beginning to emerge as important.

First and foremost, we must look at the requirements posed by the different styles of climbing. Bouldering places greater demands than lead climbing on finger, arm and upper body strength due to harder single moves, poorer holds and fewer moves. In addition, bouldering demands rapid movement and stopping of the centre of gravity to avoid swings. These two requirements are reflected in the fact that boulderers have better maximum finger strength and faster force development in the forearm muscles than lead climbers. We can assume that the same traits are important for the arm and upper body musculature, and training for those who want to specialise in bouldering must, therefore, be adapted to encourage these traits. With an increased demand for force development, muscle mass will also often follow suit, which may explain why boulderers appear to be somewhat heavier than lead climbers.

Although lead climbers also depend on strong fingers, greater demands will be placed on endurance factors, such as the ability to recover during the release phase and how long they can climb before the muscles are exhausted. Lead climbers generally score better on these parameters than boulderers, which in turn indicates that these are attributes that you must emphasise if you wish to specialise in lead climbing.

In competition climbing there has been a clear distinction between lead and bouldering during the last decade, where the boulder problems were set with moves rarely or never seen in lead competitions, while the lead competitions often had routes with up to 60 or 70 moves. This distinction made it extremely difficult to combine the two styles, and there have been only a handful of climbers worldwide who have managed to successfully combine the two disciplines internationally in recent years. Nevertheless, there is now a tendency for lead climbing to incorporate more of the dynamic elements from bouldering, and the fact that the time limit – the time one is allowed to use on a route – has decreased from 8 to 6 minutes has meant that the number of moves per route has gone down. Bouldering, for its part, has retained much of its distinctive style of route setting, but it now seems more feasible for competition climbers to combine the two styles, which is clearly an incentive from the International Federation of Sport Climbing to make lead climbing more exciting and spectacular to watch.

For those of us who do not compete at a high level, we need to look at the demands of the different styles of climbing, and thus what factors are most important if we want to specialise or train specifically for bouldering or lead for a period of time. In short, physical training for bouldering should emphasise to a greater extent maximum and explosive strength in fingers, arms and upper body, while physical training for lead climbing should focus more on the endurance elements presented earlier in the chapter. Still, as highlighted several times, climbing performance depends on far more than the physical, and there is a lot to be learned from both styles of climbing, even if you prefer one over the other.

Maddy Cope on *Snake Charmer* (E5 6c), Huntsman's Leap, Pembroke, Wales.

MOBILITY

Our mobility determines the range of motion of our joints and thus has an impact on how we solve various climbing moves. Imagine having to place your foot high to do a rockover, or reaching your foot high out to one side in a corner. These are moves that require mobility of the hip joint in several different directions. Many climbers compensate for a lack of mobility by solving moves in different ways, but this often requires more effort than is necessary. Having the mobility to be able to perform specific moves, as well as solving moves in as energy efficient a way as possible, are the main reasons why we believe it is important to do mobility training.

There are a number of factors that affect our mobility, including the anatomy of the joints, the mechanical properties of connective tissue, muscles, tendons and ligaments, and neurological factors. Mobility training methods are methods to influence these structures so that the range of motion increases.

We will now look at what training methods we can use for mobility training and which joints we think are appropriate to focus on to improve climbing performance and potentially reduce the risk of injury.

MOBILITY TRAINING CAN BE DIVIDED IN THE FOLLOWING WAY

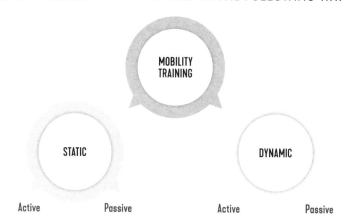

Static mobility training means pushing the joints slowly towards full range of motion either by applying your own muscular force (actively) or by using external forces such as your own body weight or a partner (passively). When you reach the point where you're no longer able to extend further, hold this position for the given time interval. This is traditionally the most common training method for mobility. It is easy to learn and implement and is proven to have a positive effect on range of motion. It is important to take into account the intensity of the stretching, as excessive force can cause damage to the muscles, joints and connective tissues. Another important issue is that static mobility training has a negative effect on the muscle's ability to produce force and power immediately after stretching, and we recommend that you do not do these kinds of exercises immediately before climbing.

Dynamic mobility training means pushing the joints to full extension several times in succession, but without holding this position over time as you do with static mobility training. It is most common to do this actively, i.e. by using your own muscle power. This can be done as a separate session in itself, or form part of a warm-up programme for climbing, as this kind of exercise has not shown the same immediate negative effects on the musculature as static mobility training has.

Below is an example programme for both static and dynamic mobility training:

METHOD	EXECUTION	FORCE	HOLD TIME	REPETITIONS	REST	TIME PER SESSION	SESSIONS PER WEEK
Static	Stretch slowly until end of range and hold position	High	20–60 seconds	2–6 per exercise	30–60 seconds	15–60 minutes	2–4
Dynamic	Repeatedly stretch until end of range and back with increasing speed	High	N/A	Over 6 per exercise	30–60 seconds	15–60 min	2–5

Mobility training to the extent described above is best done in a session on its own, but incorporating some exercises into your warm-up routine before climbing may also be appropriate. This will increase the blood circulation to and elasticity of the tissue and may help you move better as you climb. Just be aware of static stretching with a long hold time just before climbing, because, as we mentioned, this will lead to reduced muscle strength for a period of time.

As we see it, mobility in the hips, shoulders and upper back is especially important for climbing, and we will now take a closer look at mobility training for each of these areas.

HIPS

Good mobility in the hip flexor means that we can lift the knee, and thus the foot, high, and this is important for high foot placements. Lack of mobility here means that we either have to pull ourselves higher with our arms to get our feet up, or move our hips further out from the wall. Both of these options cost a lot of effort when the holds are bad, as they will become even worse when we pull ourselves higher and our centre of gravity moves out from the wall.

When fronting, we rotate the hip out so that the knee points away from the centre of the body and the inside of the thigh faces the wall. In this way, the body is held closer to the wall and the centre of gravity can be positioned directly above the foot so that the upward movement is created more by the leg than by the upper body.

In addition, it is important to be able to extend the leg straight to the side, both to reach faraway footholds, and to be able to apply pressure and gain balance with a wide platform between two footholds which are far apart.

Good mobility in this movement will, like with the hip flexor, allow you to lift your leg further to the side without using more power in the upper body than necessary.

STATIC STRETCHING

1. LOTUS

Sit on the floor with the soles of your feet facing each other and your knees pointing out to the side. Straighten your back and push your knees down to the ground. You can push your knees down with your arms, or have a partner help you. You should feel the inside of your thighs stretching up towards the groin. Hold this position for 40 to 60 seconds, release for 15 seconds and repeat two to six times, gradually stretching more every time.

Your back should be straight for all of the following exercises!

2. SPLITS

VERSION 1: Sit on the ground with your legs pointing to the side. Lie forward as if trying to push your chest down towards the floor. You should feel the stretch behind and inside the thighs. Hold the position for 40 to 60 seconds, release for 15 seconds and repeat two to six times with gradually increasing force.

VERSION 2: Stand upright, slide your feet out to each side and lower your hips towards the floor. You should feel the stretch on the inside of the thighs. Hold the position for 40 to 60 seconds, release for 15 seconds and repeat two to six times, gradually stretching more every time.

DYNAMIC STRETCHING

1. COSSACK SQUAT

Stand upright with your legs out to the side. Shift your weight towards the right and squat as deep as you can with most of your weight on the right leg. Your weight should be resting on the right heel so that the sole of your foot is in contact with the ground; you should feel it stretching the groin and the back of the thigh. Stand back up into the starting position before shifting your weight over the left leg and squatting to the left. Repeat for six sets, with four squats per leg, and hold the squat position for 10 seconds while gradually stretching more every time.

2. OPEN SQUAT

Stand up against a wall with your feet pointing out to each side, with your knees and thighs as close to the wall as possible. Lower your hips until you feel the stretch on the inside of your thighs and up towards the groin. Hold this position for 5 to 10 seconds before standing back up. Repeat three to four sets of eight to ten repetitions, gradually stretching more every time.

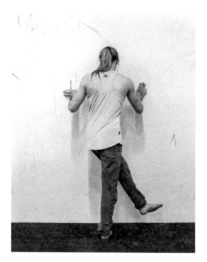  

3. LEG SWING

Stand upright facing the wall, using your arms against the wall as support. Cross your left leg in front of your right and then quickly swing it back left and up so that your toes are pointing up towards the ceiling. You should feel it stretching the back and inside of your left thigh. Repeat three to four sets of 20 repetitions for each leg, gradually stretching more every time.

SHOULDERS AND UPPER BACK

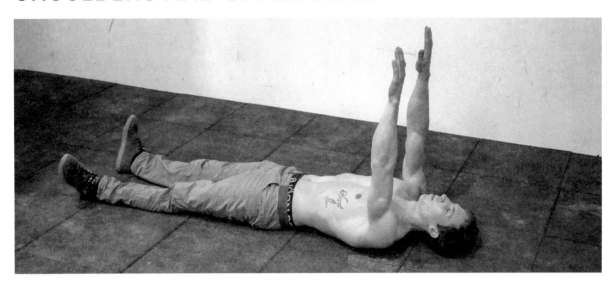

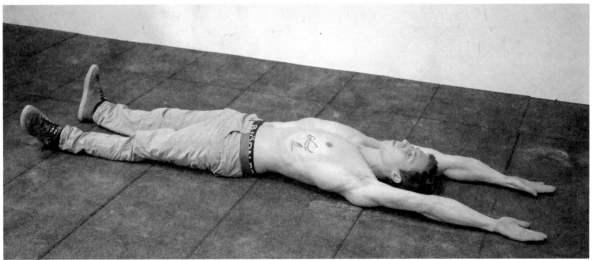

Lie down on your back and let your arms drop backwards to the floor. Are you able to touch the floor with both your hands without arching your lower back?

Shoulder mobility is important in climbing, and the shoulder is also dependent on the mobility of your thoracic spine – the upper part of your back where the ribs are attached to your spine – to function properly.

Good shoulder and thoracic mobility will allow us to reach the next hold without compensating by moving the upper body too much. This allows us to keep our body more stable when doing a move. In addition, all variations of stemming between holds and rotations for large crossover moves require good shoulder and thoracic mobility. Mobility training for the shoulders must therefore also include thoracic mobility training. We have chosen to focus on active, dynamic exercises in order to work with multiple joints at the same time.

1. KNEELING ARCH

Kneel on both knees and place your hands on your heels for support. Push your hips forwards and your shoulders back so that the insides of your arms point forwards and your chest points up towards the ceiling. Hold this position for 3 to 4 seconds before relaxing. Repeat two to three sets of 10 to 15 repetitions. You should feel it stretching the front of your hips, chest and shoulders. The exercise becomes harder the closer together your hands are, and this is adjusted by how wide you place your feet.

2. MOBILITY ON A STICK

Grab a stick with both hands. Move your arms over your head and down your backside, then back up and over again. You should feel it stretching across your chest, and the exercise is harder the closer together you grip with your hands. Do the exercise slowly, relaxed and in control all through the movement. Repeat two to three sets of 15 to 20 repetitions.

3. THORACIC ARCH

Start with your right hand on the ground behind you and both feet pointing forwards. Push your hips and chest up towards the ceiling and get up on your toes. Move your left hand behind you and to the left as if you're about to place it on the ground behind you on your left side. Hold this position for 3 to 5 seconds before returning to the starting position. Repeat two to three sets of eight to ten repetitions for each arm. You should feel it stretching the front of your hips, chest and shoulders.

4. ROTATING STARFISH

Start as if doing a push-up, and rotate up into a sideways starfish position by lifting your right arm and leg. Continue the rotation by placing your right hand and leg behind you and then lifting your left arm and leg as you continue around and back to the starting position. Complete four full rotations to each side, eight in total, for two to three sets. The exercise can be made easier by not lifting your leg as you rotate.

5. ROTATING SHOULDER PRESS

Hold a dumbbell or a kettlebell in your left hand and lift it up until your arm is straight. Keep your arm straight as you bend forwards and rotate your upper body until you can touch the floor with your right hand. Hold this position for 3 to 5 seconds and return to the starting position. Repeat for two to three sets of eight to ten repetitions. The exercise can be made more difficult by standing with your feet closer together, and harder by using heavier weights. Holding a kettlebell upside down will make it more difficult to stabilise your arm and can add an extra challenge to the exercise. You should feel the stretch in the back of your thighs and you should be actively engaging your upper arm and the muscles between your shoulders to keep the arm straight all through the movement.

REMEMBER

It's important to maintain body control during all these exercises. Even when doing a dynamic exercise like the leg swing you should feel in control of the movement and gradually increase the range of movement until you've reached the maximum range of motion of the joint. It's important to control your breathing and relax as much as possible. If you're pushing too hard and you hold your breath, it'll only be harder for you to reach full range of movement. Stretching too fast or with too much force will also increase the risk of injury to your muscle tissue, so it's important to start slowly and gradually increase the speed and how hard you're stretching as you get more familiar with the exercises.

CHAPTER 3

MENTAL TRAINING

'THE BRAIN IS THE MOST IMPORTANT MUSCLE FOR CLIMBING.'
WOLFGANG GÜLLICH,
THE FIRST PERSON TO CLIMB F9a

GÜLLICH'S QUOTE IS used in virtually all articles and books that deal with mental training for climbing. And not without reason: the quote hits the nail on the head. For example, you might have experienced getting scared and forgetting everything you know about technique as you climbed past the last bolt when leading a route, or how a lack of confidence on a climb can lead you to hesitate and fall. In the chapter on technique, we highlighted the mental aspect as an important element for doing dynamic moves, and in the physical training chapter, we emphasised the mental factors around getting pumped. Your mentality will affect every part of your climb, so it is just as important that you train your head as well as the physical and technical sides of your climbing.

In this chapter, we look at how mental techniques improve mental skills, which in turn increase climbing performance. Better mental skills mean that in the long run you will be able to make better use of your potential, and this can make the difference between whether you reach your goals or not. At the same time, it will also give you more enjoyment of the sport of climbing. Not only because you'll perform better, but also because you'll learn how to better deal with the ups and downs of climbing – and not just the literal!

Maria Davies Sandbu preparing
before an attempt in Bishop, USA.

MOTIVATION AND SETTING GOALS

Motivation is essential if you wish to become a better climber. You must be motivated to put in the effort needed when strength training, and you have to be motivated to practise precise footwork in order to improve your technique. We believe that the most important thing for motivation is that you find joy in what you are doing. If you're enjoying it, you'll pull harder during your strength training sessions and have more patience when working on technical elements. If you find pleasure in training for climbing, we recognise this as having an inner motivation to climb, train and improve. Unlike external motivation, where you are motivated by results, rewards or recognition by others, you will find joy in pursuing the activity itself and being motivated by mastery and progression. The chances of you being willing to do what it takes to progress, to cope with the harder days with a smile and continue climbing for years and years, is much greater if your motivation is intrinsically rooted. If you win a competition or get recognition for a climb, take it as a well-deserved bonus, but don't let that be the only reason you're climbing. Instead, try to feel the joy of learning a new technique or sticking yet another move on your project.

Specific
Measurable
Ambitious
Realistic
Time limited

An important technique for staying motivated is goal setting. Since motivation should come from internal factors and is dependent on progression and mastery, your goals should reflect this. Many climbers aim to climb a certain route or grade. They specifically train for a long time to send the route, and in the end, they might achieve their goal. The problem with such goals is that the road to victory can seem unrealistically long. Therefore, it may be good to set goals that let you know that you are progressing. For example, try to climb multiple routes of a particular style, get physically stronger or become less afraid of falling on lead. With these goals, each individual performance becomes less important, and it is easier to find joy in progress and not just in success.

It will be of great benefit to you if the goals you set follow the principles of SMART and are clearly defined. For example, a well-defined goal could be to climb five vertical routes graded F6b by the end of the year. This goal is specific, measurable and within a predefined time limit. At the same time, it is both an ambitious, yet realistic goal if you have just started with climbing 'in the sixes', it's early in the year and you have been training well throughout the winter.

GRADE	TOTAL							
7a	7							
6c+	18							
6c	60							
6b+	75							
6b	86							

A ticklist shaped like a pyramid shows that you've built up a good foundation of skills at lower levels. All of these routes and boulder problems can be viewed as intermediate goals on the Path of Progression, and perhaps some of these were indeed your main goal at the time?

It's beneficial to define sub-goals in addition to your main goals, as this ensures that you'll experience progression and mastery along the way. If your goal is to establish yourself on a new grade by, for example, having climbed three routes of that grade the coming season, each route can be a sub-goal on its own. In addition, another sub-goal might be to do several routes one grade below your target. To become a good climber you should always make sure your ticklist is shaped like a pyramid. In addition to the sub-goals, it's wise to set goals for the climbing session you're about to have. This is important and allows you to get a sense of achievement for each session and helps you to perform at your maximum. Such goals might be to do another move on your project or to figure out and send a sequence you've yet to complete. It could also be to achieve the feeling of really going all out in an endurance session, or doing an extra pull-up if you are doing a strength training session.

By varying the focus of your training and your goals for different periods of the year, you can more easily maintain motivation. If you have spent some time working on your technique, it can be good for your motivation to switch things up and work on your physique for a while, and vice versa. You can also have several different goals for the same period: you could focus on technical and balancy boulder problems on easy days, and arm and upper body strength on harder days. For many of us, it is the complexity of climbing which makes it so exciting, and the variety this provides in your training should be utilised to the fullest to keep your motivation up.

 Remember, grades are very subjective and routes and boulder problems can feel hard or easy for different climbers, based on their height, finger size, climbing style, and so on. It might be harder for you to climb an 'easy' route that doesn't suit you than it is to set a new personal best on a route that suits your style perfectly. Sending a new grade is therefore not a very objective way of measuring progression.

THILO SCHRÖTER:

- The quality of what you're doing is more important that what it is you're actually doing. Adjust your training according to how you feel from day to day and make sure you get enough rest. Knowing when your body needs a rest day takes more discipline and insight than the training itself.
- A good training partner is worth his or her weight in gold! Train together with people who push you and feed you with energy and inspiration – and preferably someone who's a bit better than you.

PROTIPS

PHOTO: ALEX MANELIS

Thilo Schröter playing around on *The Rhino* (Font 7b+), Rocklands, South Africa.

ADVERSITY

It's best to surround yourself with positive climbers and to be positive yourself. It's impossible not to be negatively affected by whining climbers. Try to avoid them – and don't become one!

Progression makes it easier to stay motivated, but at times motivation can and will be off on holiday. Stagnation, and even periodic decline, can be demotivating, and it is no secret that the times when you feel clumsy and weak will leave their mark on your mood and affect the quality of your workout. If you ever find yourself lacking in motivation, there are two things you can do:

- Find the reason that you feel weak. You may be in a heavy training period which will naturally reduce your performance in the short term. Remember, you're training hard now to become even stronger later. You might be experiencing a lot of stress in other areas of your life. If so, it's only natural for progression to slow down, but when you analyse why, you can be confident that you will come back even stronger. You can't be in the best shape of your life every time you put your shoes on. By accepting this, you will perform better by reducing the performance expectation for each session.

- Find pleasure in achieving other things in life. Climbing shouldn't be the only thing that defines who you are, even though it might feel like it sometimes. Remember that you are also a source of motivation for your training partners and those around you. Get psyched by others doing well, and be positive so that they can perform at their best. By being positive you'll help to create a positive training culture that will lift both yourself and others. Most of us prefer to train with positive climbing partners, so try to be one yourself too.

CONFIDENCE AND INNER DIALOGUE

Confidence is the belief that you'll be able to do whatever it is you're trying to do, whether it's your first pull-up or not slipping off that tiny foothold on the technical slab problem you're working on. Confidence is important for pushing yourself during training and when you're about to try a hard route or boulder problem. Confidence isn't something we just have; it's created by actively working with having faith in succeeding. If we do just that, we can drastically increase our chance of success. One of the true legends of bouldering, Marc Le Menestrel, once said that he needed *'A little bit of magic'* to send a boulder problem in the magical forest of Fontainebleau. Our experience is that this magic doesn't appear without the belief that it will.

Your preparations – and especially being conscious about being prepared – are important for your confidence. By trusting your preparations, you'll build faith in succeeding in the tasks at hand. Engaging in a positive inner dialogue – i.e. talking to yourself – is an important mental technique to further build your confidence. On average, 150 to 300 words per minute will be popping into your head, and these words will affect your performance. So it's important to try to control your thoughts. Tell yourself that you will accomplish what you're trying to achieve. Repeat to yourself how well prepared you are, and establish faith in your success. It is also helpful to remind yourself of previous positive experiences and relive them in your mind. For example, before doing a hard strength training session, think back to the last time you had a really good training session. When the session has started, say to yourself that you'll do that last pull-up in your programme. This will put you in the right mindset to pull hard and increase your faith in actually doing it. Before trying a really hard route, think back to the last time you climbed something hard. By reliving past successes before performing, your faith in yourself will increase. When you're on a route, practise telling yourself that you're feeling good and that you'll be able to send. Convince yourself that you're strong enough, that you won't get too pumped, and that you're climbing with good technique. Try to suppress the feeling of getting pumped, and don't allow any mistakes that you might make damage your confidence. It's imperative that anything you tell yourself is helping to boost your confidence.

Since positive experiences have a reinforcing effect on your confidence, it is important that you take care of them and spend enough time memorising them so that you can easily retrieve them at a later date. Negative experiences, on the other hand, should be analysed: find out what went wrong and why it happened, and then try to forget these experiences. Learn from the mistakes, but do not relive the experiences themselves. It is said that you need ten positive experiences to make up for one negative, and by remembering the negative, this discrepancy will be even greater. If you fail to climb a route, try smiling and laughing instead of beating yourself up – and then try again. We're not saying that you should never get mad – it's OK to vent your frustration – but you must try to avoid letting it get to you so that it affects you negatively. Remember we are falling all the time! Don't be too hard on yourself every time you fail: climbing is failing until you make it. Some climbers project routes for days, weeks and even years before sending them. When you come home after training or trying a project, you can analyse what went wrong, set a plan for how to prevent it from happening again, and then put it away.

HESITATION

You might have noticed how hesitation leads you to climb poorly, and sometimes fall.

Is my foot going to slip? Will I be able to reach the next hold? Am I going to clip the quickdraw? In the same way, you might have experienced days where you're confidently smearing on the tiniest of footholds and hitting every handhold perfectly. This is the difference between days where you have low confidence and days where you have faith in your success. A quote from one of our English climbing colleagues is, *'A weighted foot never slips'*. If you believe you're standing on the foothold, you'll also apply more pressure with your foot, maximise friction and lessen the risk of your foot slipping.

PHOTO: HENNING WANG

Maria Davies Sandbu
fighting to clip the draws
on *Kalea Borroka* (F8b+),
Siurana, Spain.

TRY, FAIL AND FAIL BETTER!

Positive thinking isn't only important when climbing hard. It is easier to learn when you're relaxed and in a positive state of mind. Positive thinking is therefore important every time you train – so focus on getting better at it. The best way to do this is to become conscious of how you're thinking. By being conscious of thinking positively and suppressing negative thoughts, you will eventually become significantly better at having a positive inner dialogue. Eventually, you'll automatically think positively, and you won't have to spend as much energy on it. Then, when you are trying hard on a route that you want to send, you can instead use your mental energy to focus on other tasks.

Be aware of when negative thoughts arise and decide if they are prudent. A simple tool for turning a negative inner dialogue into a positive one is the so-called 'thought stop'. When you notice that you're starting to think negatively – for example, 'the conditions are bad', 'my skin is bad', 'my endurance is bad' – you can perform a physical action that stops this line of thinking and turns your attention to the positive. This action can be as simple as pinching your arm or asking your climbing partner to let you know if you start talking yourself down. The most important thing is that you become aware of your inner dialogue and can turn it from a negative to a positive. Below are some tips for positive talking points which are based on the negative thoughts climbers often have.

- I'm well prepared because I've trained for what I'm about to do!
- I like challenging myself!
- I'm not too short. I can place my feet higher!
- I'm not too tall. I often don't have to place my feet high, and can reach further!
- It's OK to not have a lot of time. I'll just plan ahead and use the time more sensibly!

DARE TO TRY

In order to create positive experiences and build confidence at all, you must dare to try. Fall if you are afraid of falling. Challenge yourself with dynamic movements if you are poor at them. Don't be afraid to make a fool of yourself in front of other climbers. You must, as with all other elements of your life, extend your comfort zone and push yourself. If things go wrong, analyse them and learn from them. If you do not even try, the positive experiences will not come! Nothing will slow your progression more.

You must know your fears and why they exist. Write them down – and write down what you're doing to conquer them!

FEAR OF FALLING

Most of us have a certain degree of fear of heights, and it can feel quite unnatural and scary for us to let go of a hold and rely on gear and the belayer when climbing on lead, or a spotter and pads when bouldering. Most beginners get scared when climbing on lead, but also more experienced climbers can be impeded from performing at their best because of their fear of falling. Fear makes us move less proficiently. We stop trusting our feet, and we grip the holds more than is necessary and thus use more force than we need.

Having a basic fear of and respect for heights where the consequence of a fall is potentially serious is an important survival mechanism, and fear is, therefore, a rational response. When we know that the gear will hold, that safety checks have been completed and the belayer is ready and attentive, the fear of falling is irrational.

Fear is appropriate as it enables us to make rational choices about safety, but irrational fear should not prevent us from performing. If it does, we must actively work on it so we can better deal with it. How long it will take to become less scared will vary from climber to climber, but it will be better if you expose yourself to falling on a regular basis. Some climbers might be better off starting easy and getting used to falling gradually, while for others it'll be better to literally jump straight into the deep end. We can't say what will be the right way for you, you'll have to experiment for yourself, but you do have to expose yourself to falling.

These are some tips on how to become more comfortable with falling on lead:
1. The first fall is the worst fall. It'll get better.
2. Practise falling every time you go climbing until you're no longer afraid.
3. Visualise the fall in three segments: before falling, the fall itself, and the following swing. Go through the three parts with your belayer, and agree in advance on how long the fall should be and how much slack your belayer should give you.
4. Start with short, controlled falls indoors, where you give your belayer a heads-up before letting go. Continue with longer and longer falls indoors, and then progress outdoors. After a while, you'll be comfortable going for big moves and falling without needing to let your belayer know up front what's about to happen.
5. Start on an overhanging wall. You'll fall freely and won't have to worry about hitting anything on the way down.
6. Use an experienced belayer who knows how to give soft catches. A soft catch is important, as it lessens the swing and softens any potential impact, reducing all the forces at play.
7. As you get more comfortable falling, try giving yourself focus areas when climbing. Our experience is that we're never afraid when we have decided to send a route, because 'this is the attempt it's going to happen', and we're focusing on trying hard instead of falling. Many competition climbers feel the same way. They're never afraid during a competition, because they are too focused on the task at hand, but they might still feel fear during training. By setting a focus area you can trick your brain into not being afraid because it will be busy concentrating on something else instead.

Being aware of the potential dangers of climbing makes you alert and ensures you won't make mistakes that could have serious consequences.

Don't mess around with those who are afraid of falling! It's important for them to build confidence based on positive experiences. Giving unexpected falls or otherwise provoking the situation will only prolong their process significantly.

Maria Stangeland whipping into the weekend.

THE FIRST ASCENT OF BULDREIDIOTER by Martin Mobråten

A friend of mine, who is a safety manager for a rope access company, and I were trying to nab the first ascent of a route at Frigården outside of Trondheim, Norway. My friend fell at the third bolt and suddenly he was flat on the ground right beside me. He landed on his back on the grass right between three large rocks. He was fine, fortunately, and stood back up. As we looked up we saw the knot still dangling from the third quickdraw. It was obvious the figure of eight hadn't been completed as it should have been. The pre-climb safety check is always important and would have easily prevented the situation. We both got quite scared by the experience and have never forgotten the safety check since. We're now more aware of what can happen and are always alert when it comes to safety. We later sent the route and gave it the name *Buldreidioter* (Ed: 'Bouldering Idiots'), to reflect the fact that we mostly just do bouldering and were idiots to forget to check the knot.

PHOTO: ALEX MANELIS

'NEVER RESPECT GRADES.'
MARTIN MOBRÅTEN, 1999

Martin Mobråten sending
The Buttermilker (Font 8a+),
Bishop, USA.

FEAR OF FAILING

The fear of failing – performance anxiety – is a problem for many because it prevents them from trying moves, routes and exercises they think they will not master. This may be because they put too much pressure on themselves or experience a great deal of expectation from others. Although this fear can be devastating to both achievement and development, the fear of failure is an example of irrational fear. If this applies to you, work on it! Nothing will hinder your development more than avoiding even trying. Be pro-active and try technical, physical and mental challenges to improve. It's not the end of the world if you fail. Those who know you know how good you are, and the rest will not give it much thought if you fail. And why should you even care what others think? The climbers that impress us the most are the ones who dare to try and consider the process as helping them to develop further.

As we have mentioned many times in this book, one of the best things about climbing is the variety you can experience with different styles, walls and holds. This is what makes it a technically demanding sport and is a big part of why so many people think climbing is exciting and interesting. But this also presents a challenge. We all have a style, steepness and type of hold we prefer and are better at. Some may be lucky enough to have more than one skill, but few of us are equally good at everything. After many years as climbers and coaches, we see that some climbers prioritise most of their time in the style they are best at. And, in all honesty, so do we. Success gives us positive feedback, and it can be difficult to prioritise techniques that we are initially bad at. This can turn into a negative spiral, where you gradually become more and more sceptical of trying the techniques you do not master. But it's important to break this spiral. It's the styles we do not master that are the most important for us to practise, both for technical and mental reasons. For example, if you are poor at dynamic moves and want to become a better climber, then this is what you should practise. Even though clear and obvious results might elude you at first, begin the development process and try to find joy in your progression.

When we started climbing, F8b was about the hardest grade you could do on a rope in Norway, and the unofficial testpiece of Oslo was *Marathon* at Damtjern. It was the first of its grade in Norway and had not been repeated since Per Hustad's first ascent. Martin climbed the ranks relatively quickly when he started as a 14-year-old, but nobody expected him to try *Marathon* at only 16. Such grades were reserved only for the very strongest, those who had been training hard for a number of years, and not a skinny kid who had only climbed for a few years. Martin, on the other hand, thought otherwise. He hadn't climbed that many easier routes but he thought that if others could do it, so could he. Martin projected the route for a few days and, belayed by his father, he sent it in the late autumn of 1999. We have later thought about this and conclude that his lack of respect for the grade was one of the main reasons he sent the route. There were certainly more people who could have climbed it, but not many did. Most people thought it was too hard for them and never tried it. The role of youth has often been to break with the old ways of thinking and belief in what is possible, but here we could probably all improve. The youthful *naiveté* and belief in one's own abilities is an important starting point for improving. After Martin sent the route, there were others who followed. To many, it was an eye-opener and removed some of the respect that had been there for far too long.

CONCENTRATION AND FOCUS

Concentration is important both when exercising and when trying to climb a route or a boulder problem. In order to have good concentration, it is important that we do not focus on too many things at the same time or that our minds are not occupied by unnecessary thoughts or outside disturbances. We must also be able to maintain concentration over time, while at the same time the varying challenges mean that we must concentrate on different tasks. Sports psychology usually distinguishes between inner, outer, narrow and wide concentration.

Inner concentration is when we concentrate on thoughts, feelings and feedback from physical movements, and when we make plans. Inner concentration is central when preparing to climb a route, when we are laying down the tactics for how to climb the next sequence on an on-sight, and when trying to calm down during relaxation exercises. During these preparations, it is often advisable to start with a wide inner concentration where we take into account all the factors that will be involved when climbing the route. All the factors are important to laying out good tactics, but before you start climbing, it is worthwhile to use a narrower concentration style focusing on routines and regulating your stress level. This is important to get you into the right mood for performance, because a wide inner style of planning the complicated tasks in front of you requires too many mental resources just before you get on the route, and can ruin the flow you need when you start to climb.

When you start climbing, you should generally put the inner concentration aside and focus on the outer elements. As long as you have prepared well before you start to climb, focusing too much on inner concentration when you are in the wall will only ruin your flow. You've probably experienced overthinking when climbing at some point. By analysing and evaluating the signals you're receiving from your body, the chances are that the route will feel harder than you expected. This is rarely of any benefit, so you should concentrate on external factors. Look at footholds to position your foot precisely, and concentrate on tasks such as flow and efficiency so you don't get too pumped too soon.

We also distinguish between wide and narrow outer concentration, and the difference is again how many simultaneous elements we take into account. In general, you should try to have a narrow outer concentration when climbing. Trying to take in all the different elements of the route as you climb will only have a negative effect. This will slow down your movements and you'll lose the flow you normally would have when you're 'just climbing'. It's better to focus on a single task such as precision or efficiency. The exceptions are when you are climbing on sight, don't remember the beta, or when you're working on a section of a route for future redpoint attempts. In these cases, you are often dependent on considering many external elements at the same time, such as hand and foot placements and from where to clip the next quickdraw. You'll then need a wider concentration than you would on a redpoint, as you have to take many different factors into account and not just execute the plan you have set in advance.

PLAYBOX

When you're climbing a route, you should concentrate on fewer and more specific tasks, like climbing with flow, relaxing at the rest, or really tightening up the core so you can take the swing you know is about to come. Execute – don't think!

THINKBOX

Before getting on a route or boulder problem, analyse and assess the different elements and make a plan for what you should do. Think about which hand sequence to use, which footholds are best, whether to do the crux move statically or dynamically and how you should position your body when matching the slopers. Leave the Thinkbox before starting the climb.

PHOTO: NATHAN WELTON

Rannveig Aamodt
focusing before the
next crux section.

> ## 'THINKING WHEN CLIMBING IS A CLIMBER'S WORST ENEMY. YOU'LL HESITATE AND MISS THE HOLD.'
> **MARTIN MOBRÅTEN**

You might also have to switch between inner and outer concentration when climbing on sight. You might need to plan ahead for sequences further up the route while you're at a rest, and you might need to calm down after an unexpected crux that has suddenly appeared where you didn't expect it to. At this point, your concentration is directed internally, but we believe that it's important for you to direct the concentration back to external factors before continuing the climb. The same thing goes for when you're working a route before a redpoint attempt. When you're sitting in the harness and making a plan for how to execute the next sequence, that's inner concentration, but when you tell your belayer that you're about to give it a go, you should switch to a narrow outer concentration. In this regard, climbing differs from other individual sports because the tasks at hand require us to improvise and solve problems while climbing. We alternate between inner and outer and narrow and wide concentration all the time. In most other individual sports you train to perform a known task with few unforeseen and unknown factors. This is more like a redpoint send go. You know all the moves by heart, and all that's left to do is to 'just send it'. When it's time to send, block out anything that does not fit into the narrow outer concentration.

It's difficult to have the correct concentration, and it's extra challenging when you're forced to switch between narrow and wide and inner and outer. In addition to that, you often have to change what you're focusing on within the same style of concentration. We find it useful to use a camera analogy to illustrate what we mean:

As with a camera we can zoom in or out to choose what should be in focus. If we wish to focus on details, we zoom in. By focusing only on that tiny foothold and blocking out everything else, we can increase the chance of us placing the foot correctly and it not slipping off. If we need more general focus, we zoom out. This can be flow, efficiency or precision, and is often the type of focus we need to send a route we're familiar with. To get and maintain the right focus over time it can help to give yourself tasks during a climb. It's important that these tasks are suited for the specific route or boulder problem, and they should be somewhat general. If you're climbing a vertical indoor route, try focusing on precision footwork. If, on the other hand, you're climbing a long and pumpy overhanging route, focus on dynamic flow. If a specific move requires it, zoom in, but be sure to zoom back out once the move is done.

Our experience is that you should zoom in only when strictly necessary. It can be hard to get back into rhythm if you start zooming in on details. Getting back into the right focus is a skill that can be trained, and the best way to do this is by specifying and focusing on concrete tasks when climbing. If you know you have to zoom in at a certain point during a climb, make sure to have a plan for getting your flow back. This can be as specific as planning to do the next ten moves quickly without any hesitation. By training these tasks, you'll become more conscious of how and when you lose focus, and get better at getting back on track.

THE RIGHT FOCUS

Focus on the tasks, not the results! We hear stories about athletes who say they had the wrong focus when they failed. Often this is because they were focusing on the results rather than the simple tasks they had given themselves, and that their concentration shifted from outer to inner. We too make the same mistakes. When we're finally past the crux and all we have left is easy climbing to the top, we fail because our focus shifts to how it will feel when we succeed, or we start worrying about the consequences of failing now that we are finally past the crux.

Analyse any mistakes while you are on the ground, not when climbing. It's easy to think negative thoughts if something feels harder than it did last time, or if your foot slips and you have to waste energy to hang on. If the negative thoughts are creeping in, you need to shut the door on them and turn that mental frown upside down.

Ignore unforeseen things that happen. It's easy to lose focus if you suddenly get to a wet hold, or if there are lots of people watching you, or if the friction is bad. These things happen when you climb, and it's important that you keep your thoughts from turning sour. Be selective, ignore noise and disturbances, and focus on the tasks at hand.

 Climbers with good technique often have an easier time keeping focus. They aren't as dependent on zooming in on every little detail of every move, and they can more easily maintain a wider overview.

ROUTINES AND RITUALS

Routines and rituals are important tools for increasing concentration and creating the right focus. The routines aim to make sure that the preparations in advance are as good as possible and that you are ready to perform. Examples of routines can be to warm up the same way every time, to rest for 15 minutes after the warm-up, to visualise the route or the boulder problem, and to talk to yourself in a certain way before pulling on. It can also be a song or a music genre that puts you in that try-hard mood, or closing your eyes and taking three deep breaths right before you start.

Rituals differ from routines in that they are not clearly or objectively related to the performance. They may be important to your performance, but it is far from certain that the same ritual will make sense to your climbing partner. Rituals are often associated with superstition and are often related to earlier success, seemingly, but randomly, caused by doing something in particular. Rituals are important to many climbers, as they can strengthen their faith in success. Examples of rituals can be to always put on the left climbing shoe before the right, or wearing a special pair of lucky trousers. If your belief in your success increases when you put your left shoe on before the right then that's a good thing, but it probably has no significance beyond that.

For routines and rituals to be useful, it is important that they are feasible, not too comprehensive, and that you yourself are in control of the content. If they make you dependent on others or are difficult to control, consider changing them. For example, if you need to eat a particular type of food that might be hard to get hold of before climbing, or you have to climb with a particular pair of trousers which might actually be a bit too dirty some days, consider whether this is truly necessary for you in order to perform. There are also many unforeseen factors that can be difficult to control, such as sudden rainfall just before your attempt, a shift in the competition day schedule, or a hold that breaks during the warm-up. Don't be too tied to your routines and rituals, and have a plan B ready in case of unforeseen events.

Routines and rituals don't have to be reserved for only hard attempts. By actively using them during training you will also be able to perform better there. For example, visualisation and music help give you the right level of arousal and concentration even for static and 'simple' exercises.

Most climbers have routines and rituals, although not everyone is aware of them. If you don't have any, we recommend that you think about what you tend to do and pick out two or three things to repeat from now on before climbing. Find your own routines for warming up, visualising and relaxing. You may have some rituals as well, just make sure they're possible to recreate under most conditions. How about a fist bump with your climbing partner, or slapping yourself lightly on the chest to wake up? It doesn't have to have any meaning other than that you believe in it yourself. Routines and rituals don't have to be static, you can change them, but many climbers stick to the same things for a long time. They can also be customised to the route or the boulder you are getting on. On a technical and precise route, it may be appropriate that the last thing you do is close your eyes and take some deep breaths to calm yourself down. You will lower your stress level and be better equipped to focus on precision footwork and using the small footholds. On a brutally physical boulder problem, it might be better to get psyched by tightening your muscles and breathing quickly. This will increase your stress level and make you ready to pull as hard as you can.

Maria Davies Sandbu collecting her thoughts and lowering her stress level before the technical slab top-out on a highball in Bishop, USA.

STRESS LEVEL AND CONTROL

Our stress (or arousal) level is how calm or tense we are in different situations. At a low stress level we relax and use less energy, while at a higher stress level we are ready to pull hard. On a technically challenging route that demands balance and precision, or on long, pumpy routes, it may be appropriate to lower the stress level. On short, hard and explosive boulders or routes, however, it's more appropriate to increase the stress level. An additional challenge in climbing is that there will be sections on routes and boulders that require different levels of arousal. A technically challenging section of vertical climbing can be followed by a brutal and bouldery crux through steeper terrain, and a steep and hard boulder problem might finish with a balancy and delicate top-out. So you should be able to regulate and control your stress level before a climb, and also during a climb.

'I'M FEELING NERVOUS – GOOD!'
JERRY MOFFATT

 Know yourself! Knowing what tension level you are at, and what level you should be at for a particular route, the easier it will be to adjust to the correct level. Muscles in top gear paired with a calm mental state is the best combination in our experience.

Stress levels are individual. Some climbers have a low base level and have to psyche themselves up to get into the right mood, while others have a higher base level and might need to calm down before climbing. Even though different aspects of climbing require different levels of stress, we would argue that most of us are too tense when climbing. It is usually only for individual moves that we will benefit from a high stress level, while in most cases it's better to stay more relaxed. Give this some thought the next time you go climbing. Are you too tense, gripping the holds harder than necessary, or are you relaxed and climbing with as little effort as possible? If you fall into the former category of climber, this is most likely caused by your stress level being too high.

You've probably at some point experienced butterflies before getting on a route you've been trying. This is a result of a heightened stress level caused by you wanting to send the route. For some this nervousness can be rather destructive, while for others it's exactly what they need to perform at their best. How you respond to the increased stress will decide if it's positive or not. If you want to expose yourself to situations where your stress level will rise and you get nervous, you have to also learn how to deal with it in the best way possible. For example, you could tell yourself that you're getting nervous because sending the route means something to you, that this is what you've trained for, and that you've actually reached a level where you're able to send your project. A positive inner dialogue can help you interpret your nervousness into something positive and desirable, and consequently lower your stress level to something more appropriate.

One of the more tangible tools we have for controlling our stress level both before and during a climb is our breathing. If you are nervous before climbing, or just need to lower your stress level, try focusing on taking slow, deep breaths. Slowly fill your chest and stomach with air and exhale through your nose five to six times, and notice how your pulse drops and your breathing stabilises. On the other hand, if you need to increase your stress level, take multiple short, quick breaths to increase your pulse and arousal. It's also important to notice how you're breathing while climbing. On harder sections, most climbers have a tendency to hold their breath, and even though this might be beneficial on really hard individual moves, it's important to try to maintain a slow and steady breathing pattern. And thus, focusing on your breathing during a climb can be a helpful tool for climbing naturally.

Focus on breathing faster and increasing your pulse if you know you're about to enter a brutal section, and focus on slowing your breathing and calming down when approaching a technical slab section. If you find yourself at a good place to rest, use this time to breathe and relax to make sure that you're recovering as quickly as possible. In the same way as before starting the climb, control your breathing and inhale/exhale deeply to lower your pulse and relax in the position.

Controlling the stress level is an important mental technique for optimum performance, and it will require a lot of experimentation to figure out what works best for you. Below are some tips on how you can regulate your stress level before and during a climb:

- Good routines and rituals before a climb help to set the right stress level. Vary the contents of your routines according to the appropriate stress level for what you're climbing. For example, try listening to harder music to increase arousal and calm music to lower stress.
- Use familiar warm-up routines that you know will get you in the right mood.
- Use a positive inner dialogue to build confidence and gear up/down before and during a climb.
- Be conscious of your breathing before and during a climb. Calm, deep breaths lower stress, while quick breaths increase arousal. Use this actively to gear up/down. If you're getting stressed while run out above the last bolt, try taking a few deep breaths.
- Shout and scream to gear up during a climb.
- A pre-climb fist bump helps to set the right mood and stress level.

 Dancing elegantly on small holds on vertical walls requires you to relax and trust your feet, while burly undercling moves on your mega-project require you to gear up and increase arousal.

STRESS LEVEL

Does the way we train cause us to climb with higher stress levels than necessary? Many climbers focus primarily on physical training and don't prioritise technique, tactics and mental training. By focusing only on the physical aspects, your body and mind will learn that the only way to the top is by always pulling as hard as you can. This leads you to subconsciously increase your stress level even when it's not really necessary for a particular climb. This underlines the message of *The Climbing Bible*. The physical aspects are important for climbing performance, but they are not the only ones. By spending more time training technique and the mental aspects of climbing, in time you'll learn to climb more relaxed and efficiently.

VISUALISATION

Visualisation is one of the most commonly used mental techniques for increasing performance in sports and means, in short, imagining doing the task at hand before starting it. Visualisation is used, among other things, to practise techniques, to envisage tactical plans and goal achievement, and to regulate the stress level. For us climbers, the positive effects of visualisation are:

- remembering moves and sequences
- building confidence and finding the right focus
- setting the appropriate stress level
- preparation.

VISUALISE SUCCESS

It's important that you're always visualising success. This means always visualising yourself climbing all the way to the top of the route or topping out the boulder problem. If you can't visualise yourself doing the crux, or the movie stops playing because you get too pumped at the top of the route, you need to practise visualising actually doing the whole route. If you do end up falling when trying the route, you should still visualise climbing all the way to the top as soon as you get back down to the ground. Emphasise how to get past the point where you just fell off. Rebuild faith in being able to do the route as quickly as possible and don't think too much about failing and that you might even fall at the same point again.

Getting good at visualisation requires training, but the rewards can be significant. It has been estimated that the world's best athletes in a variety of sports spend about fifteen minutes each day visualising, and although us mere mortals probably do not need to visualise to the same extent, we should practise it every time we climb. We distinguish between two types of visualisation: dissociated and associated visualisation.

Dissociated visualisation is visualising oneself in the third person. Imagine that you are a character in a movie on TV. Then create the movie in your head as you go through the different parts of the route or the boulder problem you are going to climb. Try to make it as detailed as possible. As a first step to learning this technique, begin by going through a simple task like tying yourself into your harness. Imagine picking up the rope, tying the knot and double-checking that it is tied correctly. When you feel comfortable using the technique on simple tasks, you can start trying it out on the actual climbing. Start with a route you've tried or climbed before. Before you try to climb it, you can imagine how to chalk your hands before you start, how to clip the first quickdraw, where to place your feet on the crux and how to hold the tiny crimp. Include as many details as possible and create a movie that shows the whole process of sending the route, including all the moves right to the top.

Associated visualisation is visualising oneself in the first person. You should try to see and feel what you want to see and feel when you actually climb the route or boulder problem. In other words, the movie you are about to make is more detailed than the one you would make for dissociated visualisation, and the goal is to provide as complete an experience as possible. To practise this technique, you can perform the same tasks as before, such as tying yourself in, but now in the first person. Include what you see as you do it. Also, include other sensations and consider if it's cold, what sounds you hear and how the rope feels between your hands. Once you've practised this technique on simpler tasks, it's time to do it with a climbing route or a boulder problem. Begin with a route you've tried before, so you know how the different parts of the route will feel. Start with the feeling you have before you climb. Are you excited? Nervous? Calm? Try to think of what is appropriate for this particular route. Then move on to the climb itself. Imagine how you're clipping the first quickdraw efficiently, how you're making sure you're placing your foot accurately on the slopey foothold at the crux, and how you feel when you're bearing down on the tiny crimp. Also, include the feeling of getting pumped on the last part of the route after the crux. Prepare to get pumped, but in a good way. Not the kind of pump you get when you're cold and unprepared, but the kind

Try to block out any outside noise and don't get disturbed when visualising.

where your forearms are warm, the kind you get because you warmed up well and prepared. You know that you can endure this pump for a good while and that you can climb well all the way to the top even if you are pumped.

Dissociated visualisation is the easiest form of visualisation. This is the type you should start with if you are new to visualisation, and it will be the appropriate first step in visualising routes you haven't climbed before. It gives you an initial overview of the moves, where to clip the draws and any changes in tempo. It is also the best technique when on-sighting since you're not familiar with the details of the route, and it can be difficult to use associated visualisation if you don't have much experience in climbing on sight. Once you have tried the route or the boulder problem, it is useful to use associated visualisation to learn the different moves and sections, and to create a sense of what it is like to climb them. We think this form of visualisation is the best, and should always be used whenever possible. This will give you the right focus and stress level before you start climbing. The movie you make has to be a positive one. If you can't imagine yourself succeeding, it will be difficult to succeed in practice. To achieve this, you can start by remembering your last good attempt, or any other positive experience. Then go through the entire route and prepare yourself for how you will be thinking at the different sections. Feel your body doing the moves before you start, and picture yourself succeeding. Then you are ready!

Watch a bouldering competition on YouTube and notice how the climbers read the problems in advance. They'll often do more than just plan their hand and foot placements, especially if the problems have elements that require coordination. You'll see them testing the body positions by miming them while still on the ground. It might look strange, but it works!

If you want to analyse mistakes you have made or dangerous situations that may occur on routes, you should use dissociated and not associated visualisation. Mistakes should be analysed as objectively as possible, without being clouded by too much emotion. Associated visualisation of dangerous elements on routes will only make you more afraid than what is appropriate.

When training, you should alternate between associated and dissociated visualisation. For endurance training and pure strength exercises that you're familiar with, it might be best to stick with dissociated visualisation so as not to be thinking too much about how tiring or painful it can get. You should imagine yourself being able to complete the exercises, but don't focus on how you have to feel to get there. It's going to hurt, and there is no point in thinking too much about it beforehand. When practising technique, associated visualisation is a must. You have to familiarise yourself with all aspects of the movement and pay attention to the feedback you're receiving from your senses. Imagine doing a dyno: try to picture the starting position, the jump, and how you'll land the next hold. It's hard to get a good idea of how a position will feel if you don't see it in the first person.

As we've discussed many times in this book, improvisation is an important part of climbing. With visualisation, it can be easy to get locked into climbing a sequence the way we imagine it will be solved. This is particularly true for on-sights. You've looked at the holds from the ground and come up with a solution for what seems to be the crux and figured out where to rest. Similarly, you have an idea of the sequence for your left and right hands, and where to place your feet. So what happens when this doesn't work out? Maybe it's the slab at the top of the route that is the crux, and not the steep overhang in the middle as you first thought. To allow for such unforeseen things, you should add different solutions for the various sections into your visualisation, if possible. At the same time, mentally prepare for how to respond if the climb feels different to what you anticipated. You will then be much better equipped to deal with these challenges. Sometimes you will also have to stop halfway up the route and visualise the road ahead. This can happen when you face surprising cruxes, and you have to make a whole new plan. In the section on concentration, we wrote that you should generally not switch to an inner concentration style after you have started to climb, but in this case, it is actually necessary. You need to focus away from the task you had up to this point, adopt a broader and more analytical inner concentration style, and make a plan for what is to come. If you need to do this while climbing, find a rest or a point on the route that allows you time to think, and shift your focus back to an executive task, such as flow or efficiency, when the plan has been set.

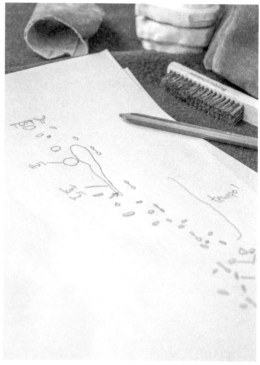

Emma Støver Wollebæk and Sunniva Øvre-Eide, two of Norway's top junior athletes, drawing a route map.

MAKING A MAP

When you're climbing in lead competitions, you won't normally get to see the other climbers on the route before it's your turn. The only information you have about the route is what you can see during the few minutes of common observation time. After the observation is over, all the climbers have to wait in the isolation area until it's their turn to climb. When we started competing many years ago, we always drew a map of the routes on a sheet of paper while waiting in isolation. We tried drawing it as accurately as we could remember while discussing how to solve the sequences. This way we made a plan on how to climb the whole route. We planned which holds to use and with which hand, where to stand, where to clip the draws, and so on. We also made a plan for where we believed we could rest, and where we had to climb fast.

As a last element, before it was our turn to climb, we used to shut our eyes, lower our pulse and stress level, and picture how we were going to feel when on the wall. We were rarely ever not psyched enough, so it was important to calm down before starting to climb. This whole routine of drawing the map and lowering the stress level made visualising easier, and in the long run, it improved our visualisation skills.

Mari Augusta Salvesen on
Master's Edge (E7 6c), Millstone Edge,
Peak District, England.

CHAPTER 4

TACTICS

TACTICS ARE IMPORTANT for performing well on a route or boulder problem, but many of the tactical elements get overlooked. The most common is to focus on how to climb the route – like how to solve the different sequences, where to clip from and where to rest. You can also be tactical in how you prepare mentally before climbing and lay down a plan for how to think during the climb. In a broader sense, tactics are strategies for when to climb, who to climb with and how many attempts to have. What follows is an overview of the different tactical elements and why they are so crucial for performance. We then look at specific examples of tactics for on-sighting or redpointing routes and boulder problems, and tactics for competition climbing.

Stian Christophersen sending *Vingsand Pirates* (Font 8a), Vingsand, Norway.

Maria Davies Sandbu
enjoying a warm sunset
wall in Bishop, USA.

'TO CLIMB DURING PRIME CONDITIONS, YOU NEED TO KNOW AT WHAT TIME
DURING THE DAY THE SUN IS ON THE WALL, AND WHAT SUITS YOU THE BEST.'

WHEN SHOULD I CLIMB?

To perform at your best, it's important to be aware of when the conditions are prime for doing just that. If you're planning a training session where you're going to try your indoor project, you should plan it for a time where you have the necessary mental and physical surplus. Are there days where your agenda is less full than others? Rushing from a hectic day of work and family life to squeeze in a short training session before moving on to other activities is seldom synonymous with being fully rested and having complete focus on performance. Choose days where you have more time and more energy, and times where your route is less likely to be busy.

With outdoor projects, you also must consider the weather and conditions. In general, you want to find the optimal balance between it being cold enough for maximum friction, but warm enough for your fingers not to go completely numb. Vertical walls, on rocks such as gritstone, granite and sandstone, are more friction dependent because of the fewer and smaller features on the wall, and therefore require lower temperatures than steeper limestone climbs which will often involve larger and better holds.

To climb during prime conditions, you need to know at what time during the day the sun is on the wall, and what suits you the best. Before going out, check the weather forecast and consider if it's supposed to be sunny or overcast, what the air humidity will be and if there's going to be any wind. By only going out on the good days, and being warmed up and ready to pull hard when the conditions are prime, you'll save both skin and energy by not wasting attempts during bad conditions. On a bigger scale, you should also consider at what time of the year to climb. It is usually better to try friction-dependent boulder problems and routes during the winter, or cooler days in spring and autumn, rather than in the middle of summer. The summer is often too hot for hard ascents unless it's really windy or the holds are relatively large. Remember that how much our hands sweat and how well we cope with climbing in the cold differs for everyone.

PHOTO: MIKE HUTTON

FRICTION

Friction is important to us climbers and is in many cases crucial to whether an attempt is successful or not. You might have experienced the difference between holding a sloper outdoors on a cold day and on a hot day. On a hot day, the hold can seem impossible to hang on to, while in cooler conditions it can feel like a pretty decent hold. Some holds have a surface that seems to always provide good friction, while others are smooth and slippery – even though they might look entirely the same. Footholds, and especially smears, can also be perceived as better when the temps are lower, and you won't slip off as easily if the footholds have a rough surface texture. So what is friction? And how can it be utilised to its full potential?

Friction is a force acting between two surfaces that are touching. To get a better understanding of how friction works, picture the surfaces as being uneven and all their tiny divots and protrusions catching on each other, hindering the surfaces from sliding. If a surface is rough, there will be more of these divots and protrusions, and the friction will be better. And likewise, the friction will also be better if the contact surface is large because a larger contact surface means more divots and protrusions. The material properties of these two surfaces can admittedly change as a result of different temperatures. This is largely a result of the materials becoming softer as they get warmer, which affects the friction.

ROCK TYPES

Rocks with round crystals have less friction than rocks with sharp crystals, and rocks with more crystals have better friction than rocks that have fewer. Plastic climbing hold manufacturers have begun to exploit this trait. Some brands offer  the same hold with either good or poor friction. The difference in friction is caused both by the manufacturer varying between a sharper or more rounded texture, and varying the amount and size of the texturising additive. By climbing on holds with varying degrees of friction you'll get better at adapting how much grip force it is necessary for you to exert. If the friction is good, you'll be able to relax more, but if the friction is bad, you'll have to grip harder. Using just the right amount of power when climbing is one of the most important techniques to master. Climbing on holds with varying degrees of friction is one of the better ways to train this technique.

PHOTO: ANDREAS EIDE

HANDHOLDS

You have probably noticed how some handholds get really slippery in the heat. This is mainly caused by your fingers sweating more. But you may also have experienced sliding off holds because it was too cold. It might feel like your skin is like glass trying to grip holds made of glass. Friction works because your skin moulds to the imperfections in the rock. This requires strong and flexible skin, and the ideal temperature is between 0° and 15° Celsius. If it's warmer, your skin will become too soft because of sweat. Your skin will catch on the protrusions of the rock, helping you grip, but it'll give and tear, and you'll slide off the hold. After a while, your skin wears down and you'll sweat even more and thereby slide even more. If, on the other hand, it's too cold, your skin will become hard and it won't be elastic enough to adapt to the texture of the hold, and again you'll end up sliding off.

Because friction is dependent on the contact surface, try to always maximise this. Let your fingers follow the shape of the hold, getting as much skin as possible in contact with the grip surface. By doing this you'll also end up not wearing down your skin as fast. A smaller contact surface will increase the pressure against the skin that is in contact with the hold. Your skin can only take so much pressure before it tears, so this is quite risky. You've probably noticed this effect when crimping small, sharp holds outdoors. Your skin wears down faster and tears.

- Most people use chalk to absorb sweat and keep their skin dry and not too soft. But too much chalk will only make things worse. It's been proven that dry, chalkless hands yield better friction than dry chalked hands. Sweaty fingers are worse though, so chalk sparingly and as needed!

- Brush the holds! The small indentations in the hold which your skin needs for friction pack up with chalk and dead skin, ruining the friction.

- Choose cooler days for sending your outdoor project. A cool breeze can also help!

Brushing the holds free from chalk and dirt is essential for optimising friction.

PHOTO: ENDRE VIK

Maria Davies Sandbu sending
Flaskeposten (Font 7b+),
Vingsand, Norway.

FOOTHOLDS

The rubber in your climbing shoes is designed to perform at its best when the temperature is between 0° and 15° Celsius. Within this interval, the rubber is flexible, yet adequately firm. At lower temperatures the rubber won't adequately mould to the texture of the foothold, and at higher temperatures it will easily deform – both of which increase the risk of your foot slipping.

We have highlighted the importance of lowering your heel to maximise friction when smearing. This is because it increases the contact surface between your shoe and the hold, so there are more features for the rubber to catch on. If the contact surface is too small the pressure will be very high and the rubber will roll and your foot will slip off.

Climbing shoes need to have both good edging properties and smearing ability. Harder rubber is better for edging, softer rubber is better for smearing. Climbing shoe manufacturers, therefore, have to compromise between the different properties climbers might demand from a shoe and its rubber.

- Wipe your shoes before climbing! Dirty shoes add considerable wear and tear to holds, and reduce friction.
- Preheat your shoes if it's cold outside. You can do this by warming them inside your jacket, or by rubbing the sole with the palm of your hand to heat the rubber; this way you'll also remove loose dirt and debris from the sole.

WHO SHOULD I CLIMB WITH?

Some climbers get along with just about anyone, while others need to surround themselves with a particular type of people in order to perform at their best. Some climb better when there are lots of people watching, while others tend to buckle under the pressure and prefer to climb in solitude. No matter what type of climber you are, we dare say you'll always perform better if you're climbing with people that make you happy and stoked. There's nothing wrong with being selective in choosing who to climb with when trying your project, and by knowing yourself well enough you can plan who to climb with. In addition to your partner getting you psyched to try hard, it's also important that you trust this person. You need to trust in their ability to belay you when you're lead climbing or know that they will move the pads and spot you if you're bouldering. If you're afraid of falling, it will be hard for you to focus on the climbing and not the falling.

It's often a good idea to have some thoughts on how time should be shared between you and the person you're climbing with. You need to know if your partner's project is close to yours, and how much time you will need for warm-ups and attempts. If you're trying different projects at different ends of the crag, you might need a plan for how much time to spend in each location, so that you know when to warm up and when to climb. Staying warm and ready to perform for a whole day is challenging, so the best solution might be to split the day in half, and start warming up for your own project after your partner has finished theirs.

PHOTO: TERJE AAMODT

Rannveig Aamodt after
one attempt too many.

HOW MANY ATTEMPTS CAN I HAVE?

There's a big difference between trying a long and pumpy route and a short and technical route. The same goes for boulder problems: some are long and drain your energy every attempt, while others have just that one really hard crux move that needs to be practised to nail it down. Also crucial to how pumped you'll get is whether the crux is at the start or the beginning; this will affect how many attempts you can expect to have before getting too tired. These route and boulder problem characteristics should be in the back of your mind when planning your strategy for the day. The same goes for sharp holds. You might only manage a couple of attempts before your skin gets too soft or cracks, so you need to make the most of every attempt.

It is therefore important to form an opinion on how many good attempts you can have on a route or boulder problem. The number of attempts with a high probability of success will set the standard for how long you should rest between each attempt. Some routes and problems can have technically difficult moves that require many attempts to figure out, and in our experience, it's better to not rest for too long, lest you 'forget' how to do the move. Still, we cannot emphasise enough how important it is to take proper rests between attempts, and many of you are sinners in this regard – especially those of you who are pebble wrestlers! On routes and longer boulder problems, it may be appropriate to rest for up to one hour between attempts. This requires a good portion of patience and self-discipline, but as long as you know what to do and spend little effort and skin on finding better solutions, it's better to rest for too long than not rest enough between attempts. With long breaks, you need to keep your body temperature up between goes. It takes a lot of effort to do a complete warm-up multiple times, but with some warm clothes on and by staying active after your first go, it can suffice to only warm up your fingers and arms before pulling back on. A portable fingerboard can be an effective aid, and you'll be able to warm your fingers up without tearing your skin.

'MARTIN USUALLY JUST SITS AND STARES AT HIS FINGERS IN CLASS.'
FROM MARTIN'S HIGH SCHOOL YEARBOOK

SKINCARE

Fingertip skin is important for climbers and can be the source of much frustration and worry. Good skin is important for optimal friction on the holds and to get the most out of a day of climbing. Unfortunately, skin wears fast, and if you're unlucky, it might even crack or tear. So, what can we do to maintain our skin, and what do we do if the skin just can't take it any more?

First and foremost we would like to point out that skin quality varies from climber to climber. Some people have hard and inelastic skin that doesn't sweat a lot, while others have softer and sweatier skin. Skin also becomes harder as it gets colder and softer when it's warmer. Hard skin is better for coarse crystals on real rock and for indoor plastic holds with lots of friction, but it is a disadvantage on smoother holds with less friction. You should get to know your own skin and how it reacts to temperature changes, as this will affect how you should go about treating it.

As a general rule, your skin needs moisture. The best way to keep your skin moisturised is to drink enough water and to use moisturiser as needed. If your skin is too dry it will grow more slowly and become less elastic. If you generally have dry fingers and relatively hard skin it's important that you use moisturiser, but this will be beneficial for most people anyway, especially if they have sore fingers. We prefer a moisturising cream that isn't wax-based, as the wax will remain on the outside of the skin without penetrating it. It can be a good idea to use moisturiser a few hours before climbing, and definitely afterwards. If your skin is soft and prone to sweating there are some creams that act as an antiperspirant which you could consider trying.

Always trim your nails before climbing if they are too long. It's also a good idea to wash your hands first, especially if you've eaten oily or greasy food or if your hands are dirty. Dirt and especially fat on your fingers will reduce the friction, you'll slide more off the holds and your skin will wear faster. When you're climbing it's important to pay attention to your skin. Consider filing down any irregularities and smoothing out rough edges. Do this with a bit of sandpaper or a file when resting between attempts. Filing your skin is especially important outdoors where the crystals tear your skin more easily than indoor plastic holds do. If you continue climbing after your skin tears, chances are that your skin is going to catch on some crystals which could rip off larger pieces of your skin. To avoid unnecessary wear and tear to your skin you should also let it rest in between attempts. Warm and sweaty skin means poorer friction and your skin will wear faster, so give it some time to cool down. Remember to also chalk your hands and to brush the chalk away from the holds in between goes. For every time a hold slips, you'll lose some of that precious skin. When you have finished climbing for the day, consider filing down any unevenness. Especially before having a rest day, it can be wise to file the skin down, so it can have time to grow while you rest.

Mia Støver Wollebøk assessing her skin before another attempt during the 2017 Norwegian National Bouldering Championships in Oslo.

If you've already climbed one move too far and your skin can't take it any more, you have two choices: you can either stop climbing for the day, often the wiser choice, or you can tape your finger and carry on. Below are three typical climber skin traumas and how to deal with them:

- A *split* is a crack across the finger, and you can get a split either at the joint or in between joints. Splits are caused by the skin being too hard and inelastic to cope with the pressure of pulling hard on a small hold. If you get a split you should file down the edges and let it rest. It can take several days for the skin to grow back to a point where you can start pulling hard moves without it splitting open again, especially if the split is near a joint, but it will take considerably longer if you don't file down the hard skin. If you have to keep on climbing you should tape your finger to stop it bleeding on the holds. Try also adding some moisturiser inside the split to soften the surrounding skin. This will reduce the chance of it splitting even further. Remember to cover the moisturised area with tape and remove any excess moisturiser from your other fingers.

- A *flapper* is when part of your skin gets torn away. This most often happens to the skin on the two innermost 'pillows' on your fingers and usually occurs on larger holds when you're pumped or when you're trying really dynamic moves. To avoid this, you should file down any hard calluses, as these will tear away more easily than softer skin. If you do get a flapper, cut the loose flapper off and tape your finger if you want to continue to climb. Since it might be painful to climb after getting a flapper, we recommend switching to less steep climbing with smaller holds that won't put so much pressure on the inner joints of your fingers.

- *Thin skin* is, as the name implies, when you've completely worn down the skin on your fingertips. Thin skin can be a consequence of having climbed on thin, sharp holds, and then wearing it down further on larger, slopey holds. To avoid it from happening, it's important to file the skin down as fast as possible if your skin starts to get small cuts and tears. It's important that the crystals don't catch and tear your already rough and torn skin any further. If you get thin skin on one finger, you most likely have thin skin on the other fingers as well, and it's time to take some rest and let the skin grow. Skin will often improve considerably with just one day of rest, though if it's very thin you might consider two days off. Thin skin is often a result of a lot of climbing, so perhaps a rest day is in order anyway. If, on the other hand, it's the last day of your climbing trip, you might want to just tape it up and go all in!

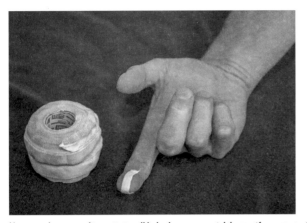 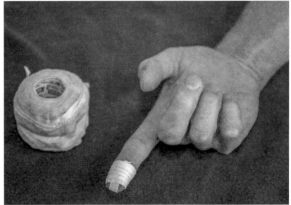

If you need to tape a fingertip, it will help the tape to stick better if you start with a small strip of tape along the finger first, before wrapping more tape around the finger.

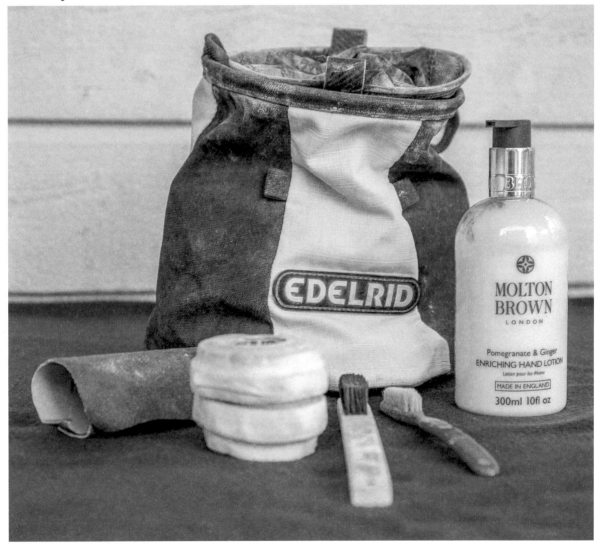

Skincare – the essentials.

HOW DO I PREPARE MENTALLY?

Having a climbing project can sometimes feel like something of a curse. Every available moment at work or before bedtime is spent thinking about the different sections of a route. Uncertainty knocks at the door: is the route even possible? Do I have the best beta for the crux? How will I manage to clip the draws when I'm pumped? In the chapter on mental performance factors, we highlighted how regulating stress and being confident are important elements, and through good mental preparation we can build confidence and find the right stress level for performing.

First and foremost you need to build a foundation of underlying belief that you're capable of sending your project. By breaking a route or boulder problem down into smaller sections and getting confident that you can do each section, it will be easier to string each section together. Visualise every single move, every foot placement, every clip. Picture how it will

 If you can do the moves, you can do the route!

feel to do the moves when you're pumped – and always picture success. There will be differences in what stress level is appropriate, depending on the route or boulder problem. If your project is a boulder problem consisting entirely of a few hard moves, you should be as psyched as possible to apply maximum effort on every attempt. If you're trying a long route, it won't be wise to go all-in at the first bolt, or you'll end up with no energy left for the top; a calmer approach and a lower stress level are required. The optimal stress level can also vary depending on the particular section of the route. Picture a technical top-out when bouldering or a tricky slab at the top of a steep route: following a few hard moves with maximum effort you must then reset, calm down, and climb slower so as to not make mistakes that will cost you the ascent. We have already covered how to train these mental factors, but there's a tactical element in choosing how to best utilise them.

As part of the mental preparations, it's good to have some routines. These routines can be anything from practical elements like when to get up in the morning, when to eat and how to warm up, to purely mental exercises like inner dialogue, visualisation and regulating stress. Good routines help you to trust in your preparations and boost confidence and your faith in your own success.

Stian Christophersen dispatches with *Lynx* (Font 8a), Vingsand, Norway.

PHOTO: MIKE HUTTON

Pete Whittaker on the second ascent of
The Jasmine Corridor (E6 6c), Millstone Edge,
Peak District, England.

HOW DO I CLIMB THE ROUTE AND THE DIFFERENT SECTIONS?

When you start the process of climbing a route or boulder problem, a good strategy can be to break it down into smaller sections. Figure out which sections are more difficult, where you can rest, and what climbing style and tempo you should apply to the different sections. By working through each individual section you can start to link them together into longer sections. Projects that might seem impossible at first, can be perceived to be far more doable if you work away at them, piece by piece.

Short and intense sections should be climbed as swiftly as possible, as your capacity for hard climbing over time is limited. Hard sections with bad feet and hard moves and body positions quickly drain your energy, so even though the total climbing time on a route can be quite long, it's important to climb these sections as quickly as possible and get to the next rest. This requires good tactical preparations. It's difficult to climb quickly and precisely without any mistakes if you haven't spent time finding the right beta and practising each section well. In addition, you need to memorise and visualise the sequences so that when you're climbing you're automatically both as technical and tactical as possible. Because you have to be fast through the hard sections and slow down for the easier ones, managing the change of pace is important. Use any available rests when you can, as they are places where you can calm down, both physically and mentally. Here you should try focusing on breathing deeply and calmly to recover as well as you can. Then you can climb with a higher tempo through the next hard section until the next rest. There will also be sections where you're forced to climb slower because the hand and foot placements need to be precise, placing high demands on balance and weight transfer. By splitting the route or boulder problem into sections where you set a predefined tempo, you're making it easier to put your tactics into practice and climb as energy efficiently as possible.

HOW TO REDPOINT A ROUTE

If you train specifically for a certain route, and you're willing to invest enough time into the project, it's very likely that you'll be able to climb it, but good tactics can drastically reduce the time it will take.

First and foremost, choose a route that motivates you to put in the effort needed. In many cases, a route is chosen because of its grade, how well it suits you and who's climbed it previously. There's nothing wrong with that, but we would challenge you to consider routes that appeal to you for other reasons. Perhaps there's a line that inspires you, a single move or section that sparks joy, or that the fact that the route actually doesn't suit you. A successful redpoint should mean something other than that you're capable of climbing a certain grade – it should also mean that you're developing as a climber and that you've had some good climbing experiences.

When you've chosen a route, figure out exactly what makes this route challenging. First, you need to figure out how to do the different moves and sections. Often you will be able to find a video or pictures of the route, but, better still, talk to others who have already either tried or climbed the route. It's a golden opportunity to discuss the beta and become better at problem-solving. A tip is to be conscious of your own climbing style and body, and don't give up if the standard beta isn't working for you! There's often more than one solution, and you should know your strengths and weaknesses in order to consider which solution will suit you the best. Try seeking beta from climbers that are roughly as tall as you and share your style of climbing. Yet there will always be individual differences regarding skill and preference, so even if you have a lot of good information, be open to finding your own solutions.

Many climbers spend too little time trying different solutions to different sections and end up failing on many attempts because they don't have the optimal beta.

There's a big difference between how the crux moves feel in isolation compared to when you've climbed into them from the ground up. Not just because you're tired, but also because you have built up a stress level that might not be optimal. We also see a lot of climbers failing or wasting unnecessary energy through the easier sections of routes. Nothing is as frustrating as falling off the easy last few moves because you didn't spend enough time figuring out the best solution. Despite moves and sections feeling manageable when you try them the first time, we recommend taking problem-solving seriously; try different alternatives before deciding which solution to go for.

Martin Mobråten finishing a triple send of *Høyspenning i Bissa* (Font 8a+), Stange, Norway.

A TALE OF HOW CHANGING THE BETA ENDED IN TRIPLE SUCCESS

Høyspenningsprosjektet was a long-standing bouldering project at Stange in Norway. Stian had spent a few unsuccessful days on it a few years back, and a friend, Kenneth, started trying it in the spring of 2015. Martin joined in, and together they worked the project for a couple of days. Kenneth and Martin got close using two different betas, but Stian couldn't make either of the two solutions work. Frustrated, he started looking for other possible solutions, and by chance he found a foothold 10 centimetres further right than the one they had been using until then. Suddenly, the crux move was considerably easier, and after a short rest Kenneth, Stian and Martin sent the problem first go with the new beta. Finding the balance between believing you have found the best beta and thus giving it all on every attempt, versus looking for new solutions, is notoriously difficult, but it's worth noting that often a small change is all it takes to make a big difference.

An important element to consider when you're working moves and sections is that you'll gradually start to tire, and your skin will soften and wear down. It might, therefore, be important to choose which sections you want to work, and then come down and have a rest before working the next section. Divide the route into sections and rank them according to difficulty. Work your way through the sections on the list one by one, starting with the most difficult. Remember to brush the chalk off the handholds and rubber off the footholds so that the friction is as good as possible.

In most cases, we choose routes that are possible within the current limits of our ability. The really big projects, on the other hand, may require you to specifically train certain qualities. You might be strong enough to do all the individual moves, but lack the endurance to link them all together. Or perhaps you need to get stronger on certain moves or types of handhold. This will require you to undertake specific training and re-evaluate the timeframe for when you can expect to climb the route. Furthermore, you need to evaluate if the route is conditions dependent, if the holds are sharp, and how the footholds are. This will help you to decide at what time of year and at what time of day is best for attempting the route, how many rest days you need to grow enough skin, which shoes to wear, and how many attempts you can have each day.

When you've found the right beta, you know what to train in order to succeed, you know what time of day you can expect the best conditions, how many attempts you can have, and how many rest days you'll need before climbing, that's when the mental preparations start. Visualise the moves so that you will remember them to the point. Picture yourself doing the crux moves, how you're going to climb before and after the crux, talk to yourself in a positive manner, and build confidence. Build up a positive expectation, look forward to going out climbing and treat being nervous as a positive thing. When you're visualising, you should feel your pulse rising and your palms sweating. Embrace all the emotions: really feel how you're not afraid of falling, that you can climb well even when pumped, and that you can still grip hard on every hold. Feel how you're applying weight on to the small footholds and convince yourself that your foot placements are rock solid.

When it's time to climb, it's important to have the right stress level and focus. Concentrate only on the tasks you've given yourself, and block out everything else. As Timothy Gallwey writes in his book *The Inner Game of Tennis*, performance equals potential minus distractions. To fully utilise your potential you must not allow yourself to be influenced by distracting thoughts or what is happening around you. Through simple tasks and a conscious focus, it will be easier to do exactly what you have planned to do. A simple way to reduce disturbances is to use a climbing partner you know well, to be prepared for the presence of other climbers at the crag, and to have a plan for what to do if the route you're trying is busy with other climbers. By being prepared, there will be less distractions, and if you're also able to block out negative thoughts, you'll have a much higher chance of success.

Naomi Buys on *Green Lipped Mussels* (F7c),
Gordale Scar, North Yorkshire, England.

Maria Davies Sandbu climbing
at Red River Gorge, USA.

An important part of the preparations is the warm-up. In addition to getting you physically prepared, the warm-up is a good opportunity to get in the right mood and at the right confidence level. You need to find your own warm-up routine, as what works best for others might not be the best for you, but it's common to stick to the same route or boulder problems every time or go through the same series of basic exercises and some fingerboarding. Many climbers also prefer to finish their warm-up on their project, trying individual moves or sections to refresh their memory and get a feel for the conditions.

All in all, we will fail more often than we will succeed, and being good at redpointing also means being good at dealing with failure. There might be days with prime conditions, when you're in great shape and your skin is good, and still you don't succeed. It is easy for the negative thoughts to come creeping in. Am I strong enough? Do I have the best beta? Should I just give up on the project and try something easier instead? There are no right or wrong answers to these questions, but if you want to succeed, you need to keep faith that you will. You also have to continuously evaluate if you have the right beta. If you keep falling at the same move, you might want to consider whether your solution is optimal or not. If you do have the best beta for the crux, perhaps you can optimise the pumpy sections leading into the crux. It's challenging to keep balancing between believing in the plan you've made, and continuously considering other and perhaps better solutions – but you have to do this every time you fall. Likewise, perhaps you failed because you had put too much pressure on yourself and were too tense when climbing? Many times you might surprise yourself with an ascent when you least expected it. For example, after giving up, you might have tried one more time even though you were tired, because what the heck. When this happens, it's usually because you've put all expectations aside and you're more relaxed, just enjoying the climb. It's therefore important that you analyse the reasons for failing as objectively as possible so that you don't lose faith in your ability to succeed. By analysing what went wrong you can think of new solutions, visualise them, test them out on the route, and be ready for the next attempt.

In order to maintain motivation we also have to appreciate the process. If we go home sad and broken every time we don't succeed, we won't find much joy or learn anything from the redpoint process. As a rule of thumb, try to always find three positives for every negative, so that for every failure you analyse you will also find a sense of achievement and accomplishment. A positive attitude towards the process will make it more rewarding and create motivation every time you're on your project, even though not every time will yield the results you were hoping for.

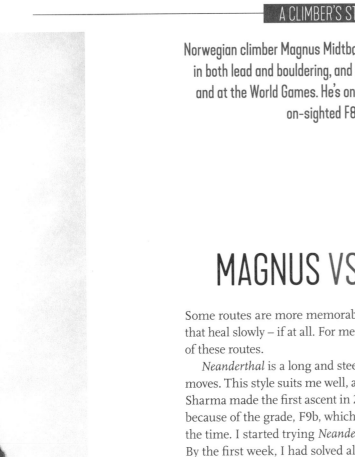

Norwegian climber Magnus Midtbø, born 1988, is a 17-time national champion in both lead and bouldering, and has had podium finishes in the World Cup and at the World Games. He's one of very few climbers worldwide to have on-sighted F8c+ and redpointed F9b.

MAGNUS VS NEANDERTHAL

Some routes are more memorable than others. Some of them leave scars that heal slowly – if at all. For me, *Neanderthal* in Santa Linya, Spain, is one of these routes.

Neanderthal is a long and steep route with relatively good holds and big moves. This style suits me well, and seeing as it was unrepeated after Chris Sharma made the first ascent in 2009, it appealed to me. And obviously also because of the grade, F9b, which made it one of the hardest in the world at the time. I started trying *Neanderthal* in 2012 and was progressing quickly. By the first week, I had solved all of the sequences and the crux, and soon I was able to do the whole route in two parts. You start by climbing a F7b+ up to a ledge where you can lay down and rest for as long as you like before the hard climbing starts right out of the gate after that. With the exception of one hold before the crux, there are no rests, with F9a/9a+ climbing up to the crux – a big dyno to a sloper. I could climb up to the crux, miss the crux move, pull back on and climb to the top after just the first few weeks of being there. I thought it wasn't going to take long before I sent it. Boy was I wrong.

After the first few weeks, there was no progression. The season in Santa Linya was coming to an end, and I had to leave for home empty-handed. Slightly disappointed, obviously, but believing I would succeed next time, I came back. And yet, as I returned the next season, history repeated itself. I was in better shape than ever, but still I couldn't do the crux move from the ground up. I would have training days in the cave where I would do multiple routes graded F8c to F9a, and I would do laps on some F9a routes, but still I couldn't do *Neanderthal*. After a while, the daily routine turned into a chore. I had one go every evening, and every time the same thing happened – I would fall on the same move without any sense of getting closer or further away than the day before. For the first time in my life, I hated climbing. I just wanted to finish the route and go home. Looking back now I realise this wasn't the right attitude to have for climbing at my limit, and I can honestly say that *Neanderthal* became more of a mental challenge than a physical or technical one.

The uncertainty and frustration led me to overanalyse everything. Are the conditions perfect? Is my skin perfect? Am I well rested? If I didn't feel like everything was perfect I would lose all faith in doing any better than I had already done. And everything being perfect is an extraordinarily rare occurrence. Voltaire said that *'Perfection is the enemy of good'*, and perhaps I should have given that some thought – not everything had to be perfect for me to be able to send the route. In hindsight, I realise I should have climbed more in other places during the time I was projecting. I had some days at other crags where I felt stronger than ever before, and it was during this time I did my first F8c+ on-sight. I should also have tried other routes of the same grade which could have given me a sense of progression, instead of banging my head against the wall on the same move every day. I think that more variation in my climbing would have made my attitude more relaxed and lessened my obsession with finishing the route so I could finally move on with my life.

Despite the adversity, I have many fond memories and learned a lot through the process. For example, I've never gotten to know a route better than *Neanderthal*. Everybody who has ever had a climbing project is familiar with focusing on the details, but with *Neanderthal* I took it to the extreme. I knew every little recess of every hand and foothold, where to stop and breathe, and on which moves I needed to hold my breath to keep body tension. To experience how well you can know a route and the flow this gave my climbing is one of the fondest memories I have. I also remember the life we had during the three seasons we spent down there. Life didn't consist of much more than eating, sleeping and climbing, and no matter how frustrating failing could be, I only did it for myself. Nobody in the whole, wide world could have made me come home before I wanted to, and it was enriching in many ways to fully focus on the one single target I had set myself. The adversity I faced was character building. Up until then, I had mostly been on a roll with my climbing. Even the hardest route I had done to date, *Ali Hulk* (F9b), took me 30 days, so there was always progress, and I have mostly accomplished the goals I have set myself. So, to first stagnate and then fail to realise something I initially thought was going to be quite doable, gave me new experiences which I later realised shaped me in a positive way.

Many people ask me if I would ever want to go back and finish the route. To this day it is still recognised as one of the hardest routes in the world. It would lift a heavy burden off my shoulders, but still, I have consistently said no. In the time after *Neanderthal*, I sought to embrace the joy of climbing and focused less on climbing hard routes and competitions because I grew tired of the focus on performance. I'm not sure I have the motivation required to shift my focus back to such a concrete performance goal as climbing *Neanderthal*. It will require a lot of training and a major shift in how I prioritise my life these days, but I also can't say that I'm *not* tempted. If I ever decide to try again, I will at least be fully committed to it, and even if I'm not at the same physical level as in the last rounds, I will at least be much better prepared mentally for the emotional rollercoaster such a project inevitably entails.

'DESPITE THE ADVERSITY, I HAVE MANY FOND MEMORIES AND LEARNED A LOT THROUGH THE PROCESS.'

Martin Mobråten climbing *Wolverine*
(Font 8b+), Vingsand, Norway.

PHOTO: BJØRN SÆTNAN

HOW TO REDPOINT A BOULDER PROBLEM

Boulder problems can be short or long, but in most cases, the moves are harder and more difficult compared to lead climbing. This means we must spend more time figuring out the beta and fine-tuning individual moves and short sections. While lead climbing is often about stringing together multiple sections in an effective way, bouldering is more about problem-solving a single move or one single section. This can be very frustrating but also very rewarding.

A boulder problem can go from being impossible for days, to suddenly being topped out in a relatively short amount of time, just because a missing piece of the beta puzzle falls into place. Since the individual moves are so important, conditions and skin play a more important role than when climbing routes, and redpointing a boulder problem often requires you to wait for prime conditions, when the chance of success is higher. If you don't have experience with this process yet, you'll be surprised at how a hold can go from totally useless to quite decent just because of lower temperatures and a cool breeze.

In the same way as when redpointing a route, you need to automate the moves and visualise the sequences. There's less margin per move than on a route, and there is no room for error, so good mental and tactical preparations are required. It is also important to regulate stress levels, and you need to decide which level is optimal.

For hard, physical boulder problems it's often advantageous to increase arousal and psyche yourself up so you'll be ready to really pull hard. Don't think about saving energy, go all in!

Adjusting to the right stress level is an art form you need to master in order to both pull as hard as you can, but at the same time be smooth and precise in your movement. You also need to account for the possibility of a delicate top-out requiring balance and precision following on from a steep and burly overhang; you will need to adjust your stress level accordingly.

Warming up on a fingerboard can be a good strategy for getting your fingers ready before getting to the boulders.

How you should warm up before climbing will also vary depending on what type of moves the boulder problem consists of. If the moves are technical and require coordination, part of the warm-up could be to practise individual moves to get the timing right before making proper attempts. If the individual moves are physically hard or the holds are sharp, it can better to warm up on other sections of the problem to optimise the beta, or on other boulder problems or a fingerboard if you're already confident on what to do when it's time to give it a go. Some problems require a high degree of flexibility, and in this case, your warm-up should include some mobility work similar to the moves you're about to do. It's important to take long enough rests in between attempts, even if they don't always seem necessary. On longer boulder problems where you fall because you're too pumped, it's obvious you need to take longer rests, but on shorter problems it might not always seem like you're too drained after an attempt. Yet you should still rest for long enough so that you're fully recovered for your next attempt, and so that your skin has a chance to cool down a bit to reduce sweating. If you're in a group of people all trying the same boulder problem, it's also important to let the holds rest after brushing off excess chalk and rubber, to lower the temperature and moisture level of the rock. It's difficult to say exactly how long you should rest for, and in our experience, it can be anywhere from ten minutes to one hour, where the latter requires you to warm your fingers up again for each new attempt. In general, longer rests are better than shorter rests when you know what to do and don't need to spend energy figuring out the beta. But still, muscle memory plays a role, and quite often the harder moves are also quite technical and require coordination. Taking long rests can therefore also be detrimental: you're well-rested, but aren't able to execute the move in exactly the same way as before your rest. One way to solve this problem is to rest for as long as you need, and then warm up again by trying that exact move or sequence to re-learn the timing of the movements.

STIAN VS EUROFIGHTER

Eurofighter at Røyken outside of Oslo isn't a fantastic problem. The crux holds are chipped, and you climb relatively low to the ground on the overhanging wall. Yet it's still the problem I've spent the longest working, and is my hardest ascent to date. What was it that grabbed my attention?

PHOTO: MARTIN MOBRÅTEN

Stian Christophersen sending *Eurofighter* (Font 8b+), Røyken, Norway.

'ONLY THEN DID I REALISE WHAT WAS STOPPING ME FROM DOING THE CRUX MOVE, AND MY FOCUS SHIFTED.'

What was it that motivated me to spend several days of my life trying to climb and training specifically for this one boulder problem? First and foremost, it was hard. It was hard enough for me to have to improve, but not so hard that it felt impossible. Also, the moves are cool, which was perhaps the most important aspect.

The problem consists of eight moves on crimps through a very steep overhang, and it's both physically and technically demanding. The third move is the crux: a long deadpoint from a three-finger crimp with the right hand up to a three-finger crimp with the left hand. The body position is very scrunched with the left foot high, and the move itself has to be done quickly and with precision. Hitting the left-hand crimp was OK, but getting the timing right to stop the momentum proved to be difficult. I lost count of how many times I tried that move, or how many different betas I tried, and the first four days when I started trying it in 2012 were spent figuring out that one move. I think I did that move maybe one or two times during that period. The next few moves to the top aren't that hard, but the second to last move was really giving me hell. Even though I was able to do the move in isolation, doing it from just two to three moves below was something entirely different. Unlike the crux move this move isn't particularly technical, but it is a lot harder physically, and it felt like I had to get stronger in my arms, upper body and fingers if I was going to have any chance at linking it all together. Or get lucky.

When I started trying *Eurofighter*, there were others who were also psyched, and we had some good days underneath that roof. But as the days passed, there were fewer of us, and finally I ended up alone. Because the crux holds are chipped they're prone to seepage, and I often had to dry them off between every attempt. Being there alone, with nobody to help get me psyched, and constantly having to dry holds, my motivation started to dwindle. At the same time, a thought was starting to creep into my mind: even if I were to do the crux, I was probably going to fall off at the top anyway. 2012 ended with me packing up all the pads and leaving the boulder, thinking I would just have to come back and complete it some other time.

Years passed and I didn't return until 2016. During that period I had my second child and I was a lot more busy with work, but thanks to a highly motivated community I had trained well over several years. I had specifically focused on finger strength, something which I hadn't really trained during my two decades of climbing. *Eurofighter* had opened my eyes to weaknesses in my climbing that I wanted to address. The spring of 2016 was a surprisingly dry one, and there was hardly any seepage on the crux holds. The first day back on the boulder I realised that much had happened in the four years since I was last there. I had significantly more margin on all the moves, and I was quick to link the moves from the crux to the top. Day two I did the crux move several times, but fell four times at the second to last move, just as I had feared four years earlier. But this time my mindset was much more positive. I was convinced that I was strong enough and that it was just a matter of time.

On 15 May 2016 I went back with two of my best friends and climbing partners, Martin Mobråten and Kenneth Elvegård. Conditions were good, I was well rested, I had slept well and my mind was calm. Most importantly, I was happy. During the last few weeks, I was having trouble sleeping, endlessly visualising the sequence. Everything was tuned, it was just a matter of doing what I had planned. After warming up and getting ready, I couldn't do the crux move. What had felt rather easy the last time, just wasn't happening. It took me about an hour before I realised I was too tense, and that I was focusing on the second to last move, and not focusing on the here and now and the crux. I was so ready to pull hard and to get the send that I couldn't find the flow to get past the technical crux move. I was starting to think, 'I just want to get this done and over with'.

Only then did I realise what was stopping me from doing the crux move, and my focus shifted. The rest of the moves didn't matter – my only goal was to do the

Stian Christophersen on the first ascent of *Eurofighter* (Font 8b+), Røyken, Norway.

crux as many times as I could that session. If I didn't send it, the boulder wasn't going anywhere. I could just try it another day. After resting for half an hour, chatting about this and that with my good friends, I sat back down beneath the starting holds.

All I was thinking about was placing my left foot precisely and accelerating through my left hip. I trusted my body to remember the rest. The crux move was easy. The next two moves were easier still. After those two moves, you cut the feet and place your left foot high before bumping your left hand up into a sidepull. The second to last move relies on getting enough height in the sidepull. All that was in my head was to get the height and pull hard until everything went dark. The second to last move never felt easier than in that last attempt, and as I grabbed the lip of the boulder I became a bit perplexed at what had just happened.

Eurofighter isn't a hard boulder problem in a global context, but for me it was challenging in many ways. I had to get physically stronger, be conscious of who I brought with me, and I needed to find the balance between being relaxed enough to do the crux and determined enough to do the last hard moves. Two things separated 2012 and 2016: first, I had become stronger, and with it had become more confident in sending my project; second, I was more relaxed about whether I would end up sending it or not. In 2012 it was more important for me to climb it, and I wasn't as interested in the process. Four years later I was more appreciative of the day-to-day progress and finding the joy in just trying it. It's a delicate balance, because if there is no will, there is no way. But it is apparent to me that I was better at that balancing act in 2016, and I realised how important it is to find motivation through mastery and not just results.

PHOTO: MIKE HUTTON

Jordan Buys on-sighting *Primal
Scream* (E6 6a), Rathlin Wall,
Fair Head, Northern Ireland.

HOW TO ON-SIGHT A ROUTE

Many of the tactical elements of redpointing are also important for on-sighting, such as at what time of day you can expect the best conditions, who you should climb with, and how to warm up. The big difference is that you don't know anything about the route apart from where the line goes and how hard it is. There's no information to be had from others regarding how to solve moves or sections, and you won't get to try any moves before the actual on-sight attempt. This requires you to picture different possible solutions based on what you can decipher from the ground. Following features, chalk marks and tick marks, you can often get an impression of which hand goes where, and where to place the feet. Many skilled climbers use binoculars to get a better look at the holds and spend a long time devising a plan for how to climb the different sections, and spot where they're likely to get a decent rest. When on-sighting it's more clear how to shift between different styles of concentration. When you find yourself at a rest you need to get an overview over the coming section. This will be the first time you get a proper look at the section, and you have to absorb and compute as much information as possible in a relatively short amount of time. A wide style of concentration is therefore crucial to the planning, but then you have to shift to a more narrow style of concentration and try to execute the moves as efficiently as possible.

Sometimes your plan will play out perfectly, but quite often you will stumble upon a surprise or two during the climb. Holds can be better or worse than anticipated, the body positions can be more challenging, and the rest you spotted from down below might turn out not to be a rest at all. You must therefore be open to using your intuition to solve the problems as they appear, and not completely lock yourself in to the initial plan. This requires a lot of experience and a large bank of movements. When we see experienced climbers on-sighting, it looks like they have already tried the route, because they execute each move with confidence and flow. Every move we do on the wall is unique, but there are many similarities, and if you're an experienced climber, it will be easier for you to recognise moves and solve new ones based on your experience.

The hardest part of on-sighting is climbing with confidence even when you're not sure if you have the right solution. Balancing between executing your plan and at the same time being open to new solutions is challenging and often leads you to become reserved, fearing you'll make a mistake and fall. It's important to build confidence in your ability to read the route, both while still on the ground and during the climb, and this confidence comes through experience. The warm-up is a good opportunity to build some of that confidence. First and foremost, stick to your regular warm-up routine, so that at least your preparations are familiar to you before you venture into the unknown. As a specific part of the warm-up, try climbing on other routes at the same crag or routes that have a similar style to the one you're going to on-sight. This can create the right stress level and will give you confidence in tackling the challenges to come, as well as familiarising yourself with the friction of the rock and the texture of the holds.

On-sighting a lot when you're at new crags or climbing walls will provide you with invaluable experience, but it's crucial that you go through your tactical and mental preparations as well as possible every time. Experience shows us that we fail far more often than we succeed when on-sighting, and so we must be proficient at analysing what went wrong and learn from our mistakes. Through trial and error we will gradually build experience and add to our movement bank, increasing our chance of success the next time.

HOW TO FLASH A ROUTE OR BOULDER PROBLEM

A flash differs from an on-sight in that you have information about how to do the moves, where the rests are, where the crux is and when the sun hits the wall. In short: you can and should collect any information that will help you succeed on your first attempt. The tactics you apply will, therefore, resemble both those for a redpoint and an on-sight; the main difference is finding confidence in the information you have.

Gathering beta is the key to a successful flash attempt. Not just figuring out the moves and sequences, but also anything regarding rests, clipping quickdraws, different climbing styles for different sections, and finding the right stress levels. You should consider who you're getting beta from. Choose climbers with roughly the same body size and shape, level, and climbing style as yourself, because most likely what works for them will also work for you. Then the mental preparations begin, with a particular focus on visualisation and stress regulation. By using visualisation techniques you can perfect the sequences in your head and then leave the climbing up to routine as your feet leave the ground. When flashing a route or boulder problem you'll know in advance where and what the character of the crux is, so you should decide whether to maintain a high level of arousal or calm down before climbing.

Practising making tactical decisions for redpoints, on-sights and flashes when training gives you valuable experience for those times when it really counts. It will at the same time increase the quality of your climbing every time you get on a new route: you'll get better at remembering moves, figuring out the beta, and building confidence in your ability to spot solutions from the ground and execute moves close to perfection first go.

Naomi Buys on *Event Horizon*
(Font 8c+), Sampson's Stones,
Lake District, England.

COMPETITION STRATEGIES

LEAD COMPETITIONS

Lead competitions consist of two qualification routes where you have one flash attempt per route. The route setters organise a demonstration of each route, and after that you can watch the other athletes ahead of you climb. Semi-finals and finals are on sight, where the athletes get to look at the route from the ground for six minutes before entering the isolation zone, from where the finalists emerge one by one without knowing how the previous climbers have performed. Whoever gets the highest up the route is crowned the winner.

In the qualification rounds it's important to know if the solutions presented are optimal for you. Differences in height, weight and climbing style can lead to different solutions, and even if it's likely that the solution presented by the route setters is the best, it is important to be open to other solutions. Take note of from which holds the quickdraws are clipped, and which sections seem the hardest. Memorise how the sections are climbed and visualise them. If possible, it can be useful to watch other climbers ahead of you to see if they are solving it the same way you were planning to, or if there are other options. Here it is important to choose climbers that you feel resemble your style, and not watch everybody. The best climbers usually get quite high on the qualification routes, but they might not be the best for you to watch if they are at a significantly higher level than you. Choose someone at roughly your level and see how they solve the route. This will give you a better idea of how your own attempt might look, and by limiting the number of other climbers you watch, you will have more time for your own preparations.

It's important to cooperate with others during the observation round before the final to get input on possible solutions. In the same way, as in the qualifiers, it's helpful to cooperate with just a few other climbers that you work well together with, and who you feel can provide valuable input. Look for footholds and positions to clip the draws from, in addition to the handhold sequences. This can give you valuable information on how to solve sections, and which sections are the most challenging. Decide what tempo to use for the different sections and where you plan to rest. There usually aren't many rests on a competition route, but sections requiring different strengths and techniques are all the more common, and this is a deciding factor when choosing the right climbing tempo. Once you have a clear mental image of the route, it can be a good idea to draw it on paper while you're waiting in the isolation zone to help you remember all the moves, holds and clipping positions. In the same way as when on-sighting outdoors, you have to believe in the plan you've made and climb confidently, but also be open to other solutions along the way.

Tina Johnsen Hafsaas topping the final route at the 2016 Norwegian Lead Championships.

COMPETITION STRATEGIES

BOULDERING COMPETITIONS

International competitions consist of qualification and semi-final rounds with five and four problems respectively: five minutes per problem, with five minutes of rest between each problem. You have no information about the problem, and get points for topping a problem or for reaching the zone hold. The climbers are ranked based on their number of tops, number of zones, and finally number of attempts to top and number of attempts to zone. The finals consist of four problems where the climbers get four minutes per problem. Before the final round starts, the route setters explain where the first problem starts and stops, and where the zone hold is. The climbers then get two minutes to observe the problem, before moving on to the next. As with lead competitions, the climbers wait in an isolation area, and aren't able to watch each other climb and see how the others solve the problems. All climbers finish a problem before moving on to the next.

The only chance you get to collaborate with others in reading the problems is in the finals. As with lead competitions, it is a good idea to be conscious of who you choose to collaborate with. Both in terms of who you enjoy being with, and to get the best possible solutions that match your level and skill set. Solving problems on your own in an international competition format requires you to be able to read the problems and spot the possible solutions. A good tactic, therefore, is to practise by doing competition simulations and reading and solving problems on your own in a given timeframe. This way you will also learn to evaluate how many attempts you can have on each problem. Four minutes on a problem is not very long, and if it's physically demanding you might only have time for two good attempts and spend the rest of the time resting. With slabs and technical coordination moves, you might have time for a higher number of attempts, as these types of boulder problems won't drain your energy as much as the burly ones.

Controlling stress levels is one of the most demanding aspects of bouldering competitions. With five and four different boulder problems per round the route setters seek to challenge the climbers on different styles – some will be physically demanding, others technical and with tricky coordination moves. This requires different levels of arousal, and the route setters know how to take full advantage of this. The first problem will often be quite technical and require slow movements and precision. If you come out of isolation all fired up you will probably be too excited to climb well. You need to plan ahead and prepare for each problem, knowing whether to be calm and patient, or to explode, take risks and be on the offensive. It's important to stick to the plan, and it is also important to be able to reset between each boulder. It's easy to dig yourself into a mental hole if the first or even the two first problems don't go so well, but remember that you still have several chances left, so keep the positivity and confidence up. There can be many tops in a bouldering competition, but sometimes the final result comes down to a single top on the last problem. As a competitor, you won't be aware of the results, so it's important to stay strong and don't give up just because you couldn't top the first problems.

Stian Christophersen competing at the 2017 National Bouldering Championships in Oslo.

TACTICAL PREPARATIONS

COMPETITION PLANS

For both forms of competition, it is important to have a competition plan. The purpose of the plan is to put you in the right mood before you perform, and when you do the same preparation every time it will be easier to recreate results. The plan should describe how your training will look up to the competition, an itinerary, and when and how to warm up. Detailed plans also include who you should be with and talking to, what focus you should have and a detailed warm-up routine.

DEALING WITH STRESS

Most people are nervous before competitions, and being nervous can be uncomfortable. You're restless, you're sweating and you have to go to the bathroom all the time. However, the increased stress should be seen as something positive. After all, you chose this yourself. You have trained for it and have prepared well. It means something to you whether it is going to go well or not, and it is a privilege to be in this situation. In order to perform, however, it is important to know how best to cope with a stressful competition situation. This is an important tactical element that greatly affects the outcome.

BINOCULARS, PEN AND PAPER

During lead competitions, binoculars can be worth their weight in gold when you need to take a closer look at the holds. Having more information about the holds can help you decide how to solve different sections and give you confidence about whether you can move dynamically to a hold or will have to do the move statically. It can also be helpful to make a sketch of the route after the observation period. This is good training for remembering moves and it's a helpful tool for visualisation of the route. This will increase your confidence, which will help alleviate some of the anxiety that characterises a competitive situation.

CHAPTER 5

GENERAL TRAINING
AND INJURY PREVENTION

TRAINING BASIC PHYSICAL skills such as strength, endurance and coordination provides us with a solid foundation for climbing-specific training and makes us more equipped to cope with the total training load.

Still – general training is not the same as specific training, and the extent to which general physical exercise directly affects climbing performance is unclear. There are countless examples of exceptionally skilled climbers who have been in shockingly poor physical shape, but today we see a greater focus on general training for climbers at all levels, and it is difficult to argue against this being a positive development. With younger climbers, we can incorporate more general training as a natural part of a training week. This ensures that they develop a versatile training base and coordination skills, as well as being able to withstand tougher and more climbing-specific training as they progress. Adult climbers can also benefit from doing general training in combination with regular climbing sessions, as a good training base allows for a higher training load and lowers the risk of injury.

There are many reasons why injuries occur, and being able to fully eliminate any and all risk of injury while also training to get better is utopian. Nevertheless, there are measures we can take to reduce the risk of injuries occurring, and the most important measures are strength training and how we manage the training load.

In this chapter, we look at how you can train general strength from an injury prevention perspective, how to manage your training load and we look at some of the most common climbing-related injuries.

'GETTING STRONG IS EASY. GETTING STRONG
WITHOUT GETTING INJURED IS HARD.'
WOLFGANG GÜLLICH

Rannveig Aamodt aiming for the
next hold in Lofoten, Norway.

GENERAL STRENGTH TRAINING

Strength training is an important method for reducing the risk of injury, and it is estimated that for a number of sports this risk can be reduced by as much as a third if we perform strength training on a regular basis. For example, the risk of a knee ligament injury in handball has been shown to be halved with specific strength training, and the risk of shoulder injury in handball can be reduced by a third with a specific exercise programme carried out twice a week. We can assume that this also applies to climbing-related injuries, and here both the specific strength training, which we presented at the beginning of the book, and more general strength training are important.

In the chapter on physical training, we presented several specific strength training exercises for the upper body, arms and fingers, and we explained why these exercises can help to take your climbing to the next level. By regularly performing these exercises we can assume that the risk of injury is reduced because the muscles, tendons, ligaments and bones become stronger, and we gradually build the strength required to endure the increased training load. This, in turn, prevents unnecessary breaks in our training caused by injury, breaks which might lead to large fluctuations in the training load. There is no reason not to do strength training.

General strength is especially important for training opposite movement patterns to those we encounter in climbing. In climbing, and through specific strength exercises, we train what are called the 'prime movers' for climbing – that is, the musculature that grips and pulls us into and up the wall. Climbing is a sport with a varied movement pattern, but this is the essence of climbing. The more we climb and train for it, the stronger the prime movers naturally become. This increases the need to strengthen the muscles that make the opposite movements – the so-called antagonists. Essentially these are muscles that push us away, rotate our shoulders outwards and pull our shoulders backwards. Important in preventing injury is creating a balance between the muscles that pull us up and into the wall, and the muscles that do the opposite.

By combining general strength training with climbing-specific exercises, you will become better equipped physically to endure an increasing training load and create a balance between the prime movers and the antagonists. Here we present a selection of the general strength exercises we believe are most important for you as a climber.

Strength training doesn't need to be complicated or time-consuming, nor does it require fancy equipment. The most important thing is that you are aware of what exercises you should do and how to do them. We have divided the exercises into exercises which use only your own body weight (including exercises using a bungee), and more traditional strength training exercises with weights, slings and other exercise equipment.

Slopestyle (Font 8b), Rogaland, Norway.

BODY WEIGHT EXERCISES

While we recommend that strength training using additional weights should be done on its own, body weight exercises can be performed as part of the warm-up or at the end of a climbing session. As with climbing-specific strength training, we recommend starting general strength training with a higher number of repetitions at lower loads so you can learn the techniques and movements. Then, as you progress, you can increase the load and reduce the number of repetitions per set. We have mainly chosen exercises that activate several muscle groups at the same time because this reflects the complexity of climbing, where we use multiple parts of the body. We have also chosen exercises that are primarily aimed at muscles that work in the opposite direction to what we encounter in climbing, so as to create balance in our training.

1. PUSH-UPS

Push-ups are a good exercise for your shoulders, arms and chest. For the elbows and shoulders, push-ups train the opposite movements to what we encounter in climbing – pushing away rather than pulling in – and can therefore help to reduce the risk of injury related to these joints. It's an easy exercise to start with, and it's also easy to make it harder and more challenging.

Begin by standing on all fours with your knees on the ground and your hands about shoulder width apart. Lower your chest to the floor and push back up again without twisting your elbows out. When you're able to do three sets of 10 repetitions, you can up the difficulty by standing on your toes instead of on your knees. Do as many as you can each set, and complete three sets with a 2- to 3-minute rest between each set. When you're able to do more than 10 repetitions for three sets on your toes, you can start to vary the exercise by adding rotations, as seen in photos 3 and 4.

2. THE LARVA

The larva is a good exercise for your shoulders, chest, abs and back. The further you walk your hands in front of you, the more you train and utilise the full range of motion in your shoulders; it is particularly at the far end of this range that you need to build strength to reduce the risk of injury to your shoulders.

Start the exercise with both hands and feet touching the floor. Walk your hands as far in front of you as you can while keeping a strong core, then walk your feet back up to the starting position. Avoid dropping your hips or arching your back – you should feel your abdomen and back muscles working to keep your core strong, stable and straight.

3. DEEP SQUATS

Deep squats are – as the name implies – squats where you go as deep down to the ground with your hips as you can. This is a good exercise for building strength for high foot placements and it's good for training your thighs, glutes and back. When climbing your knees are constantly exposed to torsional strain as you angle your legs and feet into different positions in relation to the holds. By regularly training your knees you can build strength around the knee joints and thereby reduce the risk of injury. To make the exercise harder and at the same time incorporate training for your shoulders and upper body, we recommend using a bungee and pretending you have the wings of an angel.

Start the exercise with your arms over your head and the bungee attached in front of you. Move your arms down to the side and back up again as if you're making snow angels. When your arms are back above your head, do a deep squat while keeping your arms pointing straight up; repeat the angel movement when you're standing upright again. You should feel the muscles working actively in your lower back, thoracic spine, between your shoulder blades, in your thighs and in your glutes.

4. LUNGES WITH ARM RAISE

Lunges with arm raise is a similar exercise to the deep squats, but here you are activating the muscles in your back and shoulder differently. Raising your arm up and back with added resistance is a good way to train the opposite motion to a typical climbing move. In addition to the balance element, lunges train your glutes and the fronts of your thighs. The exercise starts in an upright position with one leg in front of the other. Shift your weight forwards to the front leg and lower your hips. As you stand back up, raise your arm with your thumb pointing up. With your left foot forwards, lift your right hand, and vice versa. You should feel the muscles working actively in your lower back, thoracic spine, between your shoulder blades as well as in your thighs and glutes.

PHOTO: MIKE HUTTON

Anna Shepherd on *The Crystal Method* (Font 7b+), Caley, West Yorkshire, England.

Below is a suggestion for a strength training routine to complete after a climbing session. If you want to use some of the exercises as part of your general warm-up you can do 1–2 sets of each exercise at low loads.

PROGRAMME

EXERCISE	REPETITIONS	SETS	REST BETWEEN SETS
Push-ups	8–10	3–4	2–3 minutes
Larva	8–10	3–4	2–3 minutes
Deep squats	8–10	3–4	2–3 minutes
Lunges with arm raise	8–10 per side	3–4	2–3 minutes

SUSPENSION TRAINING

Training with slings has become a popular form of training over the last few years, and it's a good training method for combining our own body weight with unstable ground. The big advantages for climbers are that we can train close to the limit of the range of our joint mobility, it requires good muscular control over the different joints because the slings hang freely, and all the exercises challenge our core muscles.

As a general rule for all three exercises here, we recommend that if you can complete 10 repetitions for all three sets, you should increase the difficulty by standing on your toes instead of on your knees. Then work your way back up to three sets of 10 repetitions with 2 to 3 minutes of rest between each set. It's important to maintain control throughout the movements and to stabilise your shoulders and arms. The three exercises we recommend are:

1. PUSH-UPS
Begin by standing on your knees and grab the slings with your hands at shoulder width. Lower your chest to the same height as your hands and push back up.

2. CHEST FLIES

Begin by standing on your knees and grab the slings with your hands at shoulder width. Move your arms out to each side and lower your chest. Push yourself back up by pressing your arms back together.

3. SUPERMAN

Begin by standing on your knees and grab the slings with your hands at shoulder width. Move your arms straight ahead while tightening your abdominal muscles and leaning forward. Stop when your arms are aligned with your ears. Push yourself back up by pressing your arms down.

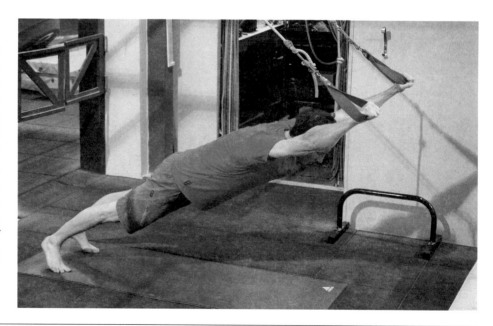

WEIGHT TRAINING

There are many good exercises which rely on your body weight alone, but we still recommend training with additional weights as a supplement to your climbing. Training with weights is an effective way to build muscle strength and will have a positive effect on both your general physique and risk of injury. The only downside of weight training is that muscle growth increases body weight, which isn't always beneficial in a sport like climbing. But still, this is a relatively small problem for most of us, and as long as weight training remains a supplement to, and not a substitute for, climbing, we see it as a positive way of building a solid base physique.

Remember to tighten your abdomen and keep your back straight throughout the exercise.

1. DEAD LIFT

The dead lift is one of the best exercises for strengthening your lower back and is a basic strength exercise for most sports. Some of you might have been told that it's harmful to your back; this myth has been debunked, though it is important to start easy with lower loads and a higher number of reps so you can properly learn the technique.

Start the exercise standing up with your arms to the sides and your feet shoulder width apart. Lift the bar straight up until you're standing upright, then lower it back down to the floor. You should feel your thighs, glutes and lower back working – and obviously your grip – when lifting heavy weights. When lifting heavy weights you can use wrist straps or an opposing grip position (one overhand and one underhand), to stop the bar rolling out of your hands.

2. OVERHEAD SQUAT

The overhead squat is a good strength exercise for your shoulders, back, glutes and thighs. In addition, it requires good mobility in your shoulders and thoracic spine to keep your arms straight when you squat.

Start the exercise standing straight with the bar on straight arms above your head. Squat as deep as you can, while keeping your back and your arms straight, and stand back up. You will feel your thighs and glutes working, but mostly you will feel it in your lower back, thoracic spine and on the backs of your shoulders.

This is a difficult exercise to master, so start easy and learn the technique before adding weight. Remember to tighten your abdomen and keep your back straight throughout the exercise.

  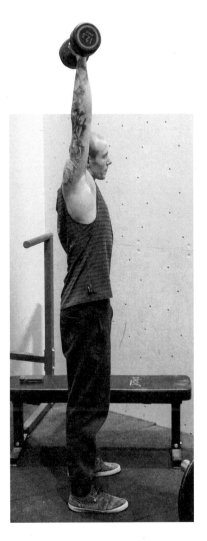

3. SHOULDER PRESS

There are many variations of the shoulder press, but the point is to add a load to the arm as we push it straight up. Here we have chosen the variation known as the Arnold press – named after its legendary inventor, Arnold Schwarzenegger – as it adds the element of shoulder rotation to the traditional shoulder press. The exercise also requires mobility in the shoulders and thoracic spine, and by correctly executing the shoulder press we can improve our mobility as well as increase our strength. To challenge the stability in your back and abdomen we recommend doing the exercise standing up, one arm at a time.

Start the exercise with your arm bent, palm facing in to your chest. Push your arm up straight above your head while rotating it so that your palm ends up facing forwards. Return to the starting position.

4. PALLOF PRESS

The Pallof press works the outside and back of the shoulder and between the shoulder blades, and it's a good way to build strength and stability around the shoulder. The exercise can be done using a bungee, but it is easier to control the progression of your training when using a weighted cable pulley system you should find at your local gym.

When training your left arm, stand with your right foot forwards, and vice versa. Start with your arm down by your side, with your forearm pointing forwards – i.e. bent 90 degrees at the elbow. Push your arm forwards, while working actively to stop it from rotating in, until it's pointing straight ahead. You should feel the muscles working on the outside and back of your shoulder and between the shoulder blades.

PROGRAMME

EXERCISE	REPETITIONS	SETS	REST BETWEEN SETS
Dead lift	8–12	3–4	More than 3 minutes
Overhead squat	8–12	3–4	More than 3 minutes
Shoulder press	8–12	3–4	More than 3 minutes
Pallof press	8–12	3–4	More than 3 minutes

This programme is a good starting point when you're just getting into weight training. By starting with a relatively high number of repetitions and sets you'll learn and practise the techniques and build a solid foundation before moving on to heavier weights. You should feel tired after every set. Adjust the number of kilos per repetition to suit the number of repetitions to ensure you are training at the right loading for your level.

If you are regularly training with weights one or more times per week, you should gradually increase the load per repetition and reduce the number of repetitions accordingly.

An example might then look like:

EXERCISE	REPETITIONS	SETS	REST BETWEEN SETS
Dead lift	3–5	3–5	More than 3 minutes
Overhead squat	3–5	3–5	More than 3 minutes
Shoulder press	3–5	3–5	More than 3 minutes
Pallof press	3–5	3–5	More than 3 minutes

We recommend keeping weight training separate from climbing sessions and preferably you should take a rest day before climbing. Strenuous strength training can come at the expense of the quality of your climbing training, and your climbing training should always take priority. If you are lifting weights several times a week, a good rule of thumb is to allow each muscle group to rest for at least two days.

Exercising using heavier weights and fewer repetitions will to a greater extent stimulate muscle activation rather than muscle growth. Therefore, after learning the exercises and training with a higher number of repetitions during the initial time period, it is advantageous for us climbers to train using heavier weights and fewer repetitions.

'TRAINING HARD ISN'T DANGEROUS. SPIKES IN TRAINING LOAD ARE.'
TIM GABBETT

LOAD MANAGEMENT

Large fluctuations in load – when periods of hard training follow immediately after periods of less exercise and at lower loads – increase the risk of injury. Continuity in your training means that you will gradually build a tolerance to more and harder training over time. It is the relationship between how hard you train and what you are trained to endure that is important. An elite climber balances on this knife-edge throughout much of the year, and it is impossible to get to the stress level these athletes are at without having trained steadily and progressively over a long period of time. Without building a good foundation, they would not have reached the level they are at. This is just as important to remember for those of us climbing at lower levels.

Going on a three-week holiday where you do not train or load your fingers will weaken your fingers' ability to withstand loads, and it is then important that when you get back to training you start gradually in order to reduce the fluctuations in load. If you wish to train hard after taking a long break, it's important that you set aside some time during your vacation to do a few sessions where you load your fingers and the rest of your body. A portable fingerboard is a fantastic tool in this regard. A couple of sessions of deadhangs, pull-ups, and core workouts per week during times when you're not climbing will leave you in much better shape as you go into a new training period.

There are several ways to manage load, and the easiest way is to look at the wall angles, climbing style and holds you use. Steep walls, bouldering and small holds increase the intensity for your upper body, arms and fingers significantly compared to vertical walls, lead climbing and larger holds. By alternating between bouldering and lead, physically and technically challenging climbing, as well as how steep the wall is, you can change which part of the body is doing most of the work and hence get enough rest even when training often and hard. Therefore, all that is required is an awareness of the type of climbing you are doing, and a simple training log, to get the most important injury prevention measure – load management – to work properly.

When managing load, it is useful to have some parameters to illustrate how hard you have been training. Exercise load is the product of volume and intensity. The volume is the amount of training you have done: this could be the number of minutes of training or the number of routes or boulder problems completed per session. The intensity is how hard you have been training and can be graded on a subjective scale of 0 to 10, where 10 is the highest intensity. In Chapter 2 we described intensity zones for endurance training where 5 was the highest intensity, and an endurance session in intensity zone 5 would then be a 10 on a 0 to 10 training intensity scale. Similarly, a maximum bouldering session, deadhangs and campus training would be close to a 10 on this scale, and the calculation may then look like this:

Training time (= 2 hours) x intensity (= 8) = 16.

The number 16 is an indicator of how high the training load was that session. If you do a calculation for each session in this way, you can get a number for the training load for the whole week. Large deviations from this sum over the next few weeks, either up or down, increase the risk of injury; knowing this, you can adjust the load up or down to flatten the curve and reduce the risk of injury. When you extract these values, the curve might look something like this:

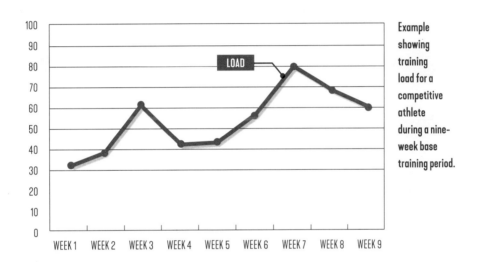

Example showing training load for a competitive athlete during a nine-week base training period.

There is one obvious challenge in counting the number of training hours, and that is that usually you will not climb continuously throughout a session. With both lead and bouldering sessions, you will have shorter or longer rests, so will not distinguish between working time and resting time by counting the hours per session. You will still get a picture of how much and how hard you have been training over the course of a week, and this is the easiest way to calculate your training load.

We would like to emphasise that this is by no means an exact science and that there are many sources of error in calculating climbing training load in this way. However, in our experience, quantifying the load for a session, a week and a period is a good tool for load management. Using the examples above, you can adapt the method to your own training so that you can easily adjust the load up or down to avoid excessive fluctuations.

WHEN THE DAMAGE IS DONE

Unfortunately, when we train to improve, there will always be a risk of injury. Despite the strength training and load management, there are several factors that can lead to injury, for example, incorrect execution of a technical move. In other cases, an acute injury may simply be due to bad luck. We may experience both acute injuries, such as a sprained ankle or a torn ligament in a finger, or chronic injuries, where we do not necessarily know why they occurred or when we first noticed the symptoms.

ACUTE INJURIES

In the case of acute injuries, it is important to seek help to diagnose what has happened and the extent of the injury so that the rehabilitation can be as good as possible. It is also crucial to find out what caused the injury in the first place. Were the crash pads poorly positioned, causing you to sprain your ankle upon landing? Did your finger go 'pop' as you desperately bore down on that crimp at the end of a two-hour-long climbing session? Was it cold outside? Did you warm up? Were you tired after too much training? Tired after not getting enough sleep? There are a number of factors that can contribute to acute injuries, and by getting a sense of why the injury may have occurred, you can reduce the risk of it happening again.

For several years, the acronym PRICE has dominated decision making when acute injuries occur. PRICE is an abbreviation of Protection, Rest, Ice, Compression, Elevation, and overall, these measures should dampen the inflammatory response that follows tissue damage, thus alleviating pain and reducing swelling. However, in recent years we have seen that Rest is rarely a good strategy and that early loading of damaged tissue is crucial to shortening the time it takes to heal – and thus how long it takes before you are back in the game. Instead, we now ask the question:

'SHOULD WE CALL THE POLICE?'

In the POLICE acronym, Rest is replaced with Optimal Loading. It's not always easy to know what optimal loading is, but it does at least point out that tissues need loading in order to heal properly. Most types of tissue in the body heal with scar tissue, and in the same way that you would want to stretch a skin wound so that the scar tissue doesn't become too short, you should do the same with muscles, tendons and ligaments. There's a big difference between complete rest versus relieving enough load so that we can utilise the injured body part without aggravating the pain and/or increasing the swelling. With a sprained ankle, we should start moving around and loading the ankle by standing and walking on it after just a few days. Although the load is reduced so that the ankle can rest, it also needs to be loaded slightly. The same goes for a finger pulley injury, where we can start with a squeeze ball, some light climbing and deadhang training relatively quickly.

CHRONIC INJURIES

Chronic injuries are different from acute injuries since we do not always know when the injury occurred or what triggered it. In most cases, a chronic injury is the result of us training:

'TOO MUCH, TOO OFTEN, TOO FAST AND WITH TOO LITTLE REST.'

If we assume that we have been training too much, too often and with not enough rest for the tissue to adapt, it is clear that the general solution to such injuries is to better manage the load. This is not the same as taking complete rest from climbing or training, but rather looking at ways we can lower the load or load differently for a period of time. An elbow that hurts from steep bouldering can be fine with some vertical lead climbing. A finger that hurts when crimping and campus training can be fine with bouldering on large holds and open grip positions. There is a lot you can still do during periods of injury, and any training you do will help maintain both your physical shape and your technique until you are ready to train normally again. As mentioned earlier, it is also important to load the body and the injured body part to steadily build up the load capacity in the tissue after an injury. If the pain persists for a long time despite efforts to relieve and adjust the load, we recommend that you seek qualified help to clarify the cause of your discomfort. Rehabilitation from an injury and returning to the level you want to climb at can be a lot easier if you get help with finding the cause and laying down a good plan for your recovery.

By figuring out what might have caused your injury, you can adjust the load for specific areas. For example, if you have been bouldering and campusing and you're starting to feel some pain in one finger, you can steer away from these training methods for a while, and instead focus more on technical bouldering and lead climbing, which are less stressful for your fingers. Then you can complete some shorter bouldering sessions and see how your finger responds. When you are comfortable with these sessions, you can gradually increase the load on the fingers for each session before trying some campusing again. So you calm the situation down, before gradually building it back up again. Rehabilitating an injury without correcting for the load that caused it is impossible.

Also consider that by training while injured you're lessening the fluctuations in training load, which reduces the risk of further injury. Let's look at an example:

Martin has injured his finger. Since he cannot train as usual, he rests for two weeks. His finger feels better after this rest, and he returns to training. His plan to gradually build his strength back up quickly disappears during his first session, and after two sessions his finger is painful again. He rests for another two weeks before the story repeats itself.

Such a response to the injury creates large fluctuations in how much the finger is loaded. Instead, Martin should have continued with easy climbing during his two weeks of rest, and then gradually increased the load. By flattening out the fluctuations, you can still train while injured, and thereby rehabilitate faster and reduce the risk of relapsing into injury.

A simple rule to remember for the treatment of chronic injury is this quote by Canadian chiropractor Greg Lehman: *Calm shit down, build shit back up.*

Mike Hutton traversing *Hamper's Hang* (Font 7a+), Stanage Edge, Peak District, England.

THE CHALLENGE OF BEING GOOD

When we have established ourselves at a certain level of climbing, we have acquired technical abilities that keep us relatively stable at this level, even after breaks in our training. Ambitious as we are, it can be a challenge to return to training at a lower level than where we left off: we are skilled enough to climb at a level that is higher than our physical condition allows. Even after relatively short breaks of just a couple of weeks, we will be significantly weakened physically, and this creates an imbalance with how much load we can withstand and what level we are able to climb at. Many climbers start their training – whether it's following an injury or an holiday, or for other reasons – at too high a level, and thereby load too much, too often and too fast. A healthy dose of self-discipline is required to be able to start slow and gradually build back up to speed, but this will most likely reduce the number of setbacks and lead to better progression in the training.

WHAT IS PAIN?

This might seem like a strange question. We have all experienced pain at some point, but the answer might be more complicated than you think. Especially if the pain lingers for longer than expected.

You can think of pain as being the siren from an alarm system which signals danger, similar to an alarm you might have in your house. Connected to most of the tissue structures in your body are nerve fibres, whose job it is to send information to your brain about the status of the tissue. Let's call them guardians, alerting the emergency response centre – your brain – if they discover something they think is dangerous. Information regarding load, or changes in temperature, pressure or length, is information that is continuously transmitted to the response centre while we are moving. This information is interpreted and evaluated before appropriate action is initiated. Our emergency response centre is programmed to take very good care of us, and if the information it receives is considered to be dangerous or harmful to us, pain is an appropriate response to avoid further harm.

Outdoors we often encounter holds that are uncomfortable to grip. The pressure from the crystals into our fingertips makes the guardians send information to the response centre, which in turn has to decide if it is dangerous for us to keep holding on. In many cases it isn't. And, after all, we want to hang on and do the move. The best option then is to disregard the information about the crystals against our fingertips and keep on gripping. The pain response is therefore dependent on how we interpret the available information, and this interpretation is based on the following three questions:

1. Am I safe?
2. Do I have enough information to predict the future?
3. Do I have enough information to influence the future?

If the answer to all three questions is YES, then pain is an unnecessary response. Answering NO to one or more of the questions increases the need for protection, and hence also the need for pain as a response to ensure this. Let's look at two examples:

EXAMPLE 1: The day after a hard strength training session your sore muscles are sending signals via your nervous system to your brain that you are picking up a bag from the floor.

'Am I safe?' YES. I was sore just last week, and I was fine.

'Do I have enough information to predict the future?' YES. All previous experience tells me my muscle soreness will go away after a few days, and I can get back to training as normal.

'Do I have enough information to influence the future?' YES. I know that if I warm up well before the next session, the soreness will go away.

The conclusion is that this is not dangerous, and there is less of a need for pain as a protective response. You might still experience muscle soreness, but you probably won't give it much thought.

EXAMPLE 2: Your fingers are aching after several hard bouldering sessions on small holds. They are sore to the touch, and gripping small holds is uncomfortable.

'Am I safe?' YES, probably. My fingers are painful, but I'm alive after all. I am however uncertain whether I should keep on climbing.

'Do I have enough information to predict the future?' NO. I don't know if this is a serious injury and whether or not I should take a longer rest from climbing.

'Do I have enough information to influence the future?' NO. Since I don't know what's wrong, I also don't know what I should do to get better.

When you are faced with a potentially dangerous situation which might have consequences in the form of a break from climbing – and perhaps a reduced quality of life – pain is an appropriate response until you know more about the situation. Pain is based both on signals from your body and how you interpret those signals based on your knowledge, experiences and memories, in which context this has happened, and what the consequences might entail. It is important to understand all of this so that you can understand the difference between pain and injury.

'THE REST OF MY TEAM ALMOST DIDN'T BELIEVE ME. I INSTANTLY
HEARD AND FELT WHAT IT WAS. AS I LEANED DOWN TO FEEL, AND
SAID THAT I HAD TORN MY ACHILLES, THEY DIDN'T BELIEVE ME.
IT WASN'T THAT PAINFUL, SO I WAS A BIT SURPRISED
TO LEARN THAT IT HAD TORN COMPLETELY.'

AKSEL LUND SVINDAL, WORLD CHAMPION AND
OLYMPIC GOLD MEDAL-WINNING SKIER

PAIN AND INJURY

Can injury exist without pain? What about pain without injury?

When Norwegian ski racer Aksel Lund Svindal tore his Achilles tendon during practice, a serious and potentially career-ending tissue injury, it wasn't particularly painful. We can question why this was the case, but it is just one of many examples of it being possible to sustain a severe injury without the accompaniment of any significant pain.

The opposite can also be the case – we can experience pain without tissue damage. A classic example of this is the story of the carpenter who stepped on a nail:

A carpenter stepped on a nail while at work. The nail went right through his shoe and into his foot. He was, naturally, in great pain, and was rushed to the hospital for further examination. With his foot still in the shoe, they took X-ray photos, but it turned out the nail had passed right between the carpenter's toes and hadn't actually damaged any part of his foot.

So, tissue damage isn't a necessary prerequisite for experiencing pain. All it takes is the potential of an injury and a situation that is perceived as dangerous. Pain is a protection mechanism and probably one of the most important survival mechanisms we have, and it is obviously vulnerable to misinterpretation.

PAIN, SENSITISATION AND LOADING

When the emergency response centre evaluates the information it receives from the guardians, it tries to assess how dangerous the situation is. After sustaining an injury, and in situations where you are unsure of the consequences of an injury, the response centre can tell the guardians to be extra alert. Consider this like the burglar alarm in your house going off when you visit the bathroom in the middle of the night – the alert system has become more sensitive.

Imagine having previously injured your elbow. The injury kept you away from climbing for a long period of time, and you have finally recuperated and are about to get back into climbing again. Are you going to be extra sensitive with how your elbow feels during and after climbing? Most of us probably would be, and this heightened alertness makes our response centre more sensitive to load, among other things. This means that it will take less load for the guardians to send information to the response centre and the siren will sound even though there's no need for protection. You're not even close to putting enough stress on your elbow to get injured, but it still hurts. Breaking this circle requires you to expose yourself to stress and learn how to interpret the pain response.

If you are sure that you're not loading your body through climbing and training to the extent of injury, you will be better equipped to answer YES to the three questions on page 275. An effective tool in this regard can be a training log:

DAY	1	2	3	4	5	6
What	Bouldering 60 minutes	Lead 45 minutes	Bouldering 30 minutes	Lead 60 minutes	Bouldering 60 minutes	Bouldering 45 minutes
Intensity	Low	Low	Moderate	Low	Low	Moderate
Pain 0–10	Before: 2 After: 4	Before: 2 After: 3	Before: 2 After: 4	Before: 2 After: 2	Before: 1 After: 2	Before: 1 After: 3

With a training log, you can see what and how hard you have trained in relation to the pain response. It's common to rate the pain response on a scale from 0 to 10, where 0 equals no pain and 10 is the worst possible pain you can imagine. An increase in load usually leads to a higher response, but if the pain goes back to its starting point within the first 24 hours it is OK to continue the training. Over time you will be able to tolerate an increased load and see that the pain response decreases. On the other hand, if the pain response gradually increases as a result of the training load, you can adjust the load down to avoid a negative trend.

To summarise, we can say that pain is an important defence mechanism, but the need for protection depends on how we interpret the information at hand. Being confident in what the pain means for you, and how you should approach the situation, is important in order for you to start loading the body part in question.

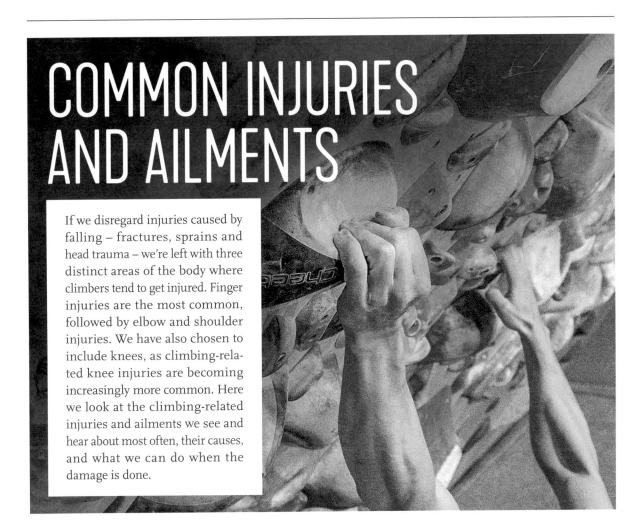

COMMON INJURIES AND AILMENTS

If we disregard injuries caused by falling – fractures, sprains and head trauma – we're left with three distinct areas of the body where climbers tend to get injured. Finger injuries are the most common, followed by elbow and shoulder injuries. We have also chosen to include knees, as climbing-related knee injuries are becoming increasingly more common. Here we look at the climbing-related injuries and ailments we see and hear about most often, their causes, and what we can do when the damage is done.

FINGER INJURIES

PULLEY INJURIES

Finger pulley injuries are the most common climbing-related injuries. There are five pulleys in each finger – A1 to A5, from the base of the finger to the tip – with the exception of the thumb, which only has two. The pulleys are ligament reinforcements which lie on top of the tendons and work in the same way as the rings on a fishing rod, keeping the tendons in place along the bones and knuckles when the finger bends. When a finger is bending, the tendon pushes against the pulley, and if the load is high enough the pulley can rupture. This usually happens when you are gripping a hold and the load suddenly increases, perhaps because your foot slips or your other hand loses its grip. Crimping is closely related to pulley injuries because this grip position can lead to tremendous pressure being exerted on the pulleys, and this is one of the main reasons you should crimp with caution.

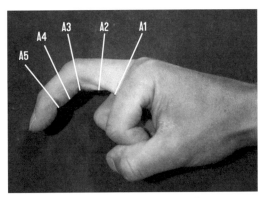

Finger injuries and painful fingers are unfortunately quite common in climbing, and it is mainly the pulleys, tendons and joints that are exposed.

Magnus Midtbø training with V-rings and a Progressor™.

When one or more pulleys rupture, either fully or partially, it's acute, and most climbers will experience a 'pop' in their finger when it happens. In many cases, the pop is also audible. You will experience pain emanating from the injured finger when you try to load it, and in many cases the injury will cause your finger to swell. It is recommended that you seek medical advice to correctly diagnose and assess the injury so that the rehabilitation can be as effective as possible.

Full and partial ruptures of one or two pulleys are always treated conservatively, while surgery is considered an option if there is damage to three or more pulleys in the same finger. Depending on its extent, an injury is immediately followed by a period of one to two weeks of moving the finger, but with a reduced load. After the first phase is over, the laborious job of rehabilitation begins; this can take anywhere from four to twelve weeks before you can expect to climb at the same level as before. During this period, it is recommended that you use open hand grips and large holds when you climb, and control the load in relation to pain and swelling during and after training.

A fingerboard can be helpful since you can more easily control the grip position and load than when climbing. A handy tip is to stand on a bathroom scale and see how much of your own bodyweight you can lift before you feel pain; this will give you a good indication of how far off you are from climbing at your normal level.

A better alternative is to use the Progressor™ mechanism from tindeq. This will allow you to measure the rate of force development for different grip positions, see how many kilos you can load before experiencing any symptoms in your finger and gradually increase the load as your finger gets better.

Even though torn pulleys do not grow back together, the prognosis is good, and most climbers recover to their previous level.

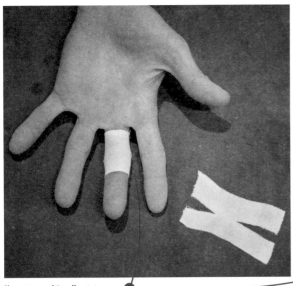

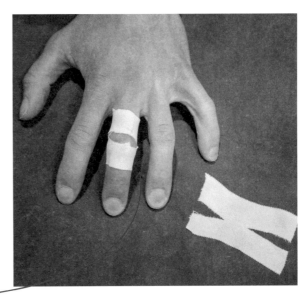

H-taping an A2 pulley injury.

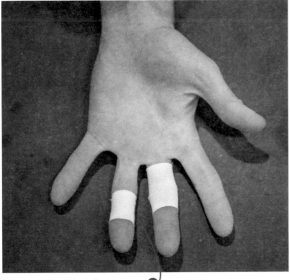

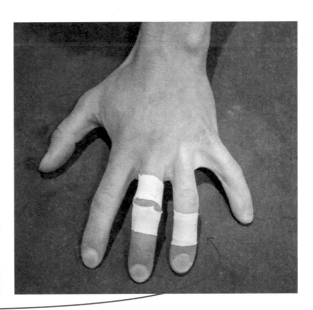

Circular taping an A4 pulley injury.

It is recommended that you support the tendon by taping the finger for the first few months following a pulley injury. H-taping is recommended for injuries to the A2 pulley, and circular taping is recommended for injuries to the A4 pulley. The tape should be tight enough to provide support, but not so tight that the blood circulation is cut off. As your finger recovers and the load can be increased, the tape won't provide the same level of support, and there is no need for taping a previously injured finger when you are back to normal loading.

TENDON SHEATH INFLAMMATION

Tendons are encapsulated within the tendon sheath which produces synovial fluids so that the tendon can glide without friction against its surroundings. As the flexor tendons are pressed against the pulleys when you close your grip, the tendon sheath is squeezed in between, and by repeated high loading of the fingers the contact point between the tendon and the tendon sheath can become irritated, which leads to an increase of fluid in the tendon sheath. Applying direct pressure or loading the finger can be painful. The pain is often localised where there is a pulley, but unlike pulley injuries there isn't an acute event that leads to the injury. In most cases the injury is caused by too much loading of the finger in a short period of time, for example at the beginning of specific finger training or campusing, or when we start to climb more after a period away from climbing. The symptoms often last for several months even if we are good at adjusting the load and using more open grip positions. However, the prognosis is good, and it's important that you continue to climb, but avoid finger-heavy training like campusing, or bouldering and lead climbing on small holds.

FLEXOR TENDON STRAIN

Whereas injuries to finger pulleys and tendon sheaths are localised to one specific area in the finger, a strained flexor tendon will feel painful all the way from the finger up into the forearm where you find the connection between the tendon and the muscle tissue. The most common mechanism of injury is a sudden load increase while hanging off an open-handed one, two or three-finger pocket. Only the outermost joint will be bent, and if your foot slips in this grip position, the fibres connecting the tendon to the muscles can tear. It's often easy to test yourself after sustaining an injury like this: if you load the outermost joint using three fingers you will feel pain, but if you engage four fingers in a half crimp grip position there is no pain. This type of injury is seldom serious enough for you to abstain completely from climbing, but climbing with an open-handed grip position might be painful for several weeks after the injury. In this case, it is important to focus on easier climbing, primarily using four fingers in a half crimp grip position. As the pain starts to decrease during the first few weeks you can begin controlled hangs using open-handed grip positions on a fingerboard or at the climbing wall. It is however important that you focus on good foot placement so as to avoid any sudden and unexpected loading, and that you grip each hold while controlling the movement.

The extent of the injury can be assessed using ultrasound; if there is no sign of significant damage to the tissue, most people will be back to regular climbing after four to six weeks. More serious injuries can take longer to heal and will require a more rigid approach; we recommend that you get a proper assessment before starting rehabilitation training.

By being aware of the risk involved when doing hard moves using open-handed grip positions, you can be more mindful of your foot placements and hitting the holds with as much control as possible to avoid acute strain injuries. The fact that finger injuries happen also when using open-handed grip positions lends weight to the argument that it is important to train climbing and deadhanging in different grip positions to be as strong as possible on all types of holds.

Flexor tendon strains usually happen when climbing on one, two or three-finger pockets.

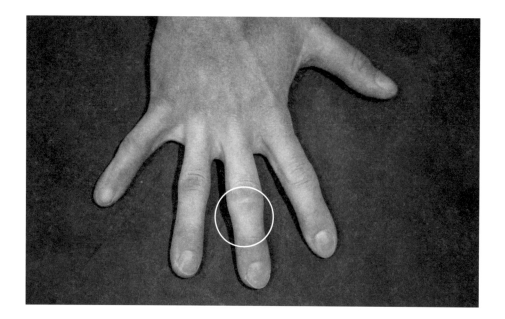

JOINT PAIN

In acute trauma, such as getting your finger stuck, or experiencing acute pain in the joint as you crimp, damage to the joint capsule and/or ligaments may have occurred. In such acute traumas, you will often experience swelling, and we recommend that these injuries are investigated by qualified medical personnel.

Far more common is diffuse pain in the joints that isn't caused by acute trauma. You might experience slight swelling, the finger can be tender to the touch and it can be difficult to bend the finger all the way into the palm of your hand. Mostly this is caused by too much heavy loading without enough time for recovery. For example, crimping places extreme stress on the middle and outermost joints of the fingers; this can lead to irritation in the joints, and more joint fluid being produced as a consequence. The joint will then swell and become tender to the touch and difficult to fully bend. This isn't dangerous but it should act as a hint for you to load your fingers less and focus more on easier climbing on better holds for a while.

While we know that the joints change with age and the number of years you have climbed, and that this is a natural consequence of loading your fingers heavily over several years, it has not been shown that these changes eventually lead to injuries that cannot heal. However, to avoid joint pain, we can assume that more care must be taken when crimping, among other things, as you get older. Even though it is not a serious injury, joint pain can still be detrimental to the quality of your climbing and prevent you from climbing as much as you want. This is yet another reminder for you to be conscious of varying your training and using as many grip positions as possible, giving you a varied load pattern on your fingers.

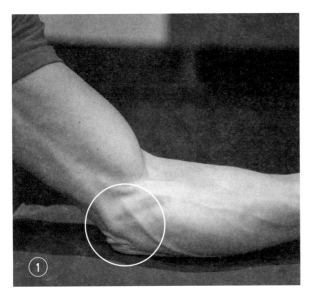

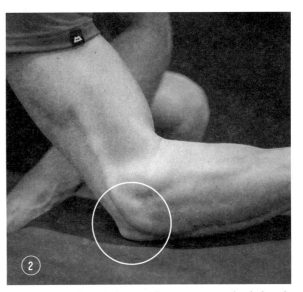

The flexor muscles of the fingers and wrist are connected to the medial epicondyle on the inside of the elbow.

The extensor muscles of the fingers and wrist are connected to the lateral epicondyle on the outside of the elbow.

ELBOW PAIN

The muscles that bend and extend the wrist and fingers are connected to the inside (photo 1) and outside (photo 2) of your elbow, respectively – the medial and the lateral epicondyles. The musculature that rotates the forearm in and out is also connected to the epicondyles. Pain on the inside of the elbow is known as golfer's elbow, or medial epicondylitis, and is related to overloading of the connection between the flexor tendons and flexor muscles of the fingers and wrists, as well as the pronator teres muscle, which rotates the forearm so that the palm faces away from us. Pain on the outside of the elbow is known as tennis elbow, or lateral epicondylitis, and is related to overloading of the connection between the extensor muscles of the fingers and wrists, as well as the supinator muscle, which, together with the biceps brachii, rotates the forearm so that the palm is facing towards us.

All of this musculature contributes when we are gripping holds, and the pain is usually caused by too much and too hard training without sufficient rest. The most important counter measure is load management, as described earlier in the chapter. For example, switching from bouldering to lead climbing to lower the intensity of the training, or climbing on walls that are less steep so that more weight is transferred from the feet to the arms and fingers than on steeper climbing. Since the pain usually stems from the connection between the muscles and the tendons, it is important to be patient during rehabilitation since tendons are notoriously slow to adapt to changes in load. A three to twelve-month time perspective is not uncommon and underlines the importance of finding ways to climb that do not provoke an excessive pain response during and after climbing. Here, a training log with pain monitoring, as described earlier, is useful for properly managing the training load. Once the load management is in place, it is advisable to start with one or two specific strength training exercises to stimulate the tendon to adapt. These exercises appear to be most effective when exercising hard, which means that you should be able to perform a set but you should feel tired for the last two repetitions – so choose weights accordingly. Some possible exercises can be found on the following pages.

1. FOREARM ROTATION

Grip the dumbbell and rotate it through 180 degrees so that your palm is facing up towards the ceiling and then down towards the floor. Allow 3 to 4 seconds for each movement for a total of 6 to 8 seconds per repetition. Complete three sets of six to eight repetitions, three times a week.

2. PINCH

Thread a rope through the bolt hole of a pinch hold and attach weights to the rope. Lift the weights off the ground by pinching the hold and bending your elbow. Allow 3 to 4 seconds on the way up, and 3 to 4 seconds on the way down, for a total of 6 to 8 seconds per repetition. Complete three sets of six to eight repetitions, three times a week.

3. WRIST CURL

Rest your forearm on a table or similar with your hand hanging off the edge and your palm facing down. Lift a dumbbell up and back. Allow 3 to 4 seconds on the way up and 3 to 4 seconds on the way down, for a total of 6 to 8 seconds per repetition. Complete three sets of six to eight repetitions, three times a week.

Exercises 1 and 2 are recommended for medial elbow pain, and exercises 2 and 3 are recommended for lateral elbow pain.

There is also a third source of elbow pain, known as climber's elbow. The pain is localised to the centre of the front of the elbow, approximately where you can feel the bicep tendon, and can be provoked by loading and bending the elbow. The pain can be related to the bicep tendon, but in most cases it is caused by overloading the brachialis muscle, which lies underneath the bicep muscle. While the bicep is dependent on the forearm being rotated so that the palm is facing up – imagine holding an undercling – the brachialis is not. This means that when you bend your elbow with the forearm rotated such that the palm is facing down – imaging doing an overhand pull-up – the brachialis has to work harder because the bicep is not in a position to exert maximum force. The pain is usually a consequence of too much training involving pull-ups, campusing and steep bouldering. Again: when pain is a result of overloading, the best countermeasure is to improve load management. First and foremost, you must identify which training methods are provoking the symptoms so that you can avoid these for a period and gain control of the situation. The easiest measures are to avoid specific strength training of the elbow flexors and do less climbing on steep walls. It's often better to compensate by doing more and easier moves instead of fewer and harder moves, and as the symptoms start to fade you can gradually climb steeper and harder.

FONT ELBOW

Climber's elbow is also known as 'Font elbow'. Most of the boulders you will find in the bouldering mecca of Fontainebleau in France have a rounded top, often with nothing more than pure friction as the only means of topping out. You must then press the palms of your hands down on the holds at the same time as bending your elbows to pull your body up. This movement pattern is central to almost all of the top-outs, independent of the level of difficulty of the boulder problem, and is repeated every day you are out climbing in Font. Many climbers will end up suffering from climber's elbow when visiting Fontainebleau, hence the name Font elbow.

SHOULDER PAIN

The shoulder has the largest range of motion of all the joints in our bodies, and we use our shoulders in a variety of ways every time we climb. Because the joint is so mobile, by nature it is relatively unstable, and great demand is placed on muscular strength and control to maintain stability of the shoulder while it is in motion. There are several possible causes of shoulder pain, and even the experts sometimes disagree on how to classify and diagnose shoulder pain. We therefore recommend seeking professional medical help if you experience shoulder pain which affects you in your climbing. However, some basic guidelines may be useful if your shoulder is painful.

With the exception of major injuries such shoulder disclocations, fall trauma and major tendon ruptures, most shoulder injuries in climbing occur due to overloading of one or more structures adjacent to the shoulder. The structures that are most frequently affected are the synovial bursae and rotator cuff tendons with their associated muscles. The rotator cuff consists of four muscles – supraspinatus, infraspinatus, subscapularis and teres minor. Collectively, these form a cuff around the shoulder joint which helps to stabilise the ball on the upper arm in the joint socket, and around this cuff lie a series of synovial bursae which ensure that the movements between the tendons and the surrounding tissue are as frictionless as possible. In simple terms, all the climbing moves we do expose the rotator cuff and bursae to loading and compression, and excessive strain over time can cause discomfort in these structures. Pain in some arm positions and during some climbing moves is a common characteristic, as is pain when lifting the arm above shoulder height and with everyday functions such as getting dressed or putting the seat belt on in the car.

Since shoulder pain in climbing is associated with overloading, it is important to adjust the load by switching exercise methods and reducing the intensity of workouts – remember Greg Lehman's quote about calming down and then building back up. After you have regained control of your training load, shoulder pain is treated primarily through various training exercises. Which exercises and how hard they should be is determined in consultation with medical professionals who are experienced in dealing with shoulder pain, and preferably someone who also has climbing experience, so that rehabilitation can be directed towards the movement pattern you are returning to. If shoulder pain is a recurring problem, we also recommend that you seek guidance from a coach who can help you identify various movement patterns and technical solutions you use that may be playing a part in causing the discomfort. You can then use climbing-specific strength and technique exercises for both rehabilitation and prevention of future injuries.

Since the shoulder is primarily stabilised by muscles, it is important to build a good physical foundation of strength surrounding it so that it can gradually endure more loading as your climbing progresses. Earlier in the chapter, we presented different exercises to help with this, and which also help to create a balance in the strength relationship between the primary movers and their antagonists.

Thilo Schrøter climbing *El Corazon* (Font 8b), Rocklands, South Africa.

PHOTO: BJØRN SÆTNAN

Mari Augusta Salvesen climbing *Pinotage* (Font 7b+), Rocklands, South Africa.

KNEE INJURIES

The knee joint is basically a stable joint, and it takes large forces to damage the various structures around it. Most climbing-related knee injuries are therefore associated with acute events on the wall or falls. When we place the knee in extreme positions such as heel hooks, twisting in and rockovers, the knee joint, the cruciate ligament and the collateral ligaments are subjected to great strain, and experience shows that most acute, climbing-related knee injuries occur in these positions.

As with all acute injuries we recommend that acute knee injuries are examined by a medical professional who can assess the damage. Severe injuries might require surgery, but most injuries involve only minor damage to ligaments and menisci, and rehabilitation focuses on building strength around the knee while the injured knee heals. It is therefore important to have the injury examined in order to choose the right path for rehabilitation.

In the selection of exercises presented earlier in the chapter, we have deliberately added strength training exercises that target the musculature around the knees. In several other sports, it has been shown that strength training can reduce the risk of acute knee injuries, and even though these injuries aren't especially common in climbing, it is a good idea to also include some strength training for the legs. Still, what is most important is to look at which positions on the wall are likely to put your knees in harm's way and then try to reduce the number of times you do these moves when training. Obviously, you will do anything within your power to get to the top when redpointing, which will include heel hooking, twisting in and rocking over, but you can reduce the risk of knee injuries if you limit these techniques in your day-to-day climbing training – or at least be aware of the risks involved when using them. And, if you feel the need to use such techniques, make sure you warm up your legs just as you would your fingers, for example, by using the exercises described in this chapter.

PHOTO: BJØRN HELGE RØNNING

Teodor Kirkebø in the 2017 Junior National
Bouldering Championship finals in Oslo.

YOUNG CLIMBERS AND THEIR RISK OF INJURY

We have chosen to define young climbers as those below the age of 16, and the most important message to this group is that until they are fully grown up they must take special care of their fingers. While the bones in the body are growing, youths are particularly prone to injury in the growth plates. The growth plate – known as the epiphysis – is a disc near the end of a bone that is softer than the rest of the bone tissue. The epiphysis allows the bone to grow and become longer, and it closes and hardens when the body is fully grown, which for some people will not happen until the age of 18. Until it has closed it is especially prone to injury. The epiphyseal plates of the fingers lie in connection at the joints in the fingers, and the middle joint in particular seems to be prone to injury when exposed to too much finger-intensive training and climbing. This is the reason why we do not recommend deadhangs and campus training for young, growing athletes, as specific finger training at this age can lead to long breaks from training and, in the worst cases, injuries that might never heal. Care should also be taken during finger-intensive climbing, and crimping should be reduced to a minimum.

In cases of pain in the fingers, such as pain before, during and after training, and swelling in the middle joints of the fingers, it is advisable to contact a qualified medical professional who can assess whether there is damage to the epiphyseal disc. Finger discomforts such as these should always lead to a reduction in training load, but if the injury can be detected through MRI or ultrasound examination, a two-month break from climbing is recommended before re-examination of the finger. If you take the symptoms seriously, your fingers will finish growing and the injury will not present any problems in the future, but if you let the condition go too far, your fingers can be afflicted with permanent, non-healing injuries, which may end your climbing career.

During puberty, both body height and body mass will increase, and during this period we must be aware of the risk of injury since an increase in body mass leads to increased body weight, and thus a higher load on the fingers. This period is estimated to be from the age of 11 to 14 for girls, and from 12 to 16 for boys. This often coincides with a time when many ambitious young climbers are gradually adding more and harder training, and this combination is not without its problems. It is important that the athletes themselves, and we as adults, are aware of this issue and organise the training in a way that does not overload the fingers. This involves using larger holds and open grip positions, avoiding specific finger training like deadhangs and campusing, and having a continued focus on versatile and varied climbing training.

For young and ambitious climbers, the increase in body weight during puberty can be difficult to deal with. Many will face a period of reduced performance and perhaps see their peers develop faster than they are doing. During this period it can be tempting to increase performance by reducing weight, and it is important to be aware of the risks involved. Reduced weight equals energy deficit. This means you are supplying your body with less energy than it consumes, and this energy deficit can have consequences for your health. Women have what is known as the female athlete triad, which describes the interrelationship of a negative energy balance, menstrual dysfunction and decreased bone mineral density. The combination of these three components can lead to permanent health damage. In some athletes, focusing too much on food and weight can lead to a disrupted eating behaviour or an eating disorder. This is a mental illness that can lead to both physical and mental health complications, and is a potentially lethal affliction. This can also happen to male athletes, and even though there is no such thing as the male athlete triad, their problems are related. Using weight reduction as a performance enhancer at a young age can lead to serious physical and mental illness forcing an early exit from climbing. In addition, it is impossible to get enough quality training over time with a constant energy deficit. Eventually, you will drastically deteriorate physically, and it is often challenging to train yourself back to your previous level. Many will lack the motivation needed to put in the effort and will end up quitting instead. It is extremely important to nurture a healthy training environment for youth climbers to develop at their own tempo, where nutrition and puberty are natural topics to talk about so that they aren't driven towards a premature focus on weight loss as a performance-enhancing tool.

These are our recommendations for reducing the risk of injury in younger climbers:
- Training should be varied and fun.
- Focus mainly on doing more moves rather than harder moves.
- Spend most of the training time learning technical skills and developing a good movement pattern on the wall.
- Train the arms and upper body, but avoid specific finger strength training. Focus on technical execution, simple training methods and slow and steady progression.
- Use general strength training for the whole body, as well as training balance, coordination and endurance.
- Be aware of symptoms in the fingers throughout puberty, but especially during periods of rapid increase in height and body mass.

Norwegian climber Rannveig Aamodt was born in 1984. She is a trained veterinary animal therapist and has a background as a teacher at a high school. She now lives in Colorado as a professional climber and photographer. On 26 April 2012 she experienced a near-fatal climbing accident.

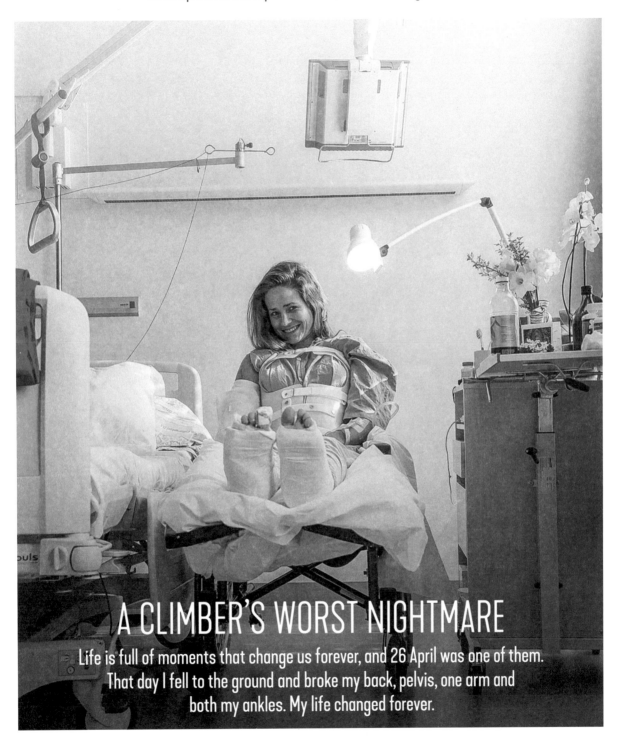

A CLIMBER'S WORST NIGHTMARE

Life is full of moments that change us forever, and 26 April was one of them. That day I fell to the ground and broke my back, pelvis, one arm and both my ankles. My life changed forever.

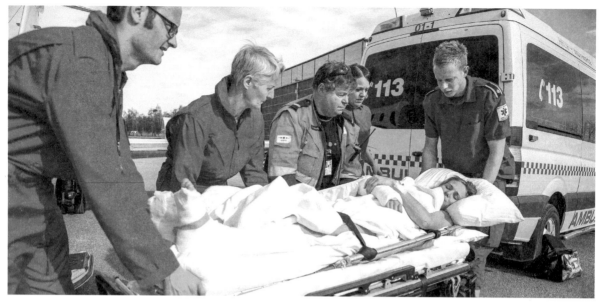

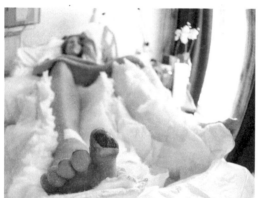

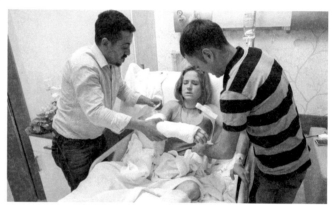

IT WAS SPRINGTIME and we were living the life in Geyikbayiri in Turkey. My husband Nathan and I were eating breakfast and drinking coffee while flipping through the guidebook and making plans for the day, as we always did. We ended up at a crag called Sarkit and started warming up as usual.

After Nathan had led a steep, athletic route, I followed on top-rope. Because another crew also wanted to top-rope the route, I brought their rope up with me, and as I unclipped our rope I clipped theirs in. I climbed easily, dancing between small footholds and large tufa. At the anchor I first clipped myself in before clipping in their rope, but because it had gotten twisted and tangled, I had to unclip their rope, untangle it and clip it back in.

And this is when it happened. A quick slip of the mind, shaped by old habits and a sense of security. I looked down at the rope clipped into every quickdraw and the anchor at the top, a common and ordinary sight. It was just that this time I wasn't on lead, and Nathan wasn't holding the other end of that rope. So when I clipped the other rope into the anchor, I unclipped my own rope, the one Nathan was holding. 'You got me?' I called down. Nathan leant back, felt the rope come tight because I was still clipped to the anchor and shouted back. I unclipped myself from the anchor – and let go.

FROM NATHAN'S DIARY:

I can still picture her falling. In a seated position, her arms making small circles in the air. Like a bird falling out of her nest. I can still feel my gut wrenching for every metre of rope that doesn't take. She made the same sound as when she accidentally dropped a plate on the kitchen floor, and I can hear the sickening sound of bones crushing and flesh tearing. The echo of my voice as I screamed for help at the empty fields below us.

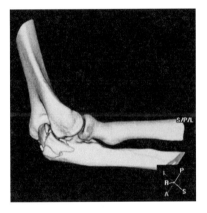
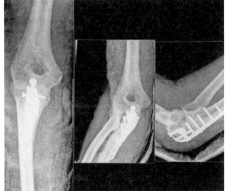
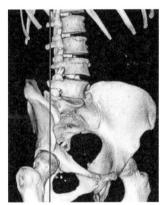

I woke up in a bubble of light, confused, but vaguely aware of what had just happened. I remember screaming and drifting in and out of consciousness. I remember moments of being awake with extreme pain in my feet, legs and back, and this went on for hours until I arrived at the hospital.

I woke up after the operation and looked down at my mummified body. I was just able to move my toes, to the great relief of those around me who feared I was paralysed. I had three compression fractures in my back, a broken pelvis, two fractured ankles, and several broken bones in my feet. I had shattered my right elbow and partially torn my tricep tendon off.

I was a healthy and strong athlete who had spent the last few years of my life climbing all over the world, and here I was: trapped in a body that didn't work and in tremendous pain. I couldn't go to the bathroom on my own, I couldn't wash myself, I couldn't even turn over in bed. Yet still, I felt enormous gratitude overwhelming everything. All the small things I had previously taken for granted were like receiving gifts – from getting my back scratched to getting my hair washed. It was like every emotion was intensified, and I was on a journey to my inner self.

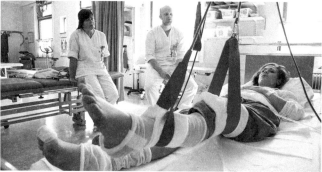

CLIMBING BACK TO LIFE

I had a lot of time with my thoughts. Will I be able to climb again? And, if so, will I be able to get back to my previous level? Will I even want to climb again?

I decided that climbing should be something I do for myself because it's something I love doing. Climbing was to be a tool of encouragement, helping me fulfil my potential and pushing me to be at my best, independent of what level I was currently climbing at. And then I had to make a distinction between who I am and what I do. Climbing is something I do. I am not a climber. Whatever I might lose, I'm still me.

Amid all the fear and anxiety this gave me a sense of clarity and calmness that let me accept my situation, and I started to think positively about what was ahead of me. It triggered a force within me, built on defiance and determination to embark on the journey ahead.

I started lifting a weight with my left arm, the one which was still working. I underwent multiple surgeries in Norway and spent weeks in the hospital and rehabilitation facilities while I continued training as much as I could. To begin with, I sat in a wheelchair and could only stretch my arms and legs and train using slings. My brother brought me kneepads so that I could start crawling on the floor, and I ended up doing alarming amounts of crawling.

After about ten weeks I could start to put some weight on my feet. I started hanging from a harness over a treadmill and progressed by lifting weights, cycling on an exercise bike and swimming. Every step forward built on what I had previously done, and the feeling I got from seeing the results of all the hard work that I had put in was extremely motivating. My biggest challenge was the pain. Previously I had used pain as an indicator for when I pushed too hard during training, but since the pain was now constant, this indicator was useless. I had to push through the pain in order to progress, but I also had to know when to rest. I learned that pain creates fear, and if you give in to this fear it limits everything.

'AFTER ABOUT TEN WEEKS I COULD START TO PUT SOME WEIGHT ON MY FEET.'

From knowing my own limits I had to jump into the deep end and learn how to swim again, and frequently I realised that my limits were much further out to sea than I had imagined.

When I finally emerged from the rehabilitation centre I started working with Stian. It marked the end of seeing myself as a fragile patient, and together we changed my focus towards dedicated training to become a better climber. I had my dreams and goals, and he helped me find ways to achieve them.

Eight months after the accident I went to Thailand, and it was then that all of my training manifested itself into climbing performance. Eight months to the day after the accident, I sent my first F8a, and I ended the trip with an additional two F8a+, two F8a, and a F7c. Now, six years after my accident, I have been back to the route where I almost died so I could look death in the eye, I climb F8b+ and I'm living as a professional climber.

However, the constant pain is exhausting to this day. Sometimes it feels like climbing and hiking takes more than it gives, which makes me question what I'm really doing. Then I have to remind myself that I am grateful. I am grateful to be able to do what I do, and just as the pain in my body after a long day in the mountains used to make me happy, I try to look at it in the same way now – to relate the pain to something satisfying and a result of having achieved something.

It has been a long journey, and it is far from over, but it has strengthened my belief that in order to realise your dreams you need to give it 100 per cent. That your criteria for success are your own. That your goals and dreams are your own and not anybody else's. Dream big and work hard to get there, because no matter what, it will lead you somewhere. Not always where you had in mind or wanted to go, but often it will take you much further than you could ever have imagined.

'DREAM BIG AND WORK HARD TO GET THERE, BECAUSE NO MATTER WHAT IT WILL LEAD YOU SOMEWHERE.'

CHAPTER 6

TRAINING PLANS

CLIMBING PERFORMANCE IS dependent on many factors. If we can place these factors in a training plan, we will see more progression than if we only do the same things every time we train. By planning our training, we can train both specifically and with variety to achieve our goals, and at the same time manage the training load so that we avoid overtraining and thereby decrease our risk of injury.

In this chapter, we look at basic training principles, training periodisation, and how we make both long-term and short-term training plans.

Planning for training is based on a few fundamental principles:

THE PRINCIPLE OF LOAD AND ADAPTATION

The body is an amazing organism that will over time adapt to any load we expose it to. This is how muscles grow and become stronger through strength training, and how we can recover better during rest phases through endurance training. This is also how moves become steadily easier through technique training, and how experience helps us deal with stressful competition situations. This happens by training – and challenging ourselves on – the elements we wish to improve. Be prepared for the adaptation to take time!

Through well-planned and varied training it is also easier to manage the training load, something which is central to reducing the risk of injury. Training load is a combination of volume, intensity and frequency – how much, how hard and how often you train. If you climb hard and often, your training load will be significant. If, on the other hand, you can reduce the volume of the more intensive sessions and the intensity of the volume sessions, it can be easier to maintain a level of training load that allows you to train a lot without overloading your body.

Different types of tissues in your body also require different amounts of time to adapt. Muscles adapt quickly, while bones, tendons and ligaments need longer to adapt to the same load. Hard and uniform training with too rapid a progression can quickly lead to the tendons being loaded more than they are trained to endure, which we know can lead to injury. Having a proper time perspective on the relationship between load and adaptation is therefore central to planning for training.

THE PRINCIPLE OF PROGRESSION

Despite the body being great at adaptation, it is by nature lazy. When we don't challenge ourselves more than what we can already endure or achieve, there is no need for the body to adapt further. Therefore, progression in training is a very important element when setting up a training plan. We create progression by gradually increasing the load or exercising an ever-increasing range of movements.

WITHOUT PROGRESSION, THERE'S ONLY STAGNATION.

THE PRINCIPLE OF RECOVERY

After training, rest is required so that the body is able to perform again. Most people who have had two consecutive days of long and hard bouldering or endurance sessions will have experienced that the second day was harder than the first. Although the recovery time will differ depending on how well trained you are initially, and what and how hard you trained, it's a general rule of thumb that after a session of hard strength or endurance training you should wait about two days before you repeat a similar session. This does not mean that you should rest completely for two days, but that you can train other things in the meantime. Recovery time depends on, among other things, general physical shape, sleep and nutrition. This explains why elite athletes in good physical shape, and who focus on sleeping and eating properly, can endure periods with a high number of extremely hard workouts. For us mortals, it is important to get enough rest between hard workouts and gradually build the foundation needed to endure more and harder workouts. Poor recovery results in poorer quality of exercise, or as the Finnish scientist Keijo Häkkinen says:

If you go too hard on your easy days, soon you will be going too easy on your hard days.

THE PRINCIPLE OF SPECIFICITY

It is a well-known fact that you become better at whatever you are training. If you want to get better at climbing long, pumpy routes, you need to simulate this in your training. If you want to become stronger to keep tension on steep climbs, you must train specifically for this – including using the exercises presented in this book, as more general strength training for the abdomen and back will not produce the same effect. As you develop as a climber, it is important to identify which areas you want to improve so that you can choose specific exercises and training methods.

THE PRINCIPLE OF VARIATION

In contrast to the principle of specificity, variation in your training is also important. For example, you should let your fingers rest the day after a finger-intensive bouldering session; instead, train endurance on better holds on day two. This way you spread the load throughout the body. Variation between types of moves, types of holds, wall angles, and indoor and outdoor climbing is also essential to building the technical skills necessary to become a better climber. In addition, new elements can increase your eagerness to train and progress further. By varying your training, you can also maintain the level of skills other than the ones you are focusing on for that period. You can, for example, focus on hard bouldering and strength for a period, but at the same time vary your training week by adding an endurance session and a more technical bouldering session, so that you maintain your level in these areas. This way you also get to train and climb more times that week, which undoubtedly will help make you a better climber.

PERIODISATION

Periodisation is a term that refers to planned variations in training to achieve specific goals, and periodisation of training is based on the training principles. We need to build a training plan that promotes progress through loading, adaptation and recovery, and with enough progression in the training to avoid stagnation; we also need to train specifically to improve on the various elements, and vary the training sufficiently to keep us motivated and include as many elements as possible.

For the physical factors – strength and endurance – it is common to start the training period with a greater focus on volume than on intensity. In strength training, this means a higher number of repetitions with a lower load per set, where the aim is to learn the exercise and build a base for harder repetitions. Eventually, the number of repetitions per set is reduced, but is replaced with a significantly heavier load per repetition. Thereafter, strength training can be focused more at rapid development of force.

The same approach can be used with endurance training. At the start of the training period, it makes sense to have a high number of moves per climbing session. So that you can complete all of these moves, they cannot be too hard, nor should you get too pumped. The goal is to build the capacity to later withstand more intensive endurance training. As the number of moves per session gradually decreases, the difficulty level per move, circuit or route can be increased, simultaneously increasing the intensity. The final part of an endurance period is about training as close to your intended performance level as possible. For a competitive climber, this means climbing a few, but very hard, routes per session, with maximum effort. If you have an outdoor project, the routes or circuits you train on can be similar to the route you are training for in the number of moves, cruxes and rests. You will also climb at maximum effort per attempt and have longer rests between each attempt.

PHOTO: ALEX MANELIS

Maria Davies Sandbu bouldering in Bishop, USA.

Planning your training in this way is called linear periodisation. Linear indicates that there is a progression from high volume and low intensity to low volume and high intensity. The challenge with such a model is that it goes on for a relatively long time, and you will prioritise some elements in your training over others. Combining a linear model with what we call conjugate periodisation allows you to incorporate training of other factors simultaneously. A conjugate model involves switching between different properties for shorter periods, and this can still be combined with the principle of progression from high volume and low intensity to low volume and high intensity. In an endurance period, around 80 per cent of your training can be built around endurance training, while the remaining 20 per cent may be aimed at bouldering and strength. In this way, it's possible to maintain strength during an endurance period and vice versa.

During each training period, it is appropriate to vary the training load over the different weeks. For example, two weeks of hard training may be followed by one easier week before another two hard weeks. This is known as load rhythm and it creates a positive relationship between load and recovery. How many hard and easy weeks you plan for during the period depends on your fitness level and what timescale you have set for when you want to be in top shape. If you have many hard weeks in a row, you will find that your physical condition gets progressively worse because you are training a lot, and thus you must lower your performance ambitions during such a period. When you are conscious of this and are confident that you will peak during easier weeks – and confident that you are actually training well even though you may feel weaker – it will be easier to live with fluctuations in fitness. The physically easier weeks are also golden opportunities to focus more on technical, tactical and mental factors. Thus, easy weeks do not mean you should not climb, and we encourage you to do as much valuable climbing as possible in the easier weeks even if the physical load is reduced.

PEAKING

The point of training will always be to make you a better climber, performing at ever-higher levels. Still, there will be times when you want to be able to give it that extra effort. If you are going on a climbing trip or trying to redpoint a route that you have been working on, you will want to engage that last percentage that separates a top from a fall, giving you the feeling of being weightless and transforming the previously impossible crux into something that is now suddenly easy. Timing peak fitness may seem easy on paper, but it takes a lot of experimentation to find the model that suits you best.

All exercise breaks the body down. After periods of hard training, you can ease up on the training load for a little longer than you normally would, creating what is called super-compensation. This means that you are raising your level for a period after training at considerably less load for a while. How much you raise the level, and how long that period lasts, depends on how hard and long you have trained and how well you have recovered.

The hardest thing about peaking is getting the timing right. In endurance sports, a peak period usually starts three weeks before reaching maximum performance, while in more strength-dependent sports, which includes climbing, the period starts two weeks in before. The most important thing is to reduce the training duration – how long each session lasts – and it is recommended to reduce the duration by 40 to 60 per cent. At the same time, the training frequency – how often you exercise – can remain unchanged, and you can train just as hard as before. Short and intense, i.e. hard, sessions are what appear to have the best effect on fitness development during such a period. The key is to load less, recover more and at the same time maintain your capacity.

If you exercise four times a week where each session is about 90 to 120 minutes, you can continue with the four sessions, but reduce their duration to 45 to 60 minutes per session at high intensity. Start with the reduction in training duration about two weeks before you plan to be at peak performance. To preserve the peak, continue with short, intense sessions – but at some point your fitness curve will start to drop and it's time to start a new training period. Therefore, it may be challenging to have multiple peaks in a short period of time, as each peak will require a pre-peak training period. You can use the same principles of load reduction if your goal is to get a small peak for the Sundays you plan to be out on your projects. Then you can do a hard workout on Monday and Tuesday, rest Wednesday and train two short, hard sessions on Thursday and Friday before resting on Saturday. The ideal method for peaking will vary between individuals, and we encourage everyone to experiment for themselves based on the recommendations above.

The last week before a bouldering trip or a competition, try doing short and hard bouldering and campus sessions every other day with two rest days before you want to start performing.

TRAINING PLANS

We often think of training plans as reserved for elite athletes who train a lot, and they do of course have a lot to gain from planning their training. But by considering the principles described above we can all get more out of our training if we have an idea of what to do, how to do it and why we should be doing it.

GOALS, REQUIREMENTS AND CAPACITY

All training plans are guided by the goals we set. We can set long-term dream goals, for example, a dream route or a competition result, or we can set more short-term, intermediate objectives along the way. Climbing a specific boulder problem, route or grade is an inspiring goal, but we recommend that you also set some broader goals. If your goal is to climb a certain F7c, you should at the same time have a goal to climb as many routes graded F7a to F7b on as many different wall angles as possible. Not only will you achieve your goal of climbing your dream route, but you will also have become a more solid climber at a higher level. It is important that your goals create both motivation for training and provide direction for what to train.

Once your goals have been set, the challenging task of planning the necessary training to achieve these goals can begin. For this task, you should consider your strengths and weaknesses – i.e. what you need to develop so you can achieve your goals. Some things will be easier to define than others. For example, it can be quite obvious to you if your fingers aren't strong enough to do a certain crux move, but it can be harder to define how technically correct you are moving or how efficiently you are clipping the quickdraws. Even when it comes to pure physical factors, it isn't always easy to define how good you must be when it comes to individual skills – i.e. how strong your fingers must be or how good your endurance must be – for you to achieve your goals. Forming a picture of where your strengths lie and where your greatest potential for development lies will therefore require effort. If you are a physically strong climber who thrives on steep terrain but you want to develop so you can climb routes and boulder problems that are more vertical and technically challenging, then these are the elements you need to prioritise in your training. Similarly, climbers who thrive on small holds and technically challenging climbing should prioritise strength training to develop as a climber. A simple exercise to start this process is to list and categorise what you see as your strengths and your potential for development in your climbing. It is a good idea to make the first draft of this list yourself, but we recommend that most climbers include their training partners or coaches in this process so it is as accurate as possible when defining where you are as a climber.

In the example opposite, we have split performance factors into technical, physical and mental, and made subcategories for each of them. As you go through each category, mark the ones you consider as strengths with green, and the ones where you need to put in more effort with red. You can use our example as a starting point, but challenge yourself to come up with and list each element on your own. This will strengthen your sense of ownership of your development plan and at the same time require you to reflect on your own strengths and potential for improvement.

TECHNICAL

Footwork	Edging	Smearing	Precision	Steep climbing	Heel hooking	Toe hooking
Wall angle	Slab	Vertical	Overhang	Roof		
Balance	Weight transfer	Flagging	Fronting	Twisting	Sidepull	
Climbing style	Static	Dynamic	Deadpoint	Dyno		
Tension	Compression	Not cutting loose on steep climbing				
Grip positions	Crimps	Slopers	Pockets	Pinches		

PHYSICAL

Finger strength	Finger-intensive bouldering	Fingerboard max		Contact strength
Arm and upper body strength	Pull-ups	Locking off	Campusing	Steep bouldering
Core	Overhangs/roofs	Swings	Not cutting loose on steep climbing	
Endurance	Power endurance	Maximum endurance	Capacity	Fingerboard endurance
Mobility	High foot placements	Splits/corners	Hips close to the wall when fronting	Stemming with the arms

MENTAL

Inner dialogue	Positive thinking	Confidence	Forgetting failure	Remembering success	
Motivated for	Outdoor climbing	Indoor climbing	Strength training	Technique training	Mental training
Visualisation	Redpoint	Reading routes/on-sight	Flash	New environments	
Performance	Outdoors	Indoors	Training		
Preparations	Routines		Time spent training		
Fear	Fear of falling	Fear of failing	Climbing in front of others		

When you have gone through each point you will have a picture of how you – and possibly others – see your strengths and weaknesses. It is, however, important to see the different properties in relation to one another. If, for example, you rate your maximum finger strength as good, yet still have problems with finger-intensive bouldering, it's probably not because your fingers aren't strong enough, but rather that you don't have good contact strength. In the same way, you can be strong when doing climbing-specific core exercises but still struggle with roof climbing. This is probably more to do with a lack of technique on that wall angle than purely a lack of strength.

Being aware of what you are already good at and what you want to develop adds to the quality of your training, where each session focuses on improving specific elements.

PHOTO: BJORNAR SMESTAD

TINA JOHNSEN HAFSAAS:

- Spend time building a solid foundation.
- Do as much climbing as possible in each training session.
- Climb every style.
- Specific training only works if you have a good foundation.
- A solid foundation gives you the best conditions for getting stronger, developing better endurance and staying away from injuries.

Seven years ago, Tina Johnsen Hafsaas, Norwegian national champion and World Cup climber, completed this exercise. By becoming aware of what she was already good at, and where she had the biggest potential for growth, it was easier for Tina to add the different elements to her daily training routine. Analysing her own skillset became habit after a while, and this has made it possible for her to develop into an elite-level climber.

WEAKNESSES	STRENGTHS
Slopers	Crimps
Big pinches	Crimpy pinches
Pulling through on bad holds	Pulling through on good holds
Roof climbing	Vertical climbing
Chalking and resting too much	Finding rests
Heel hooking	Toe hooking
Locking off	Landing holds with bent elbows
Explosive moves	Twisting in – using the legs to relieve the arms
Fear of falling	Solving sequences on the fly
Shouldery moves	Reading and planning sequences
Burly moves	Dynamic moves (as long as I am in control)
Max power	Grit
Power endurance	Creating speed

Tina's chart is more detailed than our examples and it also contains additional elements. And herein lies much of the value of this exercise: feel free to use our examples, but challenge yourself to find elements unique to your own climbing.

LONG-TERM PLANS

It makes sense to produce an overview of what will happen during the coming year. Depending upon your ambitions, long-term plans can also run for several years. For example, if you have been climbing for a few years but have the ambition to become a national champion, it's natural to consider your development over a longer period than just one year. For complete beginners, the most important thing will be to climb as much as possible without thinking too much about when to do what during the year. However, for more advanced climbers, it will be more important to define different performance periods and associated training periods which precede these.

In many countries, the year is traditionally split into an outdoor season and an indoor season, where the indoor season is characterised by indoor training while the outdoor season is all about trying – and hopefully sending – the routes and boulder problems we have dreamed about during the winter. As climbing destinations around the world have become more accessible, it is now more common to travel to places that allow climbing even in winter, and this has an effect on how we plan our training if we want to be fit to perform on these trips.

The fundamental message is that heavy training periods are rarely compatible with peak performance. You must, therefore, divide the year into different training and performance periods, and see how you can plan these around when you would like to be in top shape. If you do not have specific times of the year when you want to perform, and would rather focus on getting progressively better, it is still important to think about how different skills can be specifically developed and during which periods of the year this should happen.

Maria Davies Sandbu climbing in Hueco Tanks, USA, during winter.

PERIODIC PLANS

Based on your long-term plan you can define different periods throughout the year. The most important part of a periodic plan is to define the priority for that specific period. If one of your intermediate objectives is to become stronger in your upper body, then you must implement several sessions which target that; likewise if you wish to improve your endurance. At the same time, it is important to maintain the level of the elements that you aren't prioritising – for example, during periods of strength training you also maintain your endurance, and vice versa. A rule of thumb is to spend 80 per cent of your training time on what you wish to prioritise, and the remaining 20 per cent on the other elements. With every period you should plan for a gradual progression so that the training becomes progressively harder. It is also important to create a loading rhythm for every period so that you can alternate between harder and easier weeks and harder and easier sessions.

In the example below we have divided a 12-week period into three blocks of four weeks. Our example is for a climber who has enough time for three climbing days per week, and one day for strength training. The focus for the period is strength, so we have implemented strength training for the upper body, arms and fingers, in addition to regular climbing training. By organising the training in such a way, we have defined the types of sessions we want for each week and what they should contain. We have planned a loading rhythm per week and progressively harder training throughout the period. How the sessions are distributed throughout the week can vary based on multiple factors, so we recommend setting up the plan for each week to begin as close to the start of the week as possible.

	SESSIONS PER WEEK	LOAD RHYTHM	FOCUS
WEEKS 1–4	2 x Bouldering 1 x Lead/circuits 1 x Arm/upper body strength	Week 1: Medium Week 2: Hard Week 3: Hard Week 4: Easy	Focus for the weeks should be varied bouldering sessions, both technical, and finger intense and physical. The hard weeks involve a higher number of moves for the endurance sessions, and higher intensity for the bouldering sessions. The easy weeks involve a rest day between each session. Strength training focuses on a higher number of repetitions (8–12 x 3 sets).
WEEKS 5–8	2 x Bouldering 1 x Deadhang 1 x Lead/circuits 1 x Arm/upper body strength	Week 1: Medium Week 2: Hard Week 3: Hard Week 4: Easy	More focus on intensive bouldering and endurance sessions. The hard weeks involve finger-intensive and physically challenging bouldering sessions. The easy weeks involve more technical bouldering and lower-intensity endurance sessions. Strength training focuses on fewer repetitions (4 x 4).
WEEKS 9–12	2 x Bouldering 1 x Deadhang 1 x Lead/circuits 1 x Arm/upper body strength	Week 1: Medium Week 2: Hard Week 3: Hard Week 4: Easy	Short and hard bouldering sessions with few but hard boulder problems and longer rests between each attempt. Endurance sessions with few attempts, but high intensity per route or circuit. Strength training with three sets of 2–3 repetitions at maximum intensity.

The first four weeks focus more on quantity, while the intensity gradually ramps up during the whole period. The plan alternates between hard and easy weeks, and every week involves both endurance training and more specific technique training in individual sessions. The period ends at high intensity and with more rest to culminate in a peak in fitness.

SHORT-TERM PLANS

When you have defined the focus of a training period it will be easier to decide the contents of your training week. You can plan the contents of a training period as we did in the examples opposite, but you always have to take illness, injuries and other commitments into account when planning the training week. It is, therefore, best to decide when the different sessions should take place during the week as close to the start of the training period as possible. You should also plan your training such that the most physically demanding sessions follow a rest day, in order to maximise the training dividend from these sessions. This means that campus training and other explosive sessions should come first, then the physically demanding strength sessions, and then lastly the endurance sessions before another rest day. Below are two weeks from the periodic plan so that we can take a more detailed look at each day of the week.

	MONDAY	TUESDAY	WEDNESDAY	THURSDAY	FRIDAY	SATURDAY	SUNDAY
WEEK 3 HARD	Bouldering: 5–10 technical problems, top at least 5	Endurance: 3 x 5	Rest	Strength: pull-ups, lock-offs, hanging abdomen exercises	Rest	Bouldering: pyramids	Rest

	MONDAY	TUESDAY	WEDNESDAY	THURSDAY	FRIDAY	SATURDAY	SUNDAY
WEEK 9 MEDIUM	Endurance: 2 x 4	Rest	Bouldering: Moonboard	Strength: pull-ups, lock-offs, hanging abdomen exercises	Rest	Deadhang max + 3–5 technical problems, top at least 3	Rest

When you are planning the sessions for a week, you need to know what each session should contain and how it should play out. The latter point is one of the most important things to learn about planning your training. The most common way is to divide the session into three: the warm-up, the main part and the finish.

PHOTO LATTICE TRAINING

INTERVIEW WITH
TOM RANDALL

Tom Randall is one of the UK's top climbers and founder of Lattice Training which provides data-driven climbing assessments and training plans. A climber and coach for over 20 years, he made the first ascent of *Century Crack* (5.14b) in Utah, USA, and *The Kraken* (Font 8b) in Devon, England. He is also a former GB climbing team manager and coach. We asked Tom for his thoughts on his training philosophy and his approach to structured climbing training.

> 'YEAR AFTER YEAR, I STILL GO BACK AND TRY TO MAKE IMPROVEMENTS
> ON BASIC THINGS LIKE STRENGTH, MENTAL GAME AND TECHNIQUE.'

1. You're known for training hard and it's paid off with some incredibly hard ascents around the world. What has your personal experience of climbing-specific training taught you over the years?

I think the biggest thing for me as a climber – but also as a coach – is that the process of being very specific and structured with my training will only take me so far with my performance. Using the element of specificity, or replica training, is the method by which you can finely tune your climbing to almost perfectly match up to the demands of your goal. It often feels like it's a bit of a performance hack because it's so incredibly effective, but it's really just a method of training that's been used by most sports for decades. It's exactly the type of work that you would do in other sports during what is called a 'peak cycle' or a 'performance taper', but it has only become really popular in climbing in the last ten or so years. That being said, it should be noted that it's like the polishing of a diamond and not a magic pill for success. If what you have at the fundamental core of your climbing ability is just a lump of coal, you're not going to get a precious stone, no matter how much you rub it! That's why, year after year, I still go back and try to make improvements on basic things like strength, mental game and technique. If I don't, I find myself stagnating and getting into a cycle of endless performance polishing, trying to squeeze out that last one per cent of perfection because I'm too lazy or ill-disciplined to tackle the underlying issues.

2. Training for climbing is becoming increasingly more structured and sophisticated. Are we now closing the gap with more established/mainstream sports?

Before climbing, my background was in athletics and martial arts and I won various national titles in both, so I've spent almost all of my life in elite sport. In addition, I stay connected with other sports coaches to try and understand what's going on in the more mainstream sports and sports science literature. When I combine what I've seen and experienced in both of these areas (as a junior athlete and as a coach), I'm left with the feeling that climbing isn't actually doing that bad at all! I think the climbing population is very self-critical when it comes to training and I see us excel in many areas compared to other sports. Yes, football may have access to a lot of money, cooler sports tech and coaching resources, but when I speak to the coaches about the fundamentals of muscle physiology and the understanding of movement economy and so on, I'm rarely left with the feeling that we're decades behind. One of the things we've worked very hard at with Lattice is taking the methods used by the best in other sports and deploying them in climbing. We've been mimicking the coaching structures and education, the training methods and research, and the data-backed approach for years now.

PHOTO: JON VICKERS

PHOTO: LATTICE TRAINING

3. You founded Lattice in 2016. What is at the heart of the Lattice approach to climbing training?

Lattice is all about creating a coaching and performance ecosystem that will deliver results to teams or individuals whether they're keen amateurs or the world's elite. What I mean by this is that nothing at Lattice sits in isolation. We don't want to have coaches or data or research that sits on its own trying to bring about the best performance. Everything is designed and run so that it fits together in this big organism that works off of all of its strengths in a cohesive way and that constantly aims to feed back into the core so that everyone and everything improves bit by bit over the years. For example, the training we do must be backed by sports science expertise, so we employ sports science graduates, master's and PhDs. Then we ask them to educate and share their expertise and experience in an open and critical manner within the team. From there, we have resources and methodologies created for our clients, knowledge shared across multiple platforms of social media, and finally we'll make sure we publish papers on what we're doing for peer review. This is the approach that I've seen the elite coaching setups take elsewhere and myself and the whole team are totally driven to make this happen at Lattice.

4. What advice would you give someone who would like to start training seriously so that they can take their climbing to another level?

You've got two approaches really. You can self-educate and put a load of time into learning how to train (this book is a great place to start!) so that you can then go on your own self-coached journey. Alternatively, you can get yourself a coach who will normally be able to shortcut a lot of your time and – hopefully, if they know what they're doing – make your progression more efficient on both time and injury risk. As a summary point on both of these approaches, it's key to understand that the biggest factors that people fail to get right are training load, training specificity and consistency. When we talk about training load, we're referencing the stress that we put our bodies under, and it is directly necessary to create adaptation through overload. I have seen many climbers over the years fail to grasp that load is a function of both intensity and volume and consequently they find themselves with poor results – or they quickly get injured. In reference to training specificity, I always try to remind clients that unless the training they're doing has a high level of specificity then they're close to wasting their time if it's too big a portion of their weekly activity. Finally, consistency wins the day every time. You look at nearly all the best climbers and they're the product of years of consistent progress and they typically don't have much time out with injury. Those that do seem to be very good at creating methods of working around the problem.

'I ALWAYS TRY TO REMIND CLIENTS THAT UNLESS THE TRAINING THEY'RE DOING HAS A HIGH LEVEL OF SPECIFICITY THEN THEY'RE CLOSE TO WASTING THEIR TIME.'

WARMING UP

Warming up prepares you to perform physically, technically and mentally, and also reduces the risk of injury. The warm-up should consist of a general part and a specific part. The general part can be running, jumping, push-ups, squats and similar activities, where the goal is to activate the whole body and use the large muscle groups. The warm-up is also a good time to go through some injury prevention exercises where you train the movement patterns that are the opposite of what you do when climbing. For youths and adults, this part should last for around 10 minutes; it should last for a bit longer with kids – around 20 minutes.

The specific part should be climbing based, and the most common way to start is with easy routes or boulder problems on larger holds, before gradually making the climbing more difficult. In this part of the warm-up, you can – and should – introduce the technical elements you wish to work on.

To adequately warm up your fingers with regards to injury prevention it is recommended that you do more than 100 moves before significantly increasing the difficulty. Your warm-up should also be specifically targeted towards the contents of the main part of your training session. If steep bouldering is on the agenda, the last part of the specific warm-up should involve steep climbing and you should make sure that your fingers, arms, upper body and core are warm. If you are doing vertical lead climbing, your warm-up should be characterised by warming up the fingers and incorporating some hip mobility training. In addition to preparing you physically, warming up should also prepare you mentally to perform. Because the specific part of the warm-up is like what you are going to do in the main part, this will have a positive effect on how prepared you are mentally for what will come next.

WARM-UP TIP

Begin by traversing on good holds or by doing some easy top-roping. Then move on to making the movements more dynamic. A simple exercise for this is to do double dynos between good holds while keeping your feet on the wall. Remember, climbing is about having fun and freedom of movement, so try to let loose mentally, be dynamic and play with dynos to get more flow in your movements. Our experience is that many climbers move better during the main part of their session if they take this approach during their warm-up.

MAIN PART

As the name implies, it is in this part that you conduct the training which you have planned. If you have planned to do bouldering pyramids, you should decide in advance which problems to try. If you have planned to do circuits, you can use the warm-up to test moves and sequences of different sections of the circuits, so that every attempt in the main part is as good as it can be. With technical sessions, you should predefine focus areas and what technical challenges each boulder problem or route should offer. If you want to work on weight transfer and balance, choose less-steep wall angles and holds that will not allow you to pull hard. You must either have set the problems in advance or have an overview of the various problems and routes at your gym – and you must be able to stick to this plan.

Whatever you have planned to do in the main part, you should have prepared yourself mentally for what is going to happen. There is a big difference in attitude if you're going for maximum effort on individual routes or boulder problems, versus having an endurance session on routes or a technical bouldering session. For physically demanding sessions, your stress level must be higher with a goal of maximising each attempt. For technical sessions, you need to be mentally prepared for problem-solving and practising elements you are less skilled at, while for endurance sessions you must be prepared to endure the sensation of climbing with pumped forearms.

If you are going to train multiple elements in the same main part, it is important to plan in which order to train them. The explosive, physically demanding and most technically challenging parts of the session should follow immediately after the warm-up to ensure the best possible quality of execution. For example, you can start with campusing or deadhangs after the warm-up, then go on to climbing routes or boulders, and then finish with general training and injury prevention.

FINISHING

After a hard climbing session, it can be a good idea to 'cool down' on easier routes or boulder problems to finish the session, both to add some more training into your session and to shorten the recovery time. Or you can round off your training by spending 20 minutes doing some stretching or other injury-prevention training. Although many skip the final part of the session due to a lack of time, there is often a lot to be gained here, since you can work on general strength training, mobility or technical elements that are less physically demanding.

SESSION PLANS

Below are three examples of session plans for training different skillsets. With each session plan, we have added comments related to the specific contents. By planning the sessions in this way it's easier to see the relationship between the warm-up, the main part and the finish, as well as time allocated for each part.

SESSION PLAN FOR BOULDERING: MAXIMUM STRENGTH AND FINGER STRENGTH

	WHAT	TIME	FOCUS
Warm-up	General part: injury-prevention exercises.	10 minutes	Gradually increase stress levels.
	Specific part: deadhangs without added weight on good holds. Dynamic moves, good holds, easy bouldering.	20 minutes	Visualise individual moves. Mentally prepare for maximum effort.
Main part	Max deadhangs.	20 minutes	Maximum effort during hangs. Proper rests.
	Max bouldering.	30–45 minutes	Visualisation before every attempt. Positive thinking and creating belief in one's own skills.
Finish	Core training.	20 minutes	Body awareness: feel the correct muscle groups working.

This is a physically demanding workout, and this needs to be reflected in the warm-up which prepares you for the main part. The higher the intensity of the main part, the higher the intensity needs to be towards the end of the warm-up. It is especially important to warm up the fingers properly for this session, as it starts with deadhangs. Because you are combining deadhangs and max bouldering in the same session, it is important that the main part doesn't last too long, as both of these methods have a high intensity rating. Settle for four boulder problems and two attempts per problem, but make sure to maximise the quality of each attempt. The session can finish with core training, as the main part focuses mainly on the fingers, arms and upper body.

SESSION PLAN FOR ENDURANCE

	WHAT	TIME	FOCUS
Warm-up	General part: skipping rope/light jog and injury-prevention exercises.	15 minutes	Body awareness: feel the pulse rising, feel the movements gradually become more coordinated.
	Specific part: easy top-rope climbing (2 routes), easy lead climbing (1–2 routes).	15 minutes	Awareness of clipping positions and energy-efficient climbing.
Main part	3 x 5.	90 minutes	Visualise the routes, minimise errors for sequences, foot placements and clipping positions. Be conscious of the feeling of being pumped, recognising that it can come and go, and feeling in control of how tired you get during the climb.
Finish	Cooling down and mobility training.	20 minutes	Lower stress level, find the flow in the movements. Body awareness, feel the correct muscles stretching, staying relaxed when fully stretched.

The main focus of this session is endurance training, and the main part is relatively long with low intensity. This requires less time for warming up, and the transition into the main part can be quite fluid. With so many routes in one session, you have the opportunity to focus on technical and tactical elements like weight transfer, energy-efficient climbing and clipping technique. It is important to be conscious of the feeling of getting pumped so that you can control the intensity. This will also make you more confident in climbing with an increasing level of pump in your forearms. You can finish with some easier routes to shorten your recovery time, and mobility training for your hips and thoracic spine is a good match for this session as your body is already warm and your arms are tired.

SESSION PLAN FOR TECHNIQUE: FOCUSING ON BALANCE AND WEIGHT TRANSFER

	WHAT	TIME	FOCUS
Warm-up	General part: skipping rope/light jog. Active mobility training.	10 minutes	Body awareness: feel the pulse rising, and the correct muscles stretching, staying relaxed when fully stretched.
	Specific part: easy, vertical traversing. Easy, vertical boulder problems.	10 minutes	Control the stress level, feeling the movements gradually become more coordinated.
Main part	Bouldering. 10 different boulder problems requiring fronting, sidepulls, and flagging. Slabs, and vertical and gently overhanging walls with bad handholds.	90 minutes	Concentrate on specific parts of the movements. Visualise the execution of individual moves and sequences. Focus on problem-solving and practise individual moves rather than topping the problem.
Finish	Arm and upper body strength. Injury-prevention exercises.	20 minutes	Increase the stress level, focus on trying hard. Body awareness: feel that you are training the correct muscle groups.

For the general part of the warm-up, you can do active mobility training since the techniques of the main part require mobility. You can seamlessly transition from the easy bouldering in the specific part to the main part, but you should decide in advance which problems you are going to work on in the main part. A technical bouldering session requires patience and problem-solving, and none of the problems should be too physically demanding. Since the physical load has been low for the main part, you can finish the session with both specific and general strength training.

TRAVEL TIME
1 HOUR

SOCIAL MEDIA/TV
1 HOUR

FAMILY/FRIENDS
2 HOURS

WORK/SCHOOL
8 HOURS

TOTAL LOAD

It is important to be aware of the total load you are exposing yourself to. If you work full-time and have kids waiting at home and have to try hard to get a few training sessions done each week, the training load might be low, but the total load is high. The same goes for young athletes who are juggling school, friends, work, training and competitions – the total load you're exposed to each day can end up being very high. 'The 24-hour athlete' is a tool often used on young athletes, but we feel it's useful for anybody who wishes to organise their training.

TRAINING
3 HOURS

SLEEP
8 HOURS

Having kids has a big impact on the total load in your life, and is definitely a variable that needs to be considered when planning for training.

TO ILLUSTRATE WHAT IT MEANS TO HAVE A CONSCIOUS AWARENESS OF THE
TOTAL LOAD WE HAVE CHOSEN THE FOLLOWING THREE EXAMPLES:

1

STIAN CHRISTOPHERSEN **FULL-TIME JOB AND FATHER OF TWO**

Transitioning from prioritising climbing over everything to prioritising the kids was challenging and required me to totally transform the way I structured my training. First and foremost I had less time per training session, and the sessions had to be coordinated with work and family commitments. During periods of less sleep and greater total load, I had to prioritise what I wanted to work on in my training so that I could get the most out of each session. It was realistic to do two climbing sessions per week, supplemented by two sessions at home on the fingerboard. I decided to train finger strength and arm strength at home and vary the climbing between bouldering and lead, depending on what I wanted to train for. With the fingerboard at home, I got to train exactly what I needed in a relatively short space of time, and while at times it was hard to motivate myself for those sessions, they did produce good results. I also got more out of the two climbing sessions per week when I had decided in advance whether it should be a hard bouldering session, a high volume lead session or a more free session where the most important thing was being social and taking a break from everyday life.

Some of my hardest ascents to date I did after having children and dealing with an ever-increasing workload. The fact that I have managed to progress in times of high total load has given me confidence that I can continue to improve, and at the very least maintain my level, by being more structured in my training and prioritising more clearly what I want to work on every session.

PHOTO: BJRONAR SMESTEAD

TINA JOHNSEN HAFSAAS **PROFESSIONAL CLIMBER**

The biggest advantage of being a full-time climber is that I can show up for training feeling refreshed, motivated and ready to pull hard. When I was in high school and competed internationally as both a junior and a senior and had over 150 travel days, it was difficult to have the energy surplus required to train as hard as I needed in order to progress. Today I have a life where training is the priority, and everything else is planned around that.

To continue up the progression ladder I depend on having sessions of the highest quality possible, and the main risk of being a full-time climber is exercising too much. In my daily routine with 15 to 30 hours of training a week, it is important that I structure the week so that the sessions fit together, that they encompass everything I should go through, and that they're not just high-intensity sessions. It goes without saying that periods with a high training volume will include sessions of reduced quality, but this is because I have deliberately planned for a lot of training in that period. During these periods, it's important to ensure optimal recovery and that I don't lose energy as a result of a hectic daily life.

After many years of focusing on basic training, I have a body that can withstand high volume and heavy loads, but it's still important that the training doesn't become one-sided with too much attention directed to just a few elements. As long as I manage to vary the content of my training weeks and have a plan for how much I need to rest and how hard I should train during different periods of the year, it's not a problem in my everyday life that I exercise too much. I am privileged to have all the time in the world available for training.

3

MARIA STANGELAND FULL-TIME JOB, MARRIED, NO KIDS

I started climbing relatively late and immediately fell for the sport. It wasn't long before I was climbing three to five days a week, for two to three hours each time. Before, when I did other forms of training like running or hitting the gym, I usually had time for three hours a week. This is because I would spend half a day just trying to drag myself out of the door. With climbing, it's different. I'm literally running out of the door. I'm in my home office, already wearing my climbing clothes, and the moment I slam the MacBook shut I grab my bag and off I go. I have also become less worried about appearances and carry my bag with me everywhere, so I'm ready to go climbing directly from any situation. In meetings with strangers, it's often a nice icebreaker.

It helps to have three regular days with a regular partner or a regular crew. I then plan other things around this. I only change the regular days if I have a very good reason. They are also distributed in such a way that there are days off, so I can either recover, do alternative training, or squeeze in an extra climbing session, depending on what's suitable and what the total load is.

Climbing is also a very social sport, with nice people who share my passion, and so it's also become a haven where I enjoy spending time with good friends and acquaintances. I climb because I want to, not because I absolutely need to exercise. Besides, I usually plan my sessions as early as possible in the afternoon so I can go straight from work and have the opportunity to do something else afterwards. Unfortunately, early morning training is not for me, so instead I work early.

It doesn't cost me anything to squeeze in some climbing at times when I otherwise wouldn't think to train. I surround myself with people who are just as obsessed with climbing as I am, who, in addition to sticking to the same invariable plans, are also able to join a session at the spur of the moment. There are more of them than you'd think. And I tell my pack why it's so important for me to prioritise climbing. For me, it's necessary stress therapy, meditation and mental training, and it gives me an invaluable sense of achievement. It's incredible how people who care about you can be flexible and solution-oriented if they understand why you're doing something.

HOW TO MAINTAIN YOUR LEVEL WHEN THINGS ARE HECTIC

Maintaining your level requires a lot less effort than trying to raise it. Raising your level requires a lot of training over a long period of time, and at times this is not practically possible. You can still maintain the level you are at by avoiding complete breaks from climbing and loading the fingers, arms and upper body during these periods. The most important thing is to not go completely without exercise for more than two weeks. It is then that the training base you have built up will start to gradually break down and you will need to start training at a lower level to reduce the risk of injury. A simple aid is a fingerboard at home or on a trip that allows you to hang by your fingers, do pull-ups and train your abdominal and back muscles in hanging positions. Completing just a few short workouts a week makes it possible to exercise less, yet to a satisfactory level, during hectic periods. You will maintain continuity in your training, thus reducing the risk of injury and ensuring that you are well prepared for periods when you have time for more and harder training.

SUMMARY

Planning for training lets you structure your day-to-day training, define which factors to prioritise, create a balance between loading and recovery, and stimulate peaking. All in all, this will provide better quality and continuity in your training and allow you to train and climb more with a lower risk of chronic injuries.

Cecilie Skog climbing during her last session before giving birth to her daughter Vega three days later.

Norwegian climber Cecilie Skog (b. 1974) is best known for her expeditions to the poles and the Himalaya, but she's also an avid sport climber. She's a registered nurse and mother of two girls, Vilja and Vega.

CLIMBING DURING AND AFTER PREGNANCY

'Cecilie, can you write a chapter in the book about climbing while pregnant?'

My basic positive and spontaneous response to such questions is usually YES! Since the request this time also came from good friends, answering no was unthinkable. Besides, I have almost two years of experience of climbing while pregnant.

When I sat down to give my advice and recommendations, I have to admit I found it difficult. After all, I only have my own very subjective experiences.

How could I provide valuable tips without knowing who you are, what kind of pregnancy you are going through and how much you have climbed before? Nor am I a midwife or an obstetrician. I'm just a nurse.

It is amazing how vulnerable one suddenly feels when a tiny little miracle is growing inside your belly. We only want the best for the child who is trapped for nine months in somebody else's body.

The female body is genetically coded to change and adapt when pregnant. Our sense of taste and smell changes. We get more tired and tired more often. We undergo hormonal changes, blood volume increases, bloodflow increases, and ligaments become looser and softer. Our assessment of consequences also changes. We adapt to the situation with plenty of help from nature.

And the health clinic. They provide us with answers to the thousands of questions that suddenly arise. Whether they can provide in-depth answers to your questions about pregnancy and climbing is unknown. I never asked them such questions: I went to the source – my female climbing friends. Those who had climbed through one pregnancy after another. They had the answers. There were many I could ask since I was last of the bunch. Since mine was a geriatric pregnancy, because of my old age, I might as well have been a grandmother to the child I was carrying.

As I write this now, I have decided that I'm not going to preach one way or the other. I don't want to systematically set up a training programme for pregnant women or provide a definite and final answer.

But I can share my story.

During my two pregnancies, I climbed two to three days a week throughout each one. Vilja arrived a few weeks early, in week 37. The last session we 'hung out' together was the day before she came into this world. I sold my pregnancy climbing harness online just a couple of days before baby sister Vega arrived right on schedule, on my birthday, in week 36.

Climbing while pregnant meant that my patient climbing partners and I endured many long sessions. Because of all the pee breaks. As my belly grew, the climbing was interrupted more and more frequently by these necessary breaks. I could hold on for hours. All these interruptions gave me stamina and a sense of achievement that was good to carry with me during the day. For the most part, I climbed inside. I would often sneak into Vulkan, a climbing wall in Oslo, before the capital woke up and before the actual opening hours of the gym.

'THE BELLY GREW GRADUALLY. THE KILOS CAME GRADUALLY. GRADUALLY I ALSO DEVELOPED A NEW WAY OF CLIMBING.'

Actually, I like people a lot and am used to sticking my nose out and asking to be seen here and there. So I was surprised to find that I suddenly didn't like the attention as much.

Normally, without a baby in my belly, I have the body of a 14-year-old boy. No matter how exquisitely I curled my hair, all of a sudden it was my breasts and belly that entered the room first, that got the attention, the looks. A while later I would arrive. Somewhat embarrassed to learn that eye contact wouldn't be an option until several seconds later. I've always wanted adequately large breasts – who hasn't? But, when they did first grow out, I thought that these huge knockers looked really out of place on my body.

Commenting on pregnant bodies is widely accepted. This was a new discovery. Apparently, it's OK to have opinions on them, loudly and in front of others.

'Yes, now I can see you're pregnant!'

'Oh my, how big you have become!'

'Ready to burst at the seams!'

'Wow, *you're* climbing? With that belly?'

Therefore it was a privilege to climb in peace in the mornings, even though I don't really suffer from social anxiety.

I felt comfortable climbing on lead until about week 16, after which I only climbed on top rope. It would often be my breathing that was the limiting factor, not the usual pump in my forearms. I stopped bouldering quite early in pregnancy because I felt uncomfortable with falling or dropping on to the crash pads.

The belly grew gradually. The kilos came gradually. Gradually I also developed a new way of climbing. The adaptations of my climbing technique with my new body wasn't something I was focusing on consciously. It just happened. Naturally. I moved more sideways. Twisted in more to use my abdominal muscles. I had to place more emphasis on weight transfer. Literally. I had to compensate for my lack of ability placing my feet up high. I had to do more and shorter moves. I had to position myself differently.

Incredibly enough I felt good when climbing. On the ground I was stomping around like a cow – on the wall I felt completely different. It felt wonderful to stretch my back, use my arms, lessen the load on my feet. Stand on my toes. Sometimes I felt like I was dancing. Maybe it was the contrast with waddling around on the ground that made me feel like I was weightless on the wall. Sometimes I just had to exclaim my enthusiasm with a 'weee, I'm a helium balloon!'

Little joys can also be hard to hide.

After giving birth, both of them by caesarean, I waited six weeks before starting to climb again. Vilja was most excited about moving around. All the time. While on maternity leave with her we did a hundred thousand kilometres of strolling and not much climbing. Vega was apparently happy to lie on a pad marinated in chalk along with eight to ten other toddlers. Fortunately. Without hair they lay there like a nice, homogenous bunch without any motor skills, looking at the nice, colourful climbing holds. We bragged about them and said they were patient. We formed an incredible women's community on and underneath the walls. We cheered each other on. Shared beta. We breastfed. We cuddled the little ones. Our own and each other's. If somebody cried, comfort crisscrossed the group. And we drank coffee. And we gossiped. And breastfed some more. Good times. We were maternity bouldering two, three times a week. For the first few months, I paid attention to my operation wound with scar tissue and a tender abdomen. Surprisingly, although the same thing happened after the first pregnancy, I wasn't stronger in my comeback, even though I was several kilos lighter.

'AFTER A FULL YEAR OF MATERNITY LEAVE AND MATERNITY BOULDERING, I WAS STRONGER THAN EVER.'

It's possible expectations were high after all the comments about how I was going to fly up the wall after the baby was out. People I met at the climbing walls probably thought it had to be incredibly hard to vertically move a body the size of a small hippopotamus. People tilted their heads slightly as a sign of sympathy and wanted to tell me that all the exercise I put in would pay dividends. Tandem climbing was the same as using a weight vest. Slowly but surely, I adopted the expectation that gravity would cease as my girl was out.

The brutal truth was that I felt more at home on the wall with my daughter as a passenger. I felt stronger during the last two months of pregnancy than the first two as a mother. Even though I was heavier with a child, a placenta, and all the amniotic fluid, at least I had the feeling of filling my own body. Tight and firm. After giving birth I wasn't feeling very well put together. I wasn't in touch with my abdominal muscles and looked like a well-used bean bag.

Slowly but surely we got stronger. All the mothers. And the babies on the pads. We loved the feeling of mastery. Big and small. After a full year of maternity leave and maternity bouldering, I was stronger than ever. Maybe for the first time in my life I had real continuity in my climbing. In the 20 years I've been climbing, my activity level has always been a bit on and off. Something I've done between trips. Every time after a trip, I felt that I was starting all over again. Now the climbing was organised, with appointments three times a week. A motivating development. Extra motivational when it happens together.

Pregnancy climbing and maternity bouldering is a field that hasn't seen much research. I know nothing about consequences, injuries and long-term effects. As far as I know, nobody has written any papers on the subject.

If you are wondering whether to ask an open question about climbing during pregnancy in one of the many women's forums online – don't. You'll either be decapitated or crucified with arguments about how bad you will be as a mum. How selfish you are to consider doing extreme sports while pregnant, and that you should now think of others and not yourself. That last one is actually correct. But, regular physical activity improves blood circulation. By climbing you increase muscle mass which provides more oxygen throughout the body. Increased bloodflow to the mother during exercise also provides increased bloodflow to the foetus. Physical activity reduces the risk of weight gain and gestational diabetes and is probably important in preventing pre-eclampsia (pregnancy poisoning). Also, when we exercise, we secrete tons of endorphin hormones. The body's own morphine, the happiness hormone. So, for several hours after a session on the wall, we can walk around with a feeling of ecstasy. All this euphoria then trickles down the chain of command. In this case, to the baby in the belly.

Because I have had such pleasure from climbing as a pre- and post-pregnancy activity, it's hard to not want to recommend it to anybody who asks.

GOOD LUCK!

Note from the authors: We want to emphasise that neither of us are doctors, gynaecologists or midwives, or have any personal experience with being pregnant – obviously. There isn't much data on climbing and pregnancy, and we have therefore chosen not to present any absolute advice or opinions on what you should – or should not – do. Our experiences align with Cecilie's story, and with reasonable consideration regarding falling when bouldering or lead climbing, it seems most people can continue climbing for as long as they are comfortable doing so. If you have any specific questions or are unsure if there are any special precautions you need to take during your own pregnancy, please contact a doctor, midwife or your health clinic.

THE JOY OF CLIMBING

As a conclusion to this book, we would like to highlight the importance of having a good training environment. There are many factors that come into play here. Besides the purely practical elements, such as good climbing walls and outdoor crags, inclusion, participation and mastery are key words for a good training environment. By giving everyone space, participating with and praising others, you can be part of a community that creates and promotes good climbers. By helping others, there is a great chance that the training community will also help you.

For example, there is the importance of the dialogue we have with each other to improve our technique. Whenever we are bouldering indoors, we constantly discuss beta with each other. We discuss whether a move should be done statically or dynamically, and we discuss foot placements and grip positions. 'Are you pinching? I'm crimping', 'Use more speed', and 'Relax and lower your body' are all examples of statements made countless times in the course of a session. The same dialogue is also important when it comes to the mental and physical elements. By supporting each other and rationally going through what happens when the rope takes on a lead fall, we will more easily build the confidence needed to dare to fall. When we are doing pull-ups, it also helps to have a friend supporting you and pushing you. By participating in and being inclusive in such a dialogue, you will foster an environment where everyone helps each other out – and it is wonderfully motivating to be a part of such an environment.

 Don't get demotivated by strong climbers! If you're lucky enough to climb alongside stronger climbers, use them as a source of motivation – something to strive for. Chances are you'll push harder and get better because you are climbing with them.

Focus on mastery and not just on results. This applies to both yourself and your own achievements, and when rewarding those around you. A performance-oriented environment where competition and individual performance are rewarded tends to foster athletes who are afraid of failing and do not dare to take on new challenges. Such athletes often end up quitting and this builds a negative and not very inclusive training environment. By appreciating your own and others' progress instead of just achievements, you will help create an environment that you and others will thrive in. Appreciate progressing further than before on your project, or being a little closer to managing five pull-ups, or finally managing to hang from the edges on the Beastmaker. Let others know that you are happy with your own progression, and let others know when they progress.

The intention isn't that you should not be performance-oriented at all. To a certain extent, focusing on achievement is important for becoming a better climber, but it must not overshadow the joy of getting better and getting a sense of achievement. External factors, such as winning a competition or sending a difficult route, are a nice bonus, but it's often those who enjoy the little things, like getting better at pinching or sticking a move they haven't managed before, who will remain climbers for their entire lives. They are also often the ones who become the best, and definitely the ones who have the most fun.

Some people have the ability to lift their own and others' achievements. You can be this person by being inclusive, participatory, mastery-oriented and positive. In order to illustrate a good training environment, we want to highlight some periods and communities from our own climbing lives that have contributed to our development and defined our identity as climbers.

TIL NEDERLAND: Disse representerer Norge i junior-VM i Nederland. Fra venstre: Martin Mobråten
fra Asker, Jan Frederik Prytz fra Bærum, Stian Christophersen fra Asker og Nicolai Prytz fra Bærum.

Firkløver til junior-VM

Klatre - kameratene

THE BEGINNING

We were 13 to 14 years old when we started climbing. The community was much smaller than it is today, and the natural consequence of this was that anyone who started got included in this community from day one. We started at Skøyen Climbing Centre, and the community there, spearheaded by Jacob Normann, took us under its wings. We got to go climbing at Damtjern and Sørkedalen and we felt like an important part of the community. Being included in this way made us super stoked, and we climbed almost every day. We learned technique by watching others and by getting feedback – everyone helped everyone. We felt a sense of achievement, and it was an incredibly fun time with a lot of progression and experiences.

This early period created an important part of our identity as climbers, and without this good start, it's not certain that we would still be climbing. Our history is an indicator of how important it is to create a good and including environment. Especially for the young! After all, we want them to have as much fun with this amazing sport as we have.

TO HELL AND BACK

A trip that stands out is when we went to Hell when we were 15 or 16 years old. We caught a flight to Værnes, did some grocery shopping at the store next to the airport and pushed a shopping trolley with our food and luggage to the parking area near the crag where we camped below the cliff for a week. The climbers who passed by liked what we did, gave us lots of tips on routes to try and we got to know a lot of new people. After that, we competed at a Norwegian lead cup event at Dragvoll in Trondheim. Stian climbed wearing a Superman outfit, and afterwards we partied with a crazy bunch of climbers. Memories for life!

COMPETITIONS

As we got older we started climbing in a lot of competitions, both national and international. For a long time we had a coach, Miguel De Freitas, who came with us to competitions all around the world. Miguel wasn't a strong climber himself, and he didn't teach us a lot about technique, but he introduced us to several invaluable methods for endurance and strength training. He was there with us and created a sense of security and belonging, and he was good at pointing out achievements instead of results.

We were never really that good at climbing competitions, but that is probably because we longed for the lifestyle of outdoor climbers. Competitions were the path young climbers were expected to take, but were perhaps not the right path for us. Our identity was anchored in outdoor climbing from day one. And we missed the outdoor climbing community we had been a part of since the beginning. The moral of this is perhaps you will only perform at your very best and feel 100 per cent comfortable if you know you're in the right place. The minute we started focusing on outdoor climbing again, we trained harder than ever and we never doubted which path we had taken.

Mirage (Font 8a+), Driehoek, South Africa.

NOW

Jumping back to the present, we're now adults and have partially made climbing our jobs, and we still climb as much as possible every week. We sometimes climb in competitions, but we regard ourselves as outdoor climbers – who spend a frightening amount of time training indoors … ! Since the time being filled with competitions, we have mostly been climbing non-stop. There have of course been periods with less climbing because of injuries or other things in our lives, but the community has always been an important part of our identity. What still motivates us most is spending a day at the crag with good friends who all share the same passion. A new Jacob or Miguel has entered the scene on multiple occasions, shaping the path forwards and making a positive contribution to the creation of a good environment. Perhaps we have been these guys ourselves?

The last person who's had a big impact on our own training environment is Kenneth Elvegård. Kenneth started climbing in 2011 and got good fast. He arrived in an Oslo scene which many felt was overly focused on performance and not very inclusive. Coming from other sports, Kenneth wasn't accustomed to this, and by being stoked, positive and inclusive he managed to influence and change the Oslo environment he now was a part of into the good community it is today. This might sound like something of an oversimplification, but sometimes this is just the way it is. We have discussed this at length and have come to the conclusion that sometimes all it takes to turn an environment on its head is just one stoked person. Mood and attitude can be incredibly contagious – they can disarm failure and get everyone to perform at their best. They can remove negative competition, and the collective will then drive all climbers forwards.

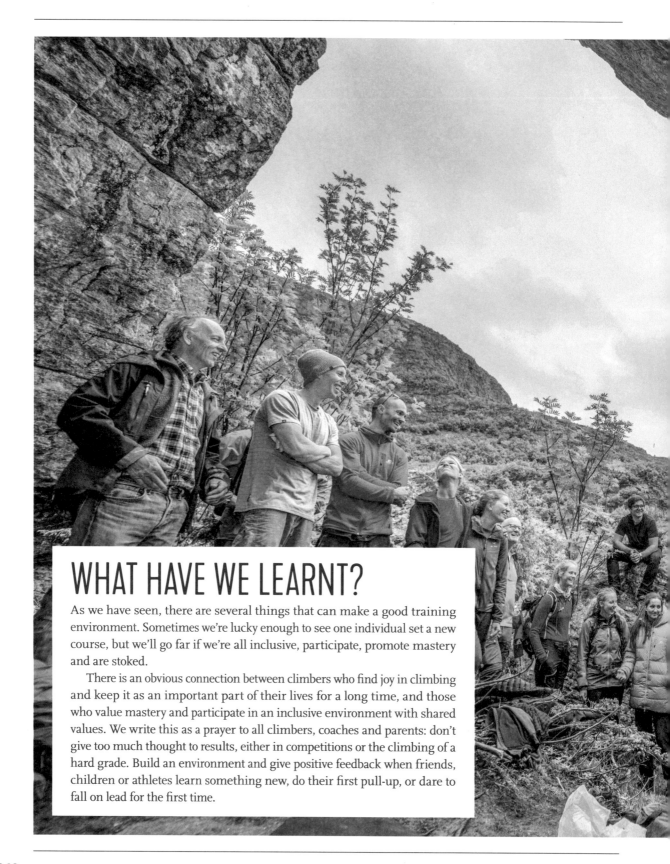

WHAT HAVE WE LEARNT?

As we have seen, there are several things that can make a good training environment. Sometimes we're lucky enough to see one individual set a new course, but we'll go far if we're all inclusive, participate, promote mastery and are stoked.

There is an obvious connection between climbers who find joy in climbing and keep it as an important part of their lives for a long time, and those who value mastery and participate in an inclusive environment with shared values. We write this as a prayer to all climbers, coaches and parents: don't give too much thought to results, either in competitions or the climbing of a hard grade. Build an environment and give positive feedback when friends, children or athletes learn something new, do their first pull-up, or dare to fall on lead for the first time.

Good vibes during the wedding of Martin Mobråten and Maria Davies Sandbu.

THE TEN COMMANDMENTS OF CLIMBING

1. You have to climb a lot to be a good climber.

2. Vary your climbing between different styles and angles – both indoors and outdoors.

3. Train technique before physical training.

4. Learn to use your feet – they will be your best friends on the wall.

5. Rid yourself of the fear of falling.

6. Train finger strength.

7. Find your strengths and weaknesses, set yourself targets and adapt your training thereafter.

8. What and how you think is crucial to your success – become just as strong mentally as you are physically and technically.

9. Create – or become part of – a supportive environment that challenges you.

10. Preserve the joy – climbing is all fun and games.

EPILOGUE

The more we learned, read and taught over the years, the more apparent it became that there was a need for a comprehensive and accessible book on the subject of training for climbing. The turning point, when the process transformed from thoughts and ideas into an actual project, came during a trip to Vingsand in January 2017, when Martin simply declared 'We're just going to do it'. The road from that day in January to now with this book in your hands has been long and extremely educational. Because – where do you start when you want to write a book?

First and foremost, we wanted to write a book that anybody who wants to read about climbing can understand, with helpful hints and tools that are easy to use, even for those with limited climbing experience. This has been a challenging process because writing simply and clearly about complicated and comprehensive topics is difficult and a bit intimidating. As Albert Einstein put it: Make it as simple as possible, but not simpler. Every chapter in this book could have been a book in and of itself. We therefore had to leave out a few elements, and simplify others, but we hope that we have still managed to capture the essence of the topics we deemed most important.

Secondly, we wished to write a book that was both educational and inspirational. We have put great emphasis on using good photography, and we want to thank all of the photographers who were generous enough to help us create a visually appealing book: Bård Lie Henriksen for the fantastic job of taking, sorting and editing all of the 4,000 photos that were the basis for the instructional pictures. Nathan Welton, Terje Aamodt, Alex Manelis, Chris Burkhard, Henning Wang, Bjørn Helge Rønning, Andy Wickstrom, Paul Robinson, Endre Vik, Ragnhild Tronvoll, Bjørnar Smestad, Bjørn Sætnan, Katrine Vandet Salling, Dag Hagen, Audun Bratrud, Mike Mullins, Ryan Waters, Jon Tore Modell and Volker Schöffl for all the other photos, which we hope inspired you as much as they did us.

To finish a book with the somewhat ambitious title of *The Climbing Bible* is not a two-man project. Our editor, Maria Stangeland, has done a fantastic job of directing two climbing nerds in the right direction with regards to content, phrasing and substance. We have also received invaluable help with proofreading and professional assessments from a number of people in different areas, and would like to thank:

Aleksander Gamme for his input in the chapters on mental, technical and tactical factors.

William Ottestad, for his input in the chapters on general training and injury prevention and physical training.

Jørgen Jevne for his input in the chapter on general training and injury prevention.

Sigurd Mikkelsen for his input and explanatory models for pain physiology in the chapters on general training and injury prevention.

Anders Krossen for his input in the chapters on physical and technique training.

Benjamin Christensen for his input in the chapter on planning for training and for valuable sparring on concepts within strength training.

Maria Davies Sandbu for her input on the chapters on physical and technique training.

Carlos Cabrera for his input in the chapters on physical and technique training.

Frank Abrahamsen for his input in the chapter on mental training.

Big thanks also to Jo Nesbø for writing the foreword to this book. This was a great honour!

To illustrate certain topics and inspire you, we added the segments we called 'A Climber's Story'. In them, Magnus Midtbø, Rannveig Aamodt and Cecilie Skog gave us fantastic depictions from their own lives as climbers. In addition, Kenneth Elvegård and Joakim Louis Sæther have both written valuable contributions on route setting and jamming, respectively. Eva López has elaborated on her thoughts on finger training, Tom Randall has given us more information about his approach to training structure, and Tina Johnsen Hafsaas, Thilo Schrøter and Hannah Midtbø have shared their pro tips with us. Thank you for taking the time to share your stories and knowledge with us.

Thanks also to Jon Tore Modell and Elisabet Skårberg at Spanish Inq for a fantastic collaboration with design and layout, and for believing in us and helping us to create exactly the book we had imagined.

More generally, we would also like to thank the wonderful climbing community that we are part of. For 20 years now we have been inspired by, challenged by and had long discussions with a number of people about this and that. All these experiences have helped in shaping this book. We are very pleased to see that climbing is a growing sport and that more and more people are experiencing the same magic that hooked us so many years ago. The future of climbing in Norway and internationally is brighter than ever.

CLIMBING GRADES – BOULDERING

V GRADE (V)	FONTAINEBLEAU GRADE
VB	3
V0-	3+
V0	4
V0+	4+
V1	5
V2	5+
V3	6a / 6a+
V4	6b / 6b+
V5	6c / 6c+
V6	7a
V7	7a+
V8	7b / 7b+
V9	7c
V10	7c+
V11	8a
V12	8a+
V13	8b
V14	8b+
V15	8c
V16	8c+
V17	9a

CLIMBING GRADES – ROUTES

USA	FRANCE	UIAA	NORWAY	BRITISH	
5.0					
5.1	1	I	1	Mod	
5.2	2	II	2	VD	
5.3	3	III	3	HVD	3c
5.4	4a	IV	4	S	4a
5.5	4b	IV+	5-	HS	4b
5.6	4c	V	5	VS	4c
5.7	5a	V+			
5.8	5b	VI-	5+	HVS	5a
5.9	5c	VI	6-	E1	
5.10a	6a	VI+			5b
5.10b	6a+	VII-	6	E2	
5.10c	6b	VII	6+		5c
5.10d	6b+	VII+	7-	E3	
5.11a			7		
5.11b	6c	VIII-		E4	6a
5.11c	6c+		7+		
5.11d	7a	VIII			
5.12a	7a+	VIII+	8-	E5	
5.12b	7b				6b
5.12c	7b+	IX-	8		
5.12d	7c	IX		E6	6c
5.13a	7c+	IX+	8+		
5.13b	8a		9-		
5.13c	8a+	X-	9-/9	E7	
5.13d	8b	X	9	E8	7a
5.14a	8b+	X+	9/9+		
5.14b	8c		9+	E9+	
5.14c	8c+	XI-	9+/10-		7b
5.14d	9a	XI	10-		
5.15a	9a+	XI+			
5.15b	9b	XI+/XII-			
5.15c	9b+	XII-			

GLOSSARY

Approach: The walk-in to the climbing area.

Anchor: Usually two bolts connected with a chain which marks the end of a route.

Arête: Outside corner/edge of two walls, like the outside corner of a building.

Back-clip: Clipping a quickdraw incorrectly, so that the rope is routed from the outside and in, rather than from the inside and out. Creates the risk of the rope unclipping if the climber falls.

Barn door: When one of your legs swings out from the wall like a crooked door because you're in an off-balance position as you move to the next hold.

Belay device: This helps you hold/control the rope when belaying your partner, and your partner either falls or asks to be lowered to the ground.

Belayer: The person belaying (holding the ropes of) the climber.

Beta: Usually describes information about moves or sequences, but can also refer to travel, accommodation, weather, and so on.

Bicycling: A version of the toe hook where you stand on the front of a foothold with one foot while toe hooking on the back with the other.

Boulder problem: A defined route up a boulder or short wall where no rope is needed. Indoors it will usually start and stop on marked holds, but outdoors it starts at the holds you can reach from the ground and finishes by topping out the rock (unless otherwise stated in the guidebook, for example sit-starts, problems which only go part way up a wall, or problems with rules).

Brush stick: A long stick with a brush at one end which allows you to brush holds beyond your normal reach.

Brush: Used to remove chalk and dirt from climbing holds. Toothbrushes have long been used for this, but in recent years a number of different brushes have been specially made for climbing. (Brushes with real bristles from boar or the like are the best.)

Brushing: cleaning chalk and dirt from the holds.

Bumping: Grabbing a hold, and then immediately using it to generate speed to grab the next hold with the same hand.

Campus board: A training device made up of wooden rungs on an overhanging plywood wall.

Chalk bag: A bag of chalk attached with a belt around your waist. There are also bigger chalk buckets placed on the ground for bouldering when you don't need to carry a bag during the climb.

Chalk: Chalk is used to prevent the sweat in your hands from ruining the friction. The chalk we use isn't actually chalk, but magnesium carbonate. You can buy regular chalk, liquid chalk or chalk balls.

Chalking up: To apply chalk to your fingers and hands or the holds before or during a climb.

Chipping: Making new or improving existing holds by using tools like a drill, chisel, hammer, glue or cement. Considered unethical and should be avoided.

Cleaning: To ready a route or boulder for climbing. This involves among other things the removal of moss and loose holds by use of a stiff brush or similar tools. Cleaning a route can also mean removing the quickdraws after climbing it.

Clip stick/beta stick/cheat stick: Specialised tool-on-a-stick that allows you to clip a quickdraw higher than you can normally reach. Often used to pre-clip the first bolt on sport climbs so as to avoid a ground fall.

Clipping: When you attach the quickdraw to the bolt hanger, or the rope through the quickdraw when lead climbing.

Clutch: Immediately moving your first hand to the next hold as your second hand lands the first hold because the first hold isn't good enough on its own.

Compression: Squeezing your hands together on two opposing holds. A prow with slopers in bouldering is known as a compression problem or fridge climbing (because it's like lifting a fridge).

Corner: AKA dihedral. The inside corner of two walls, like the inside corner of a room. Opposite of arête.

Crag: The cliff or boulders where the climbing is.

Crash pad/bouldering mat: A portable mattress filled with layers of foam. Used to soften the landing when bouldering. Usually carried like a backpack on the approach.

Crimp: Adding your thumb over your index finger to lock the grip down.

Crossing: When you cross your right hand to the left, past your left hand, or vice versa, you're crossing over. You can cross over with your foot or your hand, above or below, behind or in front, depending on the holds and your body position.

Crux: The hardest move or sequence of a route or boulder problem.

Dab: When you accidentally touch the ground, the crash pad, a spotter or anything else nearby that isn't part of the climb. Dabbing invalidates an ascent.

Deadhang: Finger strength training method where you hang from the edges of a fingerboard or similar.

Deadpoint: Stopping your body at the apex of a dynamic movement. Refers to the point in the trajectory where the motion 'dies', i.e. transitions from going up to going down, and you are practically weightless.

Dogging: Stopping and hanging on the rope at each bolt when lead climbing so you can figure out the beta.

Dry-fire: When you slip off a hold because your fingers are either too dry or too cold for there to be enough friction. Often happens without notice; can be painful and wears skin.

Dynamic: Doing a move dynamically involves using the whole or parts of the body to create momentum and swing towards the next hold, instead of locking off and moving just the arm.

Dyno: A dynamic move where you jump to and catch a hold or holds with one or two hands while both feet cut loose.

Edge: A hold so shallow that only the outermost pads of your fingers can fit on it.

Edging: Using the side edges of your climbing shoe to stand on small edges. Stiffer shoes are better.

Elvis leg: Or sewing machine leg. When your leg starts vibrating up and down like the needle of a sewing machine, often because you are tired or stressed during a climb. Makes standing on smaller footholds difficult.

Fingerboard: A board with a selection of edges and holds for training arm and finger strength.

First ascent: When you are the first person to successfully climb a route or boulder problem, you have done the first ascent, often abbreviated to FA. It is often the person who has cleaned and/or bolted a line who does the first ascent, but not always. This person is known as the creator, and until the route or boulder problem has been climbed, it is called a project.

Flash: Climbing a route or boulder problem first go, which you've never tried before but for which you have beta on how to solve the different moves and sections.

Flick: Moving your lower hand just as your upper hand lands the next hold.

Friction: The force acting between two surfaces that are touching, such as your hand or foot on a climbing hold: good or bad friction refers to how it feels when you are holding or standing on a hold. The friction is dependent on the texture of the hold, the contact surface between the hold and your skin/boot rubber.

Frogging: Squeezing both feet in towards one other with your knees pointing outwards. Often used on arêtes, tufas or opposing footholds placed next to one other.

Fronting: Standing with the inside edge of the foot on the foothold so that the inside of the leg is facing the wall. The knee is pointing out to the side and away from the body.

Gaston: See shoulder press.

Go: Synonymous with attempt. Having a go means an attempt from the start with the intent of success.

Grade: The grade of a route or boulder problem indicates the difficulty or how challenging it is to climb. Different countries have different grading systems for routes and bouldering.

Gym: Indoor climbing wall/centre.

Harness: Usually consists of a waist belt (with gear loops), a belay loop and leg loops. The harness is what you attach your rope and/or belay device to when sport or trad climbing.

Heel hook: Hooking your heel on or behind a hold or edge.

Height-dependent: AKA morpho. Usually refers to routes or boulder problems where being tall is an advantage because of the distance between the holds. But remember, being short can also be an advantage. For example, it's not easy getting your feet high underneath holds if you're tall. Morpho can also mean it's easier for shorter climbers, but this is rarely used.

High point: The furthest up a route or boulder problem you have managed to get before a successful ascent.

Highball: A tall boulder problem.

Incut: Edges that have a positive angle in relation to the angle of the wall.

Indoor climbing: Climbing inside at a climbing wall/centre.

Jamming: Locking your fingers, hands, feet or other body parts in cracks in the rock.

Jug: A really good hold.

Kneebar: If the distance between a foothold and a large hold or opposing surface is roughly the same length as your lower leg, with your foot on the foothold you can squeeze your knee against the large hold or opposing surface. This will in many cases allow you to significantly reduce the load on your arms and fingers, and sometimes even allow you to completely let go with your hands. Recent years have seen the emergence of rubberised knee pads, which increase friction and make it possible to use smaller and poorer kneebars.

Layback: Leaning away from the holds to increase grip so you can hang on. A technique often used on cracks or arêtes where the grip surface is vertical.

Lead: Climbing on lead means clipping the rope into the quickdraws on the way up. In competitions, all quickdraws must be clipped, but outdoors only those that are necessary to avoid long or dangerous falls are used. For an ascent to be valid the route must be climbed on lead without loading the rope for a rest.

Line: Synonym for route or boulder problem, describing where to climb up the wall. We often say this or that line stands out or looks good, and this is related to which part of the rock face looks most inviting to climb.

Lock-off: When you stop all motion in your body, essentially locking it off, and move one hand to the next hold. You can train this skill by doing lock-off exercises.

Lowering: When your belayer lowers you to the ground.

Mantelshelf/Manteling: Pushing yourself up with one or two hands, and 'standing' on them with your elbows straight. Mostly used for topping out outdoors.

Matching: Placing both hands or feet on the same hold.

Moonboard: Training wall developed by Ben Moon with a specific layout of holds and problems.

On-sight: When you try a route for the first time without any prior information other than the grade.

Open hand: All grip positions where the angle of the middle finger joint is greater than 90 degrees.

Overhang: Walls where the angle is steeper than vertical.

Pendulum: When your body swings into the wall when you take a fall on lead as the rope takes, or when your body swings as you dyno to a hold and your feet cut loose on steep terrain – holding a swing like this requires strength in the fingers and upper body.

Pinching: Squeezing a hold between your thumb and fingers. A pinch is a hold that invites such a grip.

Pocket: A hole with room for one or more fingers.

Pogo: Using one leg as a pendulum to create speed and momentum to execute a dynamic move.

Power spot: Pushing a climber up and into position to try a move on a boulder problem.

Pre-clip: When falling at the start of a route is deemed too dangerous, you can pre-clip one or more quickdraws, so that the start is climbed on a top rope. Whether to pre-clip and, if so, how many quickdraws, is an ethical question, as this can change the grade and character of a route. Consensus regarding pre-clipping of the route in question usually comes down to the local norms.

Project: A route or a boulder problem you're trying. Warning: a project can easily morph into an obsession.

Outdoor routes or boulder problems that have been cleaned and bolted but have not yet had a first ascent are also known as projects. If the creator wants to climb it first, the project is closed, but if anyone can have a go at the first ascent, the project is open.

Pulling through: When you don't stop to match a hold but continue the upward motion with your other hand.

Pump: the feeling of getting tired in your forearms.

Quickdraw: Two karabiners connected together with a short sling. One karabiner is clipped to the protection or bolt, and the rope is clipped through the other karabiner.

Rack: Common term for all the gear you carry with you on a climb; usually safety gear like belay device, quickdraws, nuts and cams, slings, and so on.

Rappelling: Lowering yourself down from the top of a route.

Reading a route/boulder problem: Looking at the route and making a plan for which holds to use with which hand, and where to place the feet. Mainly used before an on-sight attempt.

Redpoint: climbing a route on your second attempt or later is known as a redpoint. The expression comes from Frankenjura, Germany, where climbing legend Kurt Albert painted a little red dot – a 'rotpunkt' – at the start of any route he had done without holding or standing on anything other than the rock.

Rest: A good hold or a good position on the wall where you can stop, rest and shake some of the pump out of your forearms. Here you can psyche yourself up or calm yourself down, depending on what comes next.

Rocking over: Sitting down on one leg by fully bending the knee. A useful technique for vertical climbing as it significantly lessens the load on the fingers and arms.

Roof: A horizontal overhang.

Rope drag: The longer the route, the more contact points the rope has against quickdraws and protrusions on the wall, and this all creates more resistance – or rope drag. Rope drag is also a result of the weight of the rope and the friction between the rope and the quickdraws and the wall.

Rope gun: Describes the strongest climber of the crew – the person leading and fixing top ropes for everyone else.

Rope team: Consists of a belayer and a climber.

Rope: Climbing ropes are made up of an elastic core and a protective sheath, and come in different lengths and thicknesses depending on the application.

Route: A route is a defined way up the climbing wall, either indoors or outdoors. It can be a bolted line or a trad line, and it starts from the holds you can reach from the ground and finishes at an anchor or by topping out.

Run-out: If the bolts are few and far between. Can lead to big falls.

Safety check: Climber and belayer check each other's gear before climbing. Always do a pre-climb safety check!

Sandbag: A route that is harder than the grade suggests. Grades differ depending on the route, the wall, the crag, or the country you're in. Some routes will feel 'soft' (easy), while others will feel 'hard'. Some destinations have been referred to as having 'holiday grades', while others are not recommended if you want to climb a higher grade. Remember that grades are only opinions and these opinions will differ depending on a climber's height/reach, finger size and strengths/weaknesses.

Sending: When you successfully climb a route or boulder problem, you've sent it.

Shoe: Short for climbing shoe. AKA rock boot. Shoes specially made for climbing, with distinctive blends of rubber compounds for maximum friction and/or durability. There are many different climbing shoes for different purposes.

Shoulder press: A vertical hold where the grip surface is facing your body can be used as a shoulder press. Also known as gaston.

Sidepull: A vertical hold where the grip surface is facing away from your body.

Sit-start: Shorter boulder problems often have a sit-start. Your bottom should be the last part of your body to leave the ground.

Skipping: When you miss clipping a quickdraw.

Slab: Walls where the angle is shallower than vertical.

Sloper: A rounded hold with a negative angle in relation to the angle of the wall.

Smearing: Standing on a rounded foothold without does not have any distinct edge. Imagine smearing the rubber on to the hold or wall, like spreading peanut butter on a sandwich. Softer shoes are better suited to smearing.

Speed climbing: A category within competition climbing, where the goal is to climb a standardised route as fast as possible on a top rope.

Spotting: Standing at the ready to brace/support a bouldering climber in the event of a fall.

Static: Doing a move statically means moving slowly and in control, without building momentum in advance.

Stemming: Pushing your hands and feet on to opposing walls in a corner/dihedral or other similar features.

System board: A training wall with a specific layout of holds.

Takes skin: A route or boulder takes skin if there are one or more sharp holds that wear skin fast. Such routes or boulders should be climbed on cold days with good friction, and you need to be careful to limit the number of attempts.

Tick/tick mark: A tick mark is a thin stripe of chalk, indicating where to grip or stand on a hold. Ticking is the act of making this stripe. Ticks should always be removed before your leave a route or boulder.

Ticklist: A list of routes and boulders you have climbed or would like to climb.

Toe hook: Hooking the upper side of your foot behind a hold or an edge.

Top rope: When you are belayed from the top of the route, either via an anchor at the top or a belayer above you, you are climbing on a top rope. It's common to start top roping before learning to lead climb.

Topping out: Synonymous with success. Usually done literally in bouldering, where you finish by climbing on to the top of the boulder.

Tufa: A tufa is a stalactite. They can often be observed as long or short vertical lines on the wall, and they are formed when carbonate minerals precipitate out of ambient temperature water running down the wall. Usually found on softer rock types like limestone.

Twisting in: Standing with the outside edge of your shoe and twisting your leg so that the outside of your hip and leg is facing the wall. Your knee is then pointing in towards the centre of your body.

Undercling: A hold where the grip surface is facing down.

Volume: Larger holds placed on indoor walls to make three-dimensional changes to the wall. Come in all shapes and sizes. Can be used both as handholds and footholds, and smaller holds can often be placed on them.

Whipper: A long fall when lead climbing.

READ MORE

There is more knowledge to be gained about both training and climbing, so we want to encourage anyone who's feeling inspired to read and learn more about the different topics to continue with the books we have listed below for each chapter. Because, as you know, a foolish man thinks he knows everything. A wise man knows he doesn't.

PHYSICAL TRAINING:

Anderson, M. and Anderson, M., *The Rock Climber's Training Manual. A Guide to Continuous Improvement*, (Fixed Pin Publishing, 2014).

Hörst, E.J., *Training for Climbing. The Definitive Guide to Improving your Performance*, (Falcon Guide, 3rd edn, 2016).

MacLeod, D., *9 out of 10 Climbers Make the Same Mistakes*, (Rare Breed Productions, 2010).

TECHNIQUE:

Anderson, M. and Anderson, M., *The Rock Climber's Training Manual. A Guide to Continuous Improvement*, (Fixed Pin Publishing, 2014).

Hague, D. and Hunter, D., *The Self-Coached Climber. The Guide to Movement, Training, Performance* (Stackpole Books, 2006).

Hörst, E.J., *Training for Climbing. The Definitive Guide to Improving your Performance*, (Falcon Guide, 3rd edn, 2016).

MacLeod, D., *9 out of 10 Climbers Make the Same Mistakes*, (Rare Breed Productions, 2010).

Matros, P. and Korb, L., *Gimme Kraft. Effective Climbing Training*, (Café Kraft GmbH, 2013).

MENTAL TRAINING:

Hörst, E.J., *Training for Climbing. The Definitive Guide to Improving your Performance*, (Falcon Guide, 3rd edn, 2016).

MacLeod, D., *9 out of 10 Climbers Make the Same Mistakes*, (Rare Breed Productions, 2010).

Moffatt, J., *Mastermind. Mental Training for Climbers*, (Vertebrate Publishing, 2019).

Orlick, T., *In pursuit of Excellence: How to win in sport and life through mental training*, (Human Kinetics, 4th edn, 2008).

INJURIES:

Hochholzer, T. and Shoeffl, V., *One move too many: How to understand the injuries and overuse syndromes of rock climbing.* (Lochner-Verlag, 3rd edn, 2016).

Hörst, E.J., *Training for Climbing. The Definitive Guide to Improving your Performance*, (Falcon Guide, 3rd edn, 2016).

MacLeod, D., *Make or Break. Don't let climbing injuries dictate your success*, Rare Breed Productions. 2015.

PLANNING FOR TRAINING

Anderson, M. and Anderson, M., *The Rock Climber's Training Manual. A Guide to Continuous Improvement*, (Fixed Pin Publishing, 2014).

Hörst, E.J., *Training for Climbing. The Definitive Guide to Improving your Performance*, (Falcon Guide, 3rd edn, 2016).

For questions regarding specific citations, the authors can be contacted at **post@klatrebibelen.com**

Climbing isn't a sport that has seen much research, neither from a performance-enhancing nor from an injury-prevention perspective, but the knowledge database is ever increasing. We recommend the website **www.ircra.rocks** for updated research papers. We also want to recommend the websites http://en-eva-lopez. blogspot.com and **www.trainingforclimbing.com**, which both produce articles on training and injury prevention with quality citations.